Contents

Introduction

The theme of the Twentieth Annual Course and Conference of the United Kingdom Reading Association, held at Worcester College of Higher Education, from 25–29 July 1983, was 'Reading: Meeting Children's Special Needs'. The Conference sought to explore, beyond 'learning to read' and 'reading to learn', ways in which children's social, emotional, developmental, intellectual and leisure needs might be met through reading. The focus was firmly on the child, and on his or her needs in terms of growing up and becoming an adult, together with the need to find a way through the maze of teachers' language and curriculum content which every child meets during compulsory schooling.

Nearly a hundred teachers, advisers, researchers, academics and publishers from all over the world contributed formally to the Conference. It is a matter of regret that we have been able to publish only a sample of the excellent papers which were presented. Many of the papers not included here will be published elsewhere but irrespective of this I should like to pay tribute to all of those who gave so willingly of their expertise and time. It is this spirit which makes attendance at Conference so worthwhile an experience.

I hope that the selection of papers contained in this volume is a fair reflection of the proceedings of this great annual conference. There is, inevitably, some unevenness in a volume such as this which seeks to represent four sorts of contribution: plenary sessions, parallel sessions, research seminars and classroom workshops, and is designed to cater for class teachers, language specialists, advisers, teacher trainers, researchers and overseas visitors. Something for everyone is the aim.

Part I includes material from plenary sessions, Part II from parallel sessions, and Part III from research seminars and classroom workshops.

Doug Dennis
President 1982–3

Reading: Meeting Special Needs

Proceedings of the twentieth annual course and conference
of the United Kingdom Reading Association,
Worcester College of Higher Education, 1983

Editor: Doug Dennis

H·E·B

HEINEMANN EDUCATIONAL BOOKS

Heinemann Educational Books Ltd
22 Bedford Square, London WC1B 3HH
LONDON   EDINBURGH   MELBOURNE   AUCKLAND
HONG KONG   SINGAPORE   KUALA LUMPUR   NEW DELHI
IBADAN   NAIROBI   JOHANNESBURG
EXETER (NH)   KINGSTON   PORT OF SPAIN

British Library Cataloguing in Publication Data
United Kingdom Reading Association. *Conference.*
(20th: 1983: Worcester College of Education).
Reading: meeting children's special needs
1. Reading—Great Britain
I. Title   II. Dennis, Doug
428. 4'07'1041   LB1050

ISBN 0-435-10200-1

109141

Phototypesetting by Mid-County Press

Printed and bound in Great Britain by
Biddles Ltd., Guildford and King's Lynn

Part I

1 Meeting teachers' special needs through collaborative research

C. Morag Hunter

The theme of the Conference is the meeting of children's special needs. For this paper the focus is on a personal view of one way of moving towards meeting children's special needs in the classroom through meeting their teachers' special needs in the teaching of reading and encouraging children to learn through reading and writing.

The first part of the paper sets out to establish what are teachers' needs and what are the qualities of effective teachers of 'normal' children. It is hypothesised that effective teachers of children with special educational needs will require these qualities to be highly developed and in addition to have other special qualities.

The second part of the paper concerns what kinds of knowledge are likely to be needed by teachers in order to meet the needs of children with reading and learning difficulties. The third and final part explores ways of acquiring the relevant knowledge and skills, suggesting the value of collaborative research. Four research projects are briefly outlined and discussed in this context.

I Teachers' special needs

Before considering teachers' *special* needs it is necessary to consider what their *usual* needs are in the professional context. Perhaps these might be thought of as needs for whatever is required *to become and remain an effective teacher*. The study of the qualities of effective teachers is not a new area of study. It is one about which many educators have debated in the past, some have speculated on the basis of personal experience and others have carried out extensive and systematic research.

On the basis of observations over years of teaching and working with teachers it was reported previously (Hunter, 1980a) that the following qualities were shown by effective teachers:

1. They are interested not only in their subject matter but also in their pupils and in teaching and learning.
2. They recognise that their role is complex and the demands which are made on them.
3. They go on seeking insights (e.g. how best to teach), yet they are flexible

1

enough to abandon patterns they discover to be less effective than they thought.

4. They observe keenly and listen attentively to their pupils. They can do this and think about it at the same time (high levels of metacognitive awareness).

5. They appear to be able to differentiate between their expectations and an awareness of what they actually observe.

6. They check, by a range of techniques, that their pupils have learned what was intended.

In summary, such teachers can read their own miscues as well as cues and are not limited to the recognition of their pupils' miscues.

Further information about the qualities of effective teachers is available on the basis of systematic research in about 60 classrooms over three years in the ORACLE study (Observational Research and Classroom Learning Evaluation) directed by Professors Simon and Galton. This study has thrown light on what happens 'Inside the Primary Classroom', revealing the complexity of the relationship between teacher style and pupil behaviour. Without, at this point, discussing the impact of different styles on pupils' reading achievements, we may note that the authors have made the following, clear statement: '... although there are common elements in the practice of successful teachers, different styles achieve these effects in different ways.' The successful teachers, it concludes, (1) 'all engage in above average levels of interaction with the pupils', (2) 'devote considerable effort to ensuring that the routine activities proceed smoothly', (3) 'engage in high levels of task statements and questions', and (4) 'provide regular feedback' while at the same time (5) 'encouraging children to work by themselves towards solutions to problems', and (6) 'making above average use of higher order interactions including statements of ideas, and more open ended types of questioning.'

In the light of these findings it may not be stretching the point concerning the success of increased interaction between teachers and pupils, to suggest that increased interaction between teachers and teachers may result in successful professional development. It would seem to be important that the collaborative element be emphasised in inservice education and it may indeed be the most important single element in bringing about increased teacher-effectiveness in meeting individual children's special needs.

Another study involving over 400 student teachers and their tutors has yielded additional information relating to the characteristics of effective teachers. This information arises as a small part of the extensive study of the *Structure and Process of Initial Teacher Education within Universities in England and Wales* (Patrick, Bernbaum and Reid, 1982). Both from answers to open-ended questions and in response to characteristics listed for rating in the written questionnaire form, there emerge nine characteristics of effective teachers that were rated by more than 70 per cent of the sample of students and staff as 'highly desirable'. These nine characteristics are as follows (in order of frequency of rating to an observable gap or cut off point at 70 per cent rating as 'highly desirable'):

1. *enthusiasm* for the subject
2. ability to keep *control* of classes
3. *patience*
4. ability to use a *variety* of teaching methods
5. *knowledge* of subject
6. clear diction
7. *sympathy* for the problems of the pupils
8. *punctuality*
9. teaching from materials *prepared* in advance of lessons

These characteristics might be said to be about how effective teachers direct their *energy, empathy* and *effort* with a view to *caring* and *communicating knowledge*. These qualities (the three Es and three Cs?) are likely to be as desirable for teachers of children with special needs as for ordinary children. There may be additional characteristics which are likely to be needed by teachers of the former. Special additional characteristics are likely to include the particular ways in which the individual teacher can direct his or her sympathy, patience, enthusiasm and knowledge towards finding *appropriate* as well as varied methods of teaching individual pupils. It is in this particular 'applied' sense that teachers of children with special needs have, themselves, to face challenges which require them to recognise their own special professional needs in the light of recognising the nature, dynamics, and limitations of their own understanding and expression of 'the three Es and Cs'. This requires a degree of self-awareness in the professional context and a self-evaluative approach or willingness to find out to what extent and in what ways one's expectations, intentions, actions and interactions influence the individual child's learning and facilitate the meeting of his or her special educational needs. It is not only a matter of knowledge about methods and materials, essential though this is, nor is it only a matter of keen observation of the child in the process of learning, but includes finding ways of becoming an effective diagnostician of one's own professional needs in order to meet the child's needs. The process requires teachers to become involved in forming hypotheses on the basis of their observations in the classroom and their reflections and experience, then to test the hypotheses systematically. It has been the writer's experience that, although teachers can do this on their own, they can be supported and encouraged by embarking on the process in the context of collaborative work with colleagues. There are further gains from explicit sharing and involvement in educational research, particularly since the relative detachment of the researcher is required in the development of the necessary 'clinical' skills whether at the descriptive level, or interpreting (diagnosing) or Special teaching (treatment). 'Detachment' is not intended to suggest lack of interest or coldness, it can be warm, concerned and yet maintaining clarity of stance.

II What special knowledge do teachers need to have?

A substantial change since the publication of the Warnock Report (1978) and the 1981 Act, is that it is now recognised that the responsibility for meeting children's special educational needs is not the province of a select group of specialist teachers, or some talented and devoted general practitioners who are to be concerned with children with special educational needs, but should be shared by all teachers. According to the Warnock Report:

> . . . a teacher of a mixed ability class of 30 children, even in an ordinary school, should be aware that possibly as many as 6 of them may require some form of special educational provision at some time during their school life, and about 4 or 5 of them, may require special educational provisions at any given time . . . .

Firstly, then, all teachers need to know the *meaning of the concept of 'special educational needs'* as defined in the Warnock Report and in the 1981 Act which states that 'a child has a special educational need if he has learning difficulty which calls for special provision to be made for him.' In this context teachers need to appreciate 'the three Warnock Principles' cited by Mr George Cooke, Vice-Chairman of the Warnock Committee:

1. that the only criterion for measuring effectiveness in meeting children's special needs, is what is being done for the individual child in the circumstances in which he finds him/herself;
2. that there should be maximum (not total) integration;
3. that there should be generous and positive discrimination in favour of those who require support.

Secondly, in order to appreciate the nature and size of the task they face in meeting childrens' special educational needs, teachers will need to *become aware of the findings of recent research* in the field (e.g. see Clark 1980). Further to the studies noted in the Warnock Report itself, there are several large scale studies supported by the D.E.S. in this field. One such study carried out at Leicester University under the direction of Bernbaum and Croll on the assessment and incidence of children with special educational needs, involved 428 junior school teachers and confirms that in practice the incidence of children with special educational needs is close to that estimated by the Warnock Report as 20 per cent. In fact, 18·8 per cent of juniors were considered by their teachers to have special needs (i.e. five or six children in an average sized class of 29 or 30). More than four fifths of these nominated pupils were considered by their teachers as having learning difficulties, most frequently including reading difficulties. About half as many (7·7 per cent), i.e. about two in the average size class, were described by their teachers as having behaviour problems. Less than one child in 20 suffered from health problems and/or sensory or physical impairment. Just over one child in 100 suffered from all three kinds of difficulty, whereas 28·1 per cent of the nominated children suffered from learning and behaviour problems, and 9·5 per cent suffered from behaviour and health problems. The findings further show that the 'incidence of special needs is seen as a result of an interplay between children's needs and difficulties, teacher definitions and attitudes and institutional policies and types of provision.'

Thus, thirdly, it might be suggested that teachers need to know about their *L.E.A. and school policy and resources as well as to know when, how and where to refer for special assistance*. Case studies of practice and provisions at the preschool and secondary level (Clark *et al.*, 1983) illustrate the importance of these issues in the practical context. It is not, therefore, merely a matter of knowing about stated policy and others' practices including thorough professional study of research in the field. There is also a need for *self knowledge*, for teachers to recognise their own professional knowledge, skills and attitudes in the practical matter of meeting the needs of the individual child in the classroom. This kind of knowledge which is inward-looking, rather than mainly outward-looking, should include recognition of special abilities and aptitudes, what is the unique nature of the individual teacher's synthesis of interests and experiences, for example having a special facility in working with the energetic or aggressively expressive child perhaps even in preference to working with the characteristically reticent child. As well as recognising the interests, aptitudes and relevant 'strengths' in professional terms, it is necessary to recognise when limits are reached and when to seek support and further specialist knowledge.

It is in this context that, surprisingly, many otherwise highly professional teachers appear to have limited *knowledge about the language development process*, what part reading, writing and indeed speaking, play in this process, what reading is, and how it can be developed beyond basic decoding. Despite the publication of the Bullock Report in 1975, placing the teaching of reading in a language context, and despite the increase in publications in the field (e.g. Gatherer's *A Study of English*) and the ongoing work of U.K.R.A. with its founder members' focus on the importance of inservice education for teachers (Dr J. Morris) there is still an alarming acceptance of inadequate initial and inservice education in this crucial area of professional education for all teachers. Without a fairly detailed understanding of the reading process, the more complex relationships between causal factors in any child's reading difficulties must remain a mystery. Teachers need to be able to relate the developmental aspects of learning to read and to apply reading, to those factors associated with the development of (1) the child's heatlth, experience, motivation and linguistic background, and (2) with the school curriculum, and (3) with the dynamics of the child's personality and learning style at home and in school (Hunter, 1982b).

Obviously it takes substantial experience, study, and the integration of research and practice to appreciate fully what has been suggested above as different kinds of knowledge that are necessary for the most effective meeting of pupils' special educational needs. A further need in order to go on doing that is the need for *personal recognition, support and inspiration*. This involves the need to feel valued professionally. It might be assumed that at such an advanced level of professional commitment, this need should not exist. Perhaps it should not, but in human terms, it usually does exist and continue to exist! It is perhaps the other side of the coin, that as well as to know, there is the need to be known. For the class teacher the relevant encouragement comes not only from the children themselves but can come from the department head and head teacher, advisory teachers and visiting specialists. The question arises, who provides the encouragement for them? Which point brings us to the main contention of this paper, that there is a *need for professional collaboration*. The role of College and University might be explored in providing support in this process of teachers acquiring and developing more specialised knowledge and skill in meeting the special needs of individual children. It is a process, rather than a product able to be developed by the end of a short course. The process involves the teacher in developing increasing awareness and ability to stand back from the particular teaching event in the classroom and to see it in a wider context. This growing ability to 'decentre' (a term used by Dr Margaret Donaldson with reference to children's cognitive development and Piaget's theoretical perspectives) makes it increasingly easier to conceptualise the teaching of learning problems, and thus to come closer to describing it clearly, reporting it precisely and working towards a fuller understanding of what is involved. This skill in being able to make a brief, clear and precise statement is required in reporting at multi-discipline meetings. In the past teachers have not always distinguished themselves in their style of reporting. What appears to be needed is practice in the following three steps:

1. Observing keenly
2. Conceptualising the problem in terms of teaching and learning
3. Reporting accurately and briefly.

The capacity to 'decentre', to become aware of what is going on while it is going on, is related to what psychologists study in the field of 'metacognition' (not just knowing things, but knowing how we know and how we can know). By engaging in metacognitive activity the teacher can recognise what prompts certain actions and, in the light of having thought ahead and predicted what alternative actions are likely to lead to, the teacher is better informed about deciding what to do or resist doing (for example, in making the choice about developing a discussion, whether and how to intervene, make facilitatory noises or speed up the pace, or change the topic). It is about increasing awareness of when and how to observe, listen and show caring or directly intervene that the professional process is involved.

III How can teachers acquire the relevant special knowledge and skills?

As well as pursuing individual study by reading, discussion with colleagues and membership of professional associations such as U.K.R.A., there are several ways of increasing knowledge and skills required for effective teaching of children with special educational needs. These include inservice courses, school-based initiatives and action research.

Courses

One of the most frequently used approaches to inservice education is the provision of courses. The need for some kind of inservice support is borne out by the Structure and Process of Initial Teacher Education within Universities in England and Wales (S.P.I.T.E.) study's findings that over 60 per cent of the post graduate certificate of education (P.G.C.E.) students claimed to have done nothing on the special educational needs of children with handicaps; almost 30 per cent claimed to have done nothing on pastoral care and counselling; almost 30 per cent claimed to have done nothing on teaching children of below average ability and 20 per cent claimed to have done nothing on the use of language in the classroom. Perhaps more shocking is the finding that of those who did work on the use of language in the classroom, only 21 per cent considered that what they did provided insights to a greater extent. (A further 55·4 per cent rated 'to some extent' and 23·5 per cent 'hardly or not at all'.)

It was further found that while P.G.C.E. students found books on aspects of behaviour problems, remedial, special education and disadvantage to be interesting and stimulating and could cite examples including Holt, Gulliford, Furneaux and Kellmer Pringle, few students had their interest caught by books on the teaching of reading.

The findings of another small study, (Brooks, 1983) carried out as part of the *Assessment and Incidence of Special Educational Needs* study, may provide some clues as to how teachers prefer to learn if given the choice between courses that are all lecture, all discussion or a mixture of both. It appears that none of the 20 teachers in the study preferred an all lecture course, 50 per cent preferred all discussion, and 50 per cent preferred a mixture of lecture and discussion. These teachers were studying the small steps course within Special Needs in Action Programme (S.N.A.P.) which is part of Coventry local education authority's inservice training initiatives in response to the 1981 Act. All of them preferred the type of 'prepackaged knowledge' course in the self-contained format with prepared materials, to *either* a course which required outside reading and independent research *or* to a mixture of both types of course.

It seems that although a wide range of courses is now available, there are two factors that emerge if they are to be successful. They should include: 1. 'prepackaged knowledge' and 2. discussion.

Teachers, it seems, may not be avid readers of professional literature but they do like discussing and do prefer discussion groups of about five or six people. The value of talking for pupils' learning is borne out by various writers and researchers including, for example, Gardner (1982), Langer (1981), Gearhart (1975 and 1983), Tonjes (1982) in their separate work on reading for learning, and study strategies, not to mention Tough (1979) whose work on analysis and classification of talking for teaching and learning is now well recognised. The theme of the importance of teachers talking together to learn, recurs throughout this paper and is supported in the development of the approach to diagnosing reading and learning difficulties through teacher discussion (Hunter, 1980a and 1982b).

School-based initiatives

Any form of inservice education can best be evaluated by its impact on the classroom. There are, increasingly, developments in inservice education which directly relate to daily work in schools and which are frequently school based. These include initiatives linked with teachers centres, L.E.A. advisory staff and, for example, the D.E.S. experimental initial teaching and inservice course-linked coursework being developed at the University of Leicester.

Collaborative Research

Collaborative research has been described by the writer (1980a) as a 'dialogue between researchers and teachers in a dynamic context'. Black and de Luca (1979) refer to it as 'a process where both parties define the problem and act together to investigate means of solving it'. Jasman and Ashby (1980) consider it to be a process in which 'a series of decisions are made, some of the decisions are made by teachers whilst others are made by researchers'. This apparent division between teacher and researcher does not exclude the teacher being the researcher but acknowledges that research skills and techniques require to be learned. 'Problems' is here intended to refer to any of the issues being studied (not only 'difficultues'). They can be explored and clarified, not necessarily resolved via the collaborative process. It is the focus on collaboration which is perhaps new in this term, collaborative research, and distinguishes it from the related terms, action research and illuminative research (only the latter two terms were mentioned by Stenhouse in his 1975 publication *An Introduction to Curriculum Research and Development*). With reference to the following brief accounts of four studies, there is reason to prefer the term 'collaborative research', although the projects were undoubtedly illuminative and involved analysis and 'improvement' of action in the classroom. It appears to the writer that in these studies the development of the individual teacher's capacity for 'decentering' and applying meta-cognitive analysis increased as a function of the collaborative endeavour. This further suggests that involvement in collaborative research can be a powerful, pleasant and supportive way to becoming a more effective teacher through systematic increase in knowledge and skill in the relevant areas of research. It must be said, however, that the success of a project will depend to some extent on the nature of the problems being studied, the clarity of their conceptualisa-tion and the abilities of those involved to work out a way of developing their dialogue (collaborating). This can take time, effort and goodwill. It is in acknowledgement of the teachers' contributions to the following studies that they are briefly reported, in each case as studies which directly affected the meeting of individual children's special educational needs in reading and writing, through increasing their teachers' knowledge and skills, particularly in teaching reading and writing.

The studies set out to answer the following relatively broad questions:

1. How can we improve remedial services?
2. How can we best help children to develop their written language?
3. How can we become more effective in teaching reading in the multi-ethnic junior school?

4. How can we improve our teaching of reading and writing to children with learning difficulties?

All of the projects had to take account of school and local authority policies as well as the individual teacher's practices in the classroom. All four projects set out to provide support for individual teachers directly, particularly through teachers' meetings and indirectly by offering the skills of the researcher and reporter as well as experience in teaching and work with children with persistent and complex learning difficulties.

Remedial services in the primary school

This two-year project was requested by the Dunbarton L.E.A. and was jointly supported by the L.E.A. and the Scottish Education Department as part of a large study on language and reading directed by Professor Margaret Clark. The part of the study in which the writer was a full time researcher aimed to study remedial services in an area of 14 primary schools with a view to making recommendations and drawing conclusions which would have relevance for the whole of the then Dunbartonshire County. Amongst the project activities, all children primary 3 and 6 (approximate ages 7–8 and 11–12) were screened and results reported to the schools, all designated remedial teachers and head teachers were interviewed using a special computer-compatible interview-schedule, and regular teacher meetings took place initially to decide on areas of shared interest and concern. A wide range of resources was introduced and evaluated, an analysis was made of timetables and notes of work, record forms and referral forms for tutorial (not remedial) work were redesigned, a procedure for analysing spelling difficulties was developed, videotapes on diagnostic testing were produced and a colour film on remedial reading was made for discussion purposes. While in some ways this 1975 miniskirt era film may be considered as out of date the issues raised (e.g. the value of 'remedial movement' or P.E. of a special kind for clumsy children) are still relevant. For some time after the project officially finished, the teachers continued to meet. At the end of the project the view was expressed that it had helped teachers with (1) focusing their attention on thinking through the problems of their daily work, (2) getting to know their children better and (3) having not only an increased sense of professional worth but also (4) demonstrably increased professional skills (S.C.R.E. paper 1980a).

Investigating a technique for developing written language

This study was supported by the Scottish Council for Research in Education and the University of Strathclyde. It aimed to determine whether the success of a particular technique for developing written language derived from the teaching skills of its originator, Richard Binns, or if the method could be employed as effectively by other teachers.

The technique has become known as a method for systematic drafting and redrafting. It was not until after the study was underway that its originator's paper 'From Speech to Writing' (Binns, 1978) became available for use by teachers. By that time we had discovered that individual teachers who had been introduced to the technique through hearing Binns speak at teachers' meetings, or who had evolved similar approaches, all had subtle but important variations in the ways they used the approach.

Four keenly interested teachers began the study, one a primary teacher, the others secondary teachers of English and science. A further five teachers joined in during the course of the first few months. The teachers were a self selected small group all known to the originator of the approach or to the coordinator as having a specific interest and having requested to join the study group. It was not a defined group in the first instance. Their common interest lay in developing written language. One science teacher was known to be sceptical about the value of the technique in the teaching of science but he was professionally concerned to find out if it actually had any value. Teachers' diaries were kept, children's work was studied and at meetings, almost very two weeks over the initial year and a voluntary further year, each teacher presented his or her use of the technique and discussed aspects of its development.

During the study we recognised that the real problem facing us was the lack of definition of the nature of progress in written language, exactly how development takes place and how it could be evaluated. The study of teacher intervention in the process of the child's writing became the main focus of our research. We tried to reconstruct ways in which particular teachers and pupils interacted in helping each other to listen to rereading aloud and checking for clarity in communicating intended meaning. We were aware of the fact that the technique, as each teacher used it, was helping individual children not only to write more but to progress at their own pace, in some instances to overcome difficulties associated with poor handwriting, poor spelling and the capacity to detach themselves from the task of writing sufficiently to be able to think about it as they developed a second, third or up to seventh draft (redrafting was done, even under examination conditions).

While the project cannot claim to have produced a definitive version of Mr Binns' technique or the whole group's discussion of the development of written language, it is clear that a substantial range of insights accrued and data was collected; some of it still requires further analysis. However, sufficient has been learned to permit Mr Binns to continue his study of the development of written language (Binns, 1980) and, for example, to recognise the importance of analysing the changing patterns of cohesive ties within successive drafts on the same theme.

Preliminary analysis bears out the fact that Mr Binns' technique does appear to make possible the increase in detachment from the content that is essential if pupils are to include reflective thoughts in their writing. In our 1979 project report to S.C.R.E., we called the encouraging of the beginnings of this process 'maieutics', which involves the teacher in the job of 'intellectual midwifery'. This process is not dissimilar to the collaborative research process as it affects the generation and clarification of ideas in the minds of the collaborating teachers.

Talking with books

This study was undertaken for mutual benefit. The writer needed a school base for student-teachers' practical work and the school staff appeared to be interested and willing to enter into a joint venture intended to provide increased support in hearing children read and in developing their spoken and written language. Further, it intended to provide a context within which individual teachers could improve their effectiveness in the teaching of reading. Schools Council support as well as L.E.A. support was sought and given.

The idea behind the title 'Talking with Books' was to develop children's interest in books through many ways of increasing the exchange of ideas and discussions about books, not necessarily reading together but noticing books, handling them, using them and enjoying talking with others about books and reading. The aim of the project was formulated as follows to encourage individual teachers to find ways of becoming more effective in:

1. meeting pupils' language needs;
2. encouraging their interest in books;
3. developing their reading abilities;
4. encouraging teachers to consolidate ideas already being developed as part of the school language policy and resources.

All seven teachers (head, deputy and teachers) and the writer, as coordinator were involved in the first year of the project which was planned to run in three phases roughly corresponding with the school term. In phase I, an exploratory-descriptive phase, there would be structured interviews with teachers, meetings and study of children's work. In phase II, a productive phase, there would be the making of books, audio and video tape, the use of various ways of developing reading and home–school liaison. In phase III, an evaluative phase, a report would be written collaboratively and talk with teachers and children would provide a context for evaluating the project as a whole.

Much of what we set out to do has been accomplished, although some of it has taken longer than planned and other developments have been developed further. The school had already recognised the importance of having a written statement of its language and reading policy. The connection between policy and practice was also being worked out.

The teachers' special needs at that time seemed to include the need for clarity about their own perspectives on the teaching of reading as these related to the views of others in the school and within the context of a language policy. Greater clarity did emerge as we worked together. There were two particular events contributing to this, firstly the process of individual interviewing and the impact of reporting collectively on the interviews, and secondly the analysis of several videotaped scenes from everyday teaching of reading in several classes. The videotapes were made originally to show parents in the context of discussions about the use of books such as those provided by the National Book League's display 'A Wider Heritage'. Some time afterwards, further study of these tapes and subsequently taped scenes prompted the writer to postulate four developmentally related stages in learning to read. These four stages appear to the writer to have some relevance beyond revealing the possible basic perspectives for teaching reading at St Peter's Junior School. As organised below, these stages may be taken as hierarchical, with each stage a prerequisite of the next in the development of effective readers, capable of enjoying as well as using reading.

Stage 1.   Kindle children's interest in the books.
Stage 2.   Encourage sharing learning through books.
Stage 3.   Build trust through extended relationships beyond enjoyment of books within schools, to their relevance in the community.
Stage 4.   Explore and share the meaning of the content of books.

Clearly only a few aspects of the study can be mentioned by way of illustration in so brief an account. The value of collaboration can perhaps be indicated not only in the way that two of the teachers continued to work on an extension of the project for a further year and were successful in gaining six weeks' secondment to work full-time on the study but also in the ways in which Post Graduate Certificate of Education student-teachers became involved beyond their agreed coursework in voluntary tutoring of individual children and small groups at St Peter's. The project provided avenues for professional development linking initial teaching and inservice education.

Learning difficulties

This two-year Schools Council supported project linked with 'Talking with Books' is currently at the end of its first year. The project involves one secondary school along with seven of its feeder primaries. A designated teacher from each of the schools and interested colleagues attend teacher meetings which take place at the local teachers' centre after school and on six half-days during the school year. The project has the full support of the L.E.A. who seconded a head teacher to work full-time on the project in its first year. Plans for the second year include the freeing of several designated teachers to be able to work full-time on the project during one school term.

The aims of the project are to describe effective use of existing resources and successful teaching of pupils with learning difficulties in the ordinary school; to develop, share and evaluate selected techniques, materials and ideas (a compendium) related to meeting children's special needs as these are perceived by their teachers; and to study and develop the collaborative research process.

The coordinating of this project is different from those previously described. There are three coordinators: the writer, a colleague, Dr Merry, and the seconded head teacher, Mr Hartshorn. The scope of this study and its links with the large scale D.E.S. study of the assessment and incidence of special educational needs provides it with a different basis in the sense that results of our preliminary screening of the children and our interviewing of teachers can be related to the statistical information collected and analysed in the large study (by kind permission of the directors of the D.E.S. study and Ms Moses).

A remarkable amount has been achieved in the first year although the 'compendium' is only in its infancy. The screening, testing and teacher interviews took place, results of testing were fed back to schools and a range of activities has been undertaken in each of the schools as well as at shared teachers' meetings. At Mr Hartshorn's initiative a newsletter has been produced and is currently in its eighth edition. It provides an additional means of drawing together a group who had little regular professional contact prior to the project. Further initiatives include a visit made to the schools in the Parent Support project at Liverpool and visiting speakers from Fife Region who described their approach to education for pupils with learning difficulties and the new Dundee College Diploma in Learning Difficulties. Local speakers included the Adviser for Special Educational Needs, the project directors and teachers from the 'Talking with Books' project.

There appear to be two distinct kinds of teachers' special needs emerging. There are the needs for more shared knowledge about particular topics, for example, speech and language difficulties, referral to speech therapy and ways of supporting the speech therapists' work, where relevant, in the classroom.

Another kind of need is the need for support for the individual teacher in carrying out day to day work with particular children with learning difficulties. We are attempting to meet both kinds of needs through the project.

Summary and conclusion

Effective teachers of children with special educational needs are likely to require to have, in rich measure, the qualities of effective class teachers and to share, additionally, the ability to devise appropriate ways of individualising and adapting their teaching. They are also likely to need to be aware of their own abilities and professional limits and to have the interest and energy to find ways of meeting the professional challenges posed by individual children with various needs.

Teachers of children with special needs are likely to have special professional needs which include the following:

1. Knowledge about the concept of special educational needs
2. Knowledge of relevant recent research
3. Knowledge of government, L.E.A. and school policy and resources
4. Self knowledge in the professional context

5. Knowledge of the language development process
6. Personal recognition, professional support and inspiration
7. Professional collaboration.

It is suggested that amongst the various ways in which the relevant knowledge and skills can be acquired, including via courses, school-based initiatives and professional association activities and publications, a particularly valuable approach is through involvement in 'collaborative' research. On the basis of brief illustrations from four studies in which the writer has been involved, it is concluded that through each of them individual teachers were provided with the chance of increased purposeful professional interaction which has proved to be helpful in defining and refining the questions and problems which they wished to study together with interested colleagues. In so doing, each teacher could test the limits of his or her knowledge, skill and attitudes and could share information which would extend beyond their immediate teaching needs, to bring about increased awareness of their own abilities and possibly special resources and professional strengths, as well as increased knowledge and understanding of the development and relationship between reading, writing and spoken language.

It is debatable to what extent courses and mixtures of research and courses can achieve these ends in ways that are as flexible and individually tailored as the collaborative research process can be. In evaluating any approach towards meeting teachers' special needs it might be suggested that it is the quality of the collaborative process that is the crucial variable.

Acknowledgments

The writer would like to acknowledge the support of: all the teachers in the Remedial Education Study, the Developing Written Language Study, the 'Talking with Books' project and the Learning Difficulties project; the various funding bodies; S.E.D. Dunbarton; S.C.R.E.; Schools Council and, indirectly, the D.E.S.; Mr George Cooke, Dr Joyce Morris, the writer's colleagues and Professors Bernbaum and Galton. Also Professor Margaret Clark whose influence through the Dunbarton study encouraged further pursuit of the collaborative approach to research and teacher education.

References

BERNBAUM, G., CROLL, P. and MOSES, D. DES Research Project *Assessment and Incidence of Special Educational Needs*. University of Leicester.

BINNS, R. (1978) *From Speech to Writing*. CITE, Moray House College of Education.

BINNS, R. (1980) 'A technique for developing written language', in M. M. Clark and T. Glyn (eds) *Reading and Writing for the Child with Difficulties, Ed. Review Occasional Paper* No. 8, University of Birmingham.

BROOKS, V. (1983) *An Evaluation of the 'Small Steps' Course* (part of the Special Needs in Action Programme). One of the Reports on the DES Research Project *Assessment and Incidence of Special Educational Needs*, University of Leicester.

CLARK, M. M., BARR, J. and McKEE, F. (1983) *Pupils with Learning Difficulties in the Secondary School*. University of Birmingham.

CLARK, M. M., ROBSON, B. and BROWNING, M. (1983) *Pre-school Education and Children with Special Needs*. University of Birmingham.

CLARK, M. M. and HUNTER, C. M. (1975) *Remedial Education in the Primary School*. Report to Dunbarton Education Committee.

CLARK, M. M. (1980) *Further 3Rs for Education: 'Rigorous, Relevant Research'*. University of Birmingham.

DES (1975) *A Language for Life* (The Bullock Report). London: HMSO.

DES (1978) *Special Educational Needs* (The Warnock Report). London: HMSO.

DONALDSON, M. (1978) *Children's Minds*. London: Fontana.

GALTON, M., SIMON, B. and CROLL, P. (1980) *Inside the Primary Classroom*. Henley: Routledge and Kegan Paul.

GALTON, M. and SIMON, B. (1980) *Progress and Performance in the Primary School*. Henley: Routledge and Kegan Paul.

GARDNER, K. (1982) 'Learning through Reading', in A. Hendry (ed.) *Teaching Reading: the Key Issues*. London: U.K.R.A. and Heinemann.

GATHERER, W. (1980) *A Study of English*. London: Heinemann.

GEARHEART, C. (1975) *Making Sense*. Newark, Del.: I.R.A.

HUNTER, C. M. (1979) *Investigating a Technique for Developing Written Language*: Interim Report to S.C.R.E.

HUNTER, C. M. (1980a) 'Becoming a Better Teacher of Children with Learning Difficulties', in M. M. Clark and T. Glyn (eds) *Reading and Writing for the Child with Difficulties, Ed. Review Occasional Paper* No. 8 University of Birmingham.

HUNTER, C. M. (1980b) *Advantages and Disadvantages of Collaborative Research* with particular reference to two studies: 'Remedial Education in the Primary School' and 'Investigating a Technique for Developing Written Language'. S.C.R.E. Seminar Paper.

HUNTER, C. M. (1982a) *Talking with Books*. Interim Report. University of Leicester School of Education.

HUNTER, C. M. (1982b) 'Reading and Learning Difficulties: Relationships and Responsibilities', in A. Hendry (ed.) *Teaching Reading: The Key Issues*. London: U.K.R.A. and Heinemann.

LANGER, J. (1981) 'Prep for Reading', in J. Chapman (ed.) *The Reader and the Text*. London: Heinemann.

PATRICK, H., BERNBAUM, G. and REID, K. (1982) *The Structure and Process of Initial Teacher Education within Universities in England and Wales*. University of Leicester.

STENHOUSE, L. (1975) *An Introduction to Curriculum Research and Development*. London: Heinemann.

TONJES, M. J. (1982) 'Selected Instructional Strategies for promoting content reading and study skills', in A. Hendry *Teaching Reading: The Key Issues*. London: U.K.R.A. and Heinemann.

TOUGH, J. (1979) *Talk for Teaching and Learning*. (Schools Council). London: Ward Lock and Drake Educational Associates.

2 Children like Frank, deprived of literacy unless . . . .

Joyce M. Morris

Although, in a sense, all children have special needs with regard to reading development, it is the obviously handicapped (the mentally, emotionally and/or physically disabled) who are usually the focus of attention and special educational provision. This paper, however, is concerned with children whose needs are often inadequately recognised, especially at a critical developmental stage and, hence, are inadequately catered for. Consequently, they remain illiterate or semi-literate to the end of their school days and beyond. In other words, they are deprived of literacy and the opportunities it gives for a full adult life.

The common needs of such children are exemplified in the case history of Frank as given on pages 281–8 of the final report on the Kent Inquiries, i.e., *Standards and Progress in Reading* (Morris, 1966). Accordingly, his life story provides the starting point for discussing some of the reasons why about 20 per cent of seemingly 'normal' pupils have a poor prognosis for literacy, and why certain courses of action must be taken to recognise and cater for their needs.

Ideally, of course, the findings of more recent longitudinal research should be used for this purpose. However, to my knowledge, no longitudinal research of similar design, scope and conduct to the Kent Inquiries has been reported, and only one similar project is in progress and that is being conducted from Harvard University. Because of this, findings of the Kent Inquiries are still used to support calls to action for literacy as, for example, in the Ministerial address by Dr Tay Eng Soon when, last August, he launched the 'National Reading Month' in Singapore.

The lack of recent longitudinal projects also means that there is no research evidence to suggest that, nowadays, the prognosis for poor or non-readers in junior classes is better than it was for children in the Kent Inquiries. In fact, it is probably at least the same because, at that time, reading standards in Kent schools were above the national average, and national standards have not significantly improved since then. In short, it is reasonable to suppose that, as before, 'the chances of second-year juniors with a reading problem eventually achieving average or normal competence is about one in eight, and at least half of them will remain very poor readers to the end of their school days'.

Frank: The worst reader at the end of the primary school course

Be that as it may, Frank was one of over 8000 children who took part in the first Kent Inquiry in 1954. After that, in the second Kent Inquiry, he was selected as one of 199 children whose standards and progress in reading were intensively studied during the last three years of their primary school course and to the end of their school days in the early 1960s. At which point, a final study was made of their reading ability in relation to the type of employment they secured.

From the collection of 199 case histories, only those of Frank and a girl called Helen were included in the final report. Both children were cases of severe reading handicap at the age of eight. But Helen recovered from a temporary hatred of school which had eclipsed her promising start in the infant department. Happily, her subsequent progress was such that she joined that small proportion of children whose reading disability did not persist to the end of their school days.

In contrast, and more typical of children who fail to master the basic mechanics of reading by the age of eight, Frank's subsequent progress was unsatisfactory to say the least. Among the selected children, he was the worst reader at the end of the primary school course. As he was then 11 years old, it was pitiful to see him struggling to read *Janet and John, Book 2* (O'Donnell and Munro, 1949) which his teacher had considered appropriate for him. He merely guessed wildly at the words in that infant primer, and was clearly unable to use any other strategy but 'guessing' to try and identify them. In short, his reading performance as in previous years, when his school reading 'diet' was confined to *Happy Venture, Book 1* (Schonell and Serjeant, 1939) reminded me of my ten years' experience as a class teacher. That is, ten years spent mainly trying to wean backward primary and secondary school pupils from their 'addiction' to guessing in embarrassing reading situations by helping them to acquire the phonic knowledge, skills and attitudes that lead to initial literacy and beyond. (Would that all reading theorists had had similar experience, especially those who describe reading as a psycholinguistic *guessing* game! Likewise, those who repeat the slogan 'children learn to read by reading' which is nonsensical for children like Frank.)

Returning now to Frank's history. Because of his inability to read, he was placed in the lowest stream of the secondary modern school to which he was allocated. The head reported that he was a well-behaved, likeable lad, but his frequent absences prevented him from making progress. He had only been at the school for nine months when he was brought before the Court for 'breaking and entering and larceny'. A fortnight later he was transferred to a small, residential, approved school.

Soon after his arrival at the approved school, Frank was found to have an IQ of 85 on an individual intelligence test, and he scored badly on tests of reading and arithmetic attainment. As a result of these tests, he was placed in a class of 15 other boys, and given much more individual attention than he had hitherto received.

When Frank returned to his former secondary school at the age of 14, the headmaster classed him as an 'average' reader, and attributed his improved ability to the fact that the boy's interest in reading had been stirred by the particularly good teaching given in the small classes of the approved school. Unfortunately, after his return home, a change in him was soon noticeable. His habit of truancy returned, and his clean, smart appearance rapidly deteriorated to that of his general home standard.

Six months' later, Frank's results on national reading tests indicated that he was 'semi-literate'. His ambition to be a motor mechanic could not be realised because his parents would not agree to him accepting an apprenticeship. They insisted that he must immediately become a wage-earner, and he therefore took a job as a factory labourer.

The history of Frank to the age of 16 is that of a boy who, in his last headmaster's words, had 'little real chance in life'. He lived with his illiterate, unmarried mother in a house which had been scheduled for demolition as slum property by the local council. His father, who was forced occasionally to take a job as a casual farm labourer in order to qualify for National Assistance, lived there with three children of his broken marriage and three more children born to Frank's mother.

There was no evidence that Frank was maltreated physically by his parents but they certainly neglected him during his early childhood. This was obvious from his dirty, ragged appearance and the fact that he wolfed enormous school dinners. They also allowed him to roam the streets late at night, and only became concerned about his truancy when the local Attendance Committee threatened prosecution. Moreover, although Frank suffered almost constantly from chronic catarrh, skin troubles and sore eyes, his parents had never taken him to a doctor for treatment, nor did they ensure his presence at school when routine medical inspections were carried out. In consequence, the boy's discomfort was prolonged unnecessarily, and his defective eyesight remained undetected until he was ten years old when a doctor examined him at the special request of his headmaster.

Frank: A 'teacher-dependent' type of child

With such parents and no reading materials in his dilapidated home apart from a daily newspaper and occasional magazines read by his father, Frank, at the age of eight, needed particularly good teachers and school conditions to encourage him to attend regularly and learn to read. He was what might be described as a 'teacher-dependent' type of child. That is, one of those unfortunate children whose parents couldn't care less about education and, therefore, would not benefit from the current, laudable trend towards encouraging parents to cooperate in school-based projects to foster their children's reading development. Indeed, such well-intentioned projects could cause children like Frank to suffer even more in that, unwittingly, they expose the shame of parental neglect.

Frank was also 'teacher-dependent' because he was not sufficiently self-motivated and verbally-gifted to teach himself to read. In other words, he was not the type of child who later becomes a teacher and, usually, cannot remember a time when he or she couldn't read or how the learning to read process was personally accomplished. This, of course, is one of the main impediments to becoming a successful teacher of reading, especially a teacher of children like Frank. It is also a root cause of inadequate pre-service training for reading which still continues despite the Bullock Report (D.E.S., 1975), the long-time efforts of U.K.R.A. members and so on. Only last month, for example, two recently-qualified teachers, with a B.A. and B.Ed. honours degree respectively, came to the Digby Stuart College Reading and Language Centre and asked if they could attend the Anne Leighton Pearce Memorial Lecture (Morris, 1983) on the history of British reading instruction and research. Their explanation for this granted request was that the teaching of reading had not been a part of their pre-service courses, and they felt they ought to make a start by getting some 'background information' which would help them if and when they managed to get a teaching post.

Frank: The pupil whose teaching needs were not met

These two young women reminded me of my own feelings of inadequacy as a probationary teacher faced with a class of 40 illiterate juniors. Like them, I could and should have been trained to teach children like Frank to read instead of having to discover, on my own, what I needed to know and be able to do in order to cope with my very difficult first assignment. What a cruel waste of time and human potential, and to think that it still goes on today!

Poor Frank! How sad it was to interview that desperate nine-year-old and see the tears coursing down his grimy cheeks as he declared, 'I can't read nothing!' How sad it was to discover that he knew the names of only five alphabet letters, had no phonic knowledge at all and, without any word attack skills, was trying to remember words in a boring, look-say primer merely by their shapes! How sad it was to find how desperately he wanted to make progress because, in his own words, 'reading affects everything you do', and how he regretted not being allowed like his classmates to 'read' comics in wet playtimes! How sad that a boy who gave further proof of his fairly extensive vocabulary and oral ability in expressing his insightful thoughts, should not have had his teaching needs met!

How dreadful that his headmaster should be aware that Frank and 17 other backward readers in his unstreamed class were being neglected, and yet was so seemingly powerless to do anything about it! How dreadful to contemplate the head's explanation for this state of affairs; that other members of staff were even less well equipped for their respective tasks than Frank's teacher was for hers and, therefore, had first claim on his practical assistance in the classroom!

No wonder that she became so discouraged that she resigned her post for one in a junior school large enough to stream its pupils! No wonder that Frank continued to play truant and, when in school, felt it necessary to draw attention to his plight, for instance, by having to be coaxed down from his precarious perch on the school lavatories' roof! No wonder that as a researcher observing the poor teaching and other unsatisfactory school conditions provided for children like Frank, I should see no reason for putting forward the hypothesis that any of the poor readers in the Kent intensive studies were suffering from that controversial, neurological disorder of constitutional origin called 'specific developmental dyslexia'! After all, such a medical diagnosis would assume that the children had difficulty in learning to read *despite* 'conventional instruction' and, certainly, their instruction was not 'conventional' in terms of what good teachers would and should have provided.

Children like Frank: 'Backward readers' or 'dyslexics'?

I remain convinced that teacher-dependent children like Frank in the Kent Inquiries could have learned to read effectively if they had not been let down by their schooling. Moreover, in spite of recent books on 'specific developmental dyslexia' and the N.F.E.R. Report, *Children with Specific Learning Difficulties* (Tansley and Panckhurst, 1981), I am still not convinced by the research evidence to date that 'word blindness', as the condition is popularly called, is an identifiable syndrome distinct from 'reading backwardness'.

Admittedly, I need a lot of convincing especially after a professional visit to Japan in 1981. There, motivated by strong official and parental support, teachers have achieved the highest rate (99 per cent) of literacy in the world. The reasons for this achievement and the rarity of dyslexia were given to me by leading researchers, including the renowned neuropsychiatrist, Professor Makita, who wrote a landmark article on 'The rarity of reading disability in Japanese children' (Makita, 1968). These reasons include organised systematic teaching from the beginning in accord with the specificity of the Japanese language and scripts (Hiragana, Katakana, Kanji) and a plentiful supply of appropriate materials.

Meanwhile in Britain, North America and Australia, secondary remedial departments grow in size, private schools and dyslexia institutes multiply, and government-sponsored adult literacy schemes are virtually a permanent feature of the educational scene. Sadly this situation will continue as long as the 'Chinese' method of look and say (or 'guess') continues to flourish, despite the alphabetic nature of the English writing system and overwhelming evidence favouring a code-emphasis approach. Sadly it will continue to affect most children like Frank who do not have parents willing and/or able to fight for their children's special educational needs to be met; in contrast to children classified, albeit unofficially, as 'dyslexic' as a result of parental pressure, who have not only their articulate parents but film stars like Susan Hampshire to broadcast their needs.

Bearing all this in mind, I wonder whether the fate of children like Frank, who have followed a similar path down the years, would have been better if the final Kent Report (Morris, 1966) and the subsequent Tizard Report (D.E.S., 1972) had been less rigorous in considering the question of 'specific developmental dyslexia'. Certainly that term and 'word blindness' have not disappeared from the educational scene despite offical preference for the term 'specific reading difficulties'. On the contrary, nowadays the media delight in such headlines as 'One in ten children suffers with word blindness disability' (Tasker, 1983).

What is more, when one studies what the 'dyslexia lobby' is pressing for, it is precisely what children like Frank also need. For example, at a recent meeting of the newly-formed Ealing Dyslexia Association, the packed audience were told that the Education Act 1981 (D.E.S.) places more emphasis than hitherto on tailoring educational provision to individual needs. The main speaker, Bill Watkins, then explained how this was done at East Court, a private school for dyslexic children in Ramsgate where he teaches, and is one of two resident psychologists. He also provided each of us with a document headed *East Court School Written Language Curriculum: A Guide* (1983).

Briefly, the East Court Guide emphasises the importance of individualising instruction, and that the teaching should be enjoyable with an additional component in the idea of overteaching and overlearning. It states that 'The dyslexic must be taught precisely what is difficult for him. This requirement leads to the first principle, that of a *sound phonetic basis* to written language learning. This implies a detailed teaching of sound-symbol correspondence rules, spelling/word patterns and rules. Given the nature of our alphabet this cannot be avoided. Other important principles are that the programme should be *structured, sequential, cumulative and thorough.*' After that, details are given of what the programme involves, how the pupils' needs are answered, what the aims of the multi-sensory teaching are, and the specific techniques used, such as the 'Kinaesthetic Training Technique' devised by Fernald (1943).

Studying the East Court Guide and listening to the discussion about dyslexia, I wondered what would happen if the D.E.S. agreed that, officially, all children with reading difficultues should be described as 'dyslexics'. Would the British Dyslexia Association approve this, and continue to bring pressure to bear on society so that, eventually, children like Frank would also have the type of remediation provided at schools like East Court? Or better still, as prevention is better than cure, an early intervention programme such as that developed in New Zealand by Clay (1979). Since 1977, the British Dyslexia Association has had formal links with the D.E.S., and regular meetings are held twice yearly to discuss developments. Surely, at these meetings, a thought could be spared for children like Frank who suffer just as much as children called 'dyslexics'.

Children like Frank, deprived of literacy unless . . .

After a professional lifetime spent teaching children like Frank, giving lectures to teachers of reading, and researching into the variables that promote and prevent literacy both here and on foreign soil, I believe that revolutionary action in Britain is long overdue. Unless various courses of action are taken now, more children like Frank will be deprived of literacy at a time when the employment prospects for school leavers are at an all time low. Accordingly, I would suggest starting with politicians as they have the power to make changes or at least to publicise the need for them.

1. Unless British politicians call a halt to complacency

Ever since 1953, when I began conducting research on behalf of the N.F.E.R., I have read government reports declaring that there is no room for complacency about illiteracy and standards of literacy. Yet what have British politicians done about complacency except talk a great deal about equal opportunities for all, and about how they approve the modern trend towards greater parental involvement in children's schooling?

What a difference politicians would make if they announced that, nationally, about 20 per cent of children cannot read on entering junior classes, their prognosis is very poor, and thousands of school leavers have joined the functionally illiterate in the adult population which has just been estimated as being well over the previous official estimate of two million (Simonite, 1983). What a difference they would make if, like Professor Swan (1982) at last year's World Congress on Reading, they called adult illiteracy the 'School's Unfinished Business', and voted in Parliament and Local Councils to support measures to help schools 'finish their business' instead of cutting allowances for books, not reducing pupil-teacher ratios in primary schools and so on. Unfortunately, it would seem that Professor Swan is right when, referring to Western Countries, he says, 'In an age of mass communication when minority problems have a way of awakening majority sympathy almost overnight, Adult Illiteracy must rank close to proverbial motherhood and apple pie, as things *not* to be against!'

In view of all this, last year in Singapore it was refreshing to hear Dr Tay Eng Soon, Minister of State for Education, openly declare that the fact that over 600,000 Singaporeans are illiterate can no longer be tolerated and, therefore, a massive training programme has been set in motion. How stimulating to witness the determination of politicians (backed by the English Inspectorate and teaching profession) to ensure the success of such a programme! What is more, the determination to ensure that such a programme is never needed again by improving English teaching from the beginning of children's schooling, and by fostering a reading habit throughout.

Never before, in any country, have I been so impressed by a national drive to eradicate adult illiteracy and to promote literacy in schools. Short of war or other national disaster, it will continue and be successful if the will to succeed is as important as popular psychology would have us believe. Indeed, as I said at this year's I.A.T.E.F.L. Conference (Morris, 1983), 'Singaporeans could well be the first nation to match the Japanese rate of literacy and, remarkably, in English as a second language'.

2. Unless reading 'experts' stop acting as though they had invented the wheel

One of the basic problems in Britain as in other native English-speaking countries is that some reading 'experts' put forward their ideas as though they had just invented the wheel, and this has a disastrous 'bandwagon' effect on classroom practice. Whereas history shows that whatever 'innovations' there are today, except in terms of the new technologies, they are usually old methods, techniques or whatever, brought up to date with new knowledge from relevant disciplines such as linguistics and psychology. For example, the recent move to encourage parent participation in school reading projects which, with other Trustees, I have supported in the making of a new Cadmean Trust film on the subject, is an old idea resuscitated in modern guise. Thus, it is salutary to remember that in *Reading without Tears* (1901), the famous school primer series published here over 80 years ago, the preface is actually addressed to parents (with a note on the need for reading readiness and engaging children in talk), while the 'Notice to Teachers' takes second place. Moreover, the first primer contains pictogram alphabets which, like the 18th and 19th century *Chapbook ABC's* (Stockham, 1974) may usefully be compared with *The Pictogram System* devised by Lyn Wendon (1973) and discussed at this Conference as being appropriate for today's children with special needs.

It is also salutary to remember that in *Songs the Letters Sing* (S.N.D., 1919), which was still being reprinted in 1958, the author's main idea may be compared to *Breakthrough to Literacy* (Mackay *et al.*, 1970) in that 'the blackboard, reading sheets, loose letters and words, and other apparatus should be used first (and for revisal all through), and then the books put into children's hands to be used individually'. Besides individualisation, the same old primer series contains the 'modern' notion of children being 'agents of their own learning' but calls this 'auto education'. The author also unknowingly prepares the way for my own analysis of sound-symbol correspondence in English-English which has led to the linguistics-informed system called 'PHONICS 44'. Her estimate of regularity is 80 per cent, whereas my data yield approximately 90 per cent regularity, depending on the particular vocabulary analysed.

However, what is especially significant about the author of *Songs the Letters Sing* (S.N.D., 1919) is that she assumes that, in 1919, children's needs will already have been met and, hence, the problem of illiteracy will have been solved. This is what she writes:

'It is hoped that, on account of the methodical plan and the unusual number of rules included, the Primers will be useful with late entrants and backward children in Senior Departments, should such exist in these enlightened days.'

I wonder what that author would have thought if she could have heard a group of remedial teachers recently discussing the proportion of children with reading difficulties in their suburban area. The proportion at high school level is 14 per cent and includes this year in one school, for instance, a six foot tall English boy, aged thirteen, who knows absolutely nothing about the alphabet etc.

What we need nowadays is not a constant repetition of old slogans like 'reading for meaning from the beginning' which have been around all my life, but a detailed description of how to get children like Frank to the stage of being able to read for meaning. We also need video-recordings of first class teachers showing how they do this, so that inexperienced teachers can study what is required if children are not to be deprived of literacy.

3. Unless publishers provide appropriate literacy materials

We need the cooperation of publishers too. Thirty years ago they began to ask N.F.E.R. officers to estimate from research findings what percentage of the school population would need proposed books and schemes. It was then very difficult to persuade them to publish for the relatively small percentage of backward readers. Even Stott's *Programmed Reading Kit* (Stott, 1962), though so carefully researched and highly recommended for publication by me, went the rounds of all the major publishers before being taken up successfully by Holmes of Glasgow.

The situation for minority groups gradually improved in the 1960s and 1970s but, recently, it has begun to deteriorate. For instance, Betty Root (1983) recently stated that, 'In the field of reading and language more than 150 new series of books have been published during the last 12 months. Not one of these is designed to help slow readers apart from the occasional and welcome addition to established series (e.g. *Spirals, Bull's Eye, Alpha*).' She then observes, 'In view of all the concern for children with special needs following the publication of the Warnock Report, it is surprising that publishers have seemingly ignored this area of growth. The existing provision is already extremely sparse, and becoming more so as many books disappear from catalogues'.

On top of this, remedial teachers tell me that some schemes urgently need gaps to be filled. But probably also because of the economic situation, there are no signs of this happening. For example, the teachers reported that, although *Hit the Word!* (Cox, 1979), the first book in *The Dorcan Scheme*, is very useful for backward readers in high schools, no further provision to develop rudimentary word-attack skills is made in subsequent books, and the gap is well nigh impossible to bridge. One hard-pressed high-school teacher even begged me to try and do something about materials for older 'remedials', and to incorporate PHONICS 44 in a series for 'remedial remedials' as she called non-readers. 'Please act swiftly if you can', she added, 'to stop us all climbing up the wall with frustration.'

With regard to younger pupils, there is a need for more linguistics-informed material like *Breakthrough to Literacy* (Mackay *et al.*, 1970) and *Language in Action* (Morris, 1974). Until this is provided, teachers have a wide selection of British-made schemes from which to choose what should be the English-English *core* of their developmental programmes. It is therefore unfortunate that publishers import large developmental schemes with admittedly attractive books for the middle school range, but with hopeless look-say primers for infants, at least as far as children like Frank are concerned. In these difficult financial times, it is doubly unfortunate that teachers find this to be the case *after* using up much of their capitation allowance, and they are now understandably invited to purchase the 'extras' which have resulted from their criticisms.

4. Unless teacher-trainers recognise the need for 'explicit' linguistic knowledge

Of course, if children like Frank are not to be deprived of literacy, the critical evaluation of classroom materials should form an essential part of pre-service courses. As a necessary prelude to this and the consideration of methods and media, teacher-trainers should meet the basic need for students to have 'explicit' knowledge of the nature of English and the linguistic processes of listening, speaking, reading and writing. Regrettably, to date, as Mike Riddle (1983), Chairman of the Committee for Linguistics in Education, has pointed out, 'The teacher education system has signally failed to provide its students with adequate knowledge of the linguistic systems (phonetic, syntactic, pragmatic etc.).' He then goes on to say, 'Teachers of reading and language have endured a double deficit: their training has given them no precise and consistent knowledge about language, and their education has conditioned them not to know that such knowledge exists.'

Happily, inservice-training has not been so deficient in this regard. But really only for that very small proportion of teachers who have taken the advanced diploma courses which have been established in a few universities, polytechnics and colleges of education during the last ten years. Even here, there is cause for concern in that the Open University (1982) has announced that its Reading Diploma will end in 1985. Basically, this is because the Open University's first and, to date, only diploma has to be 'self-financing', and there is just not enough money around to keep it going. Hopefully, some substantial funding will be secured for a 'New Improved Language and Reading Course'! Meanwhile, the situation seems to indicate that, in some influential circles, in-service education for the teaching of reading, and *ipso facto* for children like Frank, is well down the list of priorities.

5. Unless 'teacher-dependent' children are detected early

With the possible exception of geniuses, all children need to be taught by knowledgeable, professionally-trained teachers if they are to achieve their reading potential. Those who have supportive parents are fortunate, but no amount of campaigning for parental involvement in education will affect uncaring, inadequate parents. It is important, therefore, to detect early those children who are 'teacher-dependent', and to keep a look-out for signs of physical problems normally taken care of by parents. (Remember how Frank's defective eyesight remained undetected until he was ten years old!) Such children are also more likely to have emotional and cognitive problems. (Frank had the most of all the selected children.) Again early diagnosis and treatment is essential with the aid, in very difficult cases, of the School Psychological Service.

Teacher-dependent children naturally want a lot of individual attention and, like Frank on the roof top, will often go to great lengths to signal this want. For them, especially, there has to be a careful matching of a programme of work to need in terms of their main areas of weakness or relative strengths. In short, children like Frank will be deprived of literacy unless they have experienced, successful teachers who are particularly sensitive to the needs of teacher-dependent pupils.

6. Unless inspectors and advisers demonstrate what is needed

Meeting the teaching needs of children like Frank is, assuredly, a tall order. Moreover, as the Kent Inquiries show, there is a tendency for good readers, who usually have favourable home circumstances, to be given the best teachers. Of course, in an ideal world, all teachers would be good teachers. As it is, something has to be done to ensure that school teaching staffs are suitable for the education of their pupils.

To this end, the British Government has recently published a white paper on *Teaching Quality* (D.E.S., 1983) which, amongst recommendations for improved teacher education etc., draws attention to the future role of H.M. Inspectors in keeping the qualifications of school teaching staffs under review. At present, there is also a hotly debated local authority plan to have senior teachers monitor, for three years, the progress of colleagues who are new recruits to the teaching profession.

Personally, I think that what is greatly needed is for inexperienced teachers to be given practical assistance in the classroom. If head teachers have not sufficient time to do this for every staff member in need of help, as in the case of Frank's primary school headmaster, there should at least be a language post holder who can do so as an 'officially' recognised part of the job. Even more important, in my view, is that inspectors, advisers and teacher-trainers with students on school practice should be able and willing to demonstrate what is needed in classrooms where they think children's teaching needs are not being met.

7. Unless the mass media support teachers for literacy

Undoubtedly, school teaching is a complex, difficult task, especially teaching children like Frank in large classes. In my view, the mass media and, especially, television could do a lot more to help the cause of literacy. Admittedly, there are reading programmes on educational TV, but these often try too hard to be a part of 'show biz'. Probably, what would help the cause of literacy more would be if television generally projected a more favourable image of schools and teachers as well as a more desirable image of literacy itself. Why can't we have more plays in which the ability to read and write of the main character is the key to the happy ending of an exciting drama? Why can't we have more successful people telling us how reading has enriched their lives? Does it always have to be show business people who claim to be or have been 'dyslexic'? After all, some children like Frank could think with some justification, 'Why bother with reading when you can apparently climb the ladder of fame without being able to read properly?'

Next year, at the 21st Anniversary Conference of U.K.R.A. the theme 'Reading and the New Technologies' will provide opportunities for detailed discussion of the contribution that television, microcomputers and so on can make to the cause of literacy. Meanwhile, let us not forget the teacher-dependent children like Frank, who will be deprived of literacy unless the various courses of action outlined by me and other speakers are taken or, at least, tried and tested. Unless also, we all speak on behalf of children like Frank whenever the opportunity arises, and so help to ensure that their special needs are adequately recognised and adequately catered for.

Frank said, 'Reading affects everything you do', and what that sadly-neglected boy said, did and was has affected my professional life ever since. I hope that the story of a boy who had 'little real chance in life' has also touched a responsive chord in yours.

References

CLAY, M. M. (1979) *The Early Detection of Reading Difficulties: A Diagonostic Survey with Recovery Procedures*. London: Heinemann.

COX, J. (1979) *Hit the Word! The Dorcan Scheme*. Walton-on-Thames: Thomas Nelson and Sons.

D.E.S. (1972) *Children with Specific Reading Difficulties* (The Tizard Report). London: HMSO.

D.E.S. (1975) *A Language for Life* (The Bullock Report). London: HMSO.

D.E.S. (1981) *Education Act 1981*. London: HMSO.

D.E.S. (1983) *Teaching Quality*. London: HMSO.

EAST COURT SCHOOL (1983) *Written Language Curriculum: A Guide*.

FERNALD, G. M. (1943) *Remedial Techniques in Basic School Subjects*. New York and London: McGraw Hill.

MACKAY, D. *et al.* (1970) *Breakthrough to Literacy*. London: Longman.

MAKITA, K. (1968) 'The rarity of reading disability in Japanese children'. *American Journal of Orthopsychiatry*, 28, pp. 599–614.

MORRIS, J. M. (1966) *Standards and Progress in Reading*. Slough: N.F.E.R.

MORRIS, J. M. (1974) *Language in Action*. London: Macmillan.

MORRIS, J. M. (1983) 'Teaching children to read and write in Japan and Singapore: A comparison of motives, incentives, and the provisions made to meet basic needs', in *Proceedings of the 17th International Conference of IATEFL* (in press).

MORRIS, J. M. (1983) *Reading without Tears: British reading instruction and research 1921–1982*. The first Anne Leighton Pearce Memorial Lecture. Digby Stuart College (in press).

O'DONNELL, M. and MUNRO, R. (1949) *Janet and John, Book 2*. London: Nisbet.

OPEN UNIVERSITY (1982) 'Demise of the Diploma'. *Readabout No. 4*.

Reading without Tears (1901) London: Longmans, Green and Co.

RIDDLE, M. (1983) 'Signal Failure'. *Times Educational Supplement*, 22 July.

ROOT, B. (1983) 'Leading readers along the right path'. *Times Educational Supplement*, 1 July.

SCHONELL, F. J. and SERJEANT, I. (1939) *Happy Venture Book 1*. Edinburgh: Oliver and Boyd.

SIMONITE, V. (1983) *Literacy and Numeracy – Evidence from the National Child Development Study*. London: Adult Literacy and Basic Skills Unit.

S.N.D. (1919) *The Songs the Letters Sing*. Glasgow: Grant.

STOCKHAM, P. (1974) *Chapbook A B C's*. New York: Dover Publications.

STOTT, D. H. (1962) *Programmed Reading Kit*. Glasgow: Holmes.

SWAN, D. (1982) *The School's Unfinished Business: A Study of Adult Illiteracy in Western Countries with particular reference to Ireland*. Paper presented at the Ninth World Congress on Reading, Dublin.

TANSLEY, P. and PANCKHURST, J. (1981) *Children with Specific Learning Difficulties*. Slough: N.F.E.R.-Nelson.

TASKER, I. (1983) 'A new teaching hope for dyslexic children'. *Ealing Gazette*, 1 July.

WENDON, L. (1973) *The Pictogram System*. Cambridge: Pictogram Supplies.

3 Method and mythod in modern reading philosophy: the handicapping effects of clichéd theory in schools

Chris Nugent

'Teaching reading is a whole lot of fun but reading about reading is a pain in the neck.'
Censored statement from a fed-up teacher, September, 1982.

This address adopts a rather irreverent attitude towards reading, a subject that tends to be hallowed by almost every other speaker in the field. I cannot help this. Like the fed-up teacher just cited I enjoy teaching reading too but I become terribly depressed when *reading* about reading. The seriousness, sophistry and pseudo academy of it all has finally got to me and I feel like I want to break out and talk commonsense.

So my speaking, like my thinking, has increased its leaning towards irreverence and in any event I can find no valid reason for maintaining traditional gentlemanly decorum when both my intellect and my teaching instinct revolt at the para-academic gobbledegook that is paraded and practised by some under a disguise that is called modern reading theory.

THEORY
after
all
is
THEORY

and the cost of a theory that is misapplied is all too often the basic reading skills of the child.

Most of the popular reading theories and their corresponding teaching practices are imported to Australia and to England from America. S.R.A. (a subsidiary of the giant American I.B.M. corporation) provides us with most of our relentless behaviouristic stuff in phonic instruction. Goodman (an American) and Smith (who exported himself from England then Australia to America) provide us with the somewhat 'wobbly' reading process theory which gives us pseudo-benign excuses for relentlessly interrogating children in the belief that *language* experience will produce *reading* experience.

Series R, Reading 360 and even *Young Australia* were all originally American *Look-Say* reading systems that were dressed up with a number of ill considered phonic instructional afterthoughts or with a couple of kangaroo or hedgehog stories and then promoted for local consumption. Donald Graves is an American too.

In summary then we have in the main:
American Based Phonic Systems
American Based Look-Say Systems
American Based Reading Theorists (and Australian and English disciples)
an American Based Language Experience Procedures.
We may yet well be short, however, on . . .
American Based *reading* experience systems.

This is not to decry America. Indeed it is to be congratulated for the size, wealth and efficiency of its publishing machine as well as for the even greater efficacy of its promotion campaigns. Any country that can sell *pet rocks*, for example, has got to be good!

Unfortunately, however, this same wealth and business acumen and ingenuity has lent its talents in recent years to the promotion of methods, materials and philosophies for LITERACY development. These materials, methods and philosophies are often lacking in comprehensiveness, and charismatic envoys seem triennially despatched to spread their incomplete gospels. It is this *incompleteness* that I object to, because it is children who ultimately bear the cost.

Charismatically converted experimenters in schools: Monotheories versus common sense

The obvious *feature* of monotheoretical extremes in teaching fashions is that children are invariably the victims and we tend to notice this feature only after we have (over) zealously implemented the 'new' theory and then counted the *data* at the end of the experiment. Each item of 'data', however, has a smile to offer you if you'd only care to trace its source . . . and I often wonder whether the smile reveals an experimental success story or whether it masks an experimental failure.

SAFEGUARDS for *children* should be built into EVERY trial of a new educational philosophy.

Teacher CONSULTANTS also fall prey to fashion. Indeed, consultants appear more susceptible than classroom teachers to fashion trends if only because they are not usually constrained by the necessity to teach a small group of children upon a *regular* day-to-day basis over a full school year. Hence, recently I had a brief discussion with a teacher consultant who was extolling the virtues of the Donald Graves approach to *writing* as an equally viable approach to the teaching of MATHEMATICS! The discussion with this consultant WAS brief. There was no point in long discussion with fanaticism. I regretted that the person was an adviser to classroom teachers.

There are other extremes too. The 'DAN CAN FAN THE MAN' experts, straight out of the strict behaviourist school, clearly do not appreciate that the development of the child's ability to read CANNOT be described so completely in terms of *graded exercises in phonic analysis*. Many children appear to leap-frog over reading hurdles simply because their intelligence or oral language competence seems to permit them to guess accurately upon the basis of only a small amount of the visual/auditory information on the page.

Such GOOD readers, however, ALL have phonic back-up competencies to fall back on in the event that their guesswork is inaccurate. If children do not have these back-up competencies they are NOT good readers because they do not possess the FULL array of competencies that *all* good readers have. They are therefore DISABLED readers in at least those survival reading settings where text or context does not provide sufficient 'clues' to permit them to guess accurately. Examples of survival literacy tasks include street signs, names, shopping lists and dictionary head words.

Phonic competencies are therefore NOT ONE BIT LESS IMPORTANT than comprehension competencies. The child can have as much oral language competence as you please . . . but if he cannot 'filter' this oral language competence through the (grapho) phonic barrier then he is totally stumped and *without any other recourse* in a very large number of reading settings. It is the responsibility of the teacher to make sure that the child can cope with reading in pretty nearly ANY setting not just those settings where prediction or guesswork can prevail.

And Janet might not be able to read either . . . .

Any approach to rational discussion of phonic competence must be preceded by attempts to break down the barrier of suspicion that often accompanies this subject. In particular this 'barrier breaking' attempt involves putting to serious question the *extent* to which a number of popular notions on reading can actually survive rational scrutiny from alternative perspectives.

In order to labour the point I have labelled each popular notion as a MYTH . . . and I state here and now that my viewpoints do NOT necessarily invalidate the 'myths': they merely challenge the extent to which these popular notions can be *seen to apply* over a large number of reading tasks and reading instructional settings. If there is a theme that I would like to get to in reading education then it would be the one that is epitomised by the expression HORSES FOR COURSES.

Witches and wizards spells slogans and myths

The clichéd views or 'myths' that I refer to are relatively popular among curriculum support agencies and among publishers' sales representatives throughout Australia. From preliminary chats with your people I understand that they are gaining in impetus here too. When writing critical evaluations of these views I faced the dilemma of deciding whether or not I would *name* the specific point or person of origin for each of the 'myths'. I decided against this because the paper then read more like a witch hunt than a series of alternative views on aspects of modern teaching of reading philosophy. We all know too that one person's witch is another person's wizard and there is no point in offending people whilst we question the practicalities.

Here then are some myths and counter-myths where the 'goodies' only are mentioned by name.

Myth 1: Poor learner readers rely too heavily on phonics

The *poor* learner readers that I personally test as a reading consultant, also tend to know A LOT LESS about their phonics than the *good* learner readers that I test. When children KNOW their phonics they do not *need* to rely on them because they *know* them (Nugent, 1977). Additionally, research by Juel (1980) shows firstly that GOOD learner readers actually read what is put in front of them whereas the POOR learner readers tend to *guess more from context than do good learner readers.* Juel suggested that this was probably because the poorer readers did not know sufficient about the conventions of print to do otherwise.

Myth 2: Good learner readers rely more on context and less on phonics

Stanovich in a later edition of Reading Research Quarterly (1980) states that good readers are separated from poor readers MORE by their superior word recognition skills and phonic skills than by their ability to 'use' context. Additionally Jorm and Share (1982) show that good readers are by far better than poor readers at using *phonic skills as an independent* SELF-TEACHING *device*, and which of ALL teachers would NOT like to foster children's independence in reading?

Myth 3: There is only one reading process

Actually the so called Reading Process (singular) quite clearly involves a *number* of processes such as visual processing, semantic processing, syntactic processing, phonological (speech sound) processing and motor (articulatory) processing. There is also an argument for the involvement of a further 'higher' level of processing that we can call intellectual processing and at this level of processing, we are stimulated to think about much more than the mere semantics on the page that we have just read. Reading in this sense is much more than that which meets the eyes.

The point that I want to make, however, is that there are MANY processes in the so called reading process and to make a reference to the reading process without specifying *which* of the reading processes you are referring to, is probably incomplete academy.

Myth 4: Reading is an integrated process

As I have explained above, reading is more probably an integrated GROUP of processes. This is not semantic nit-picking. If we recognise that reading (rather like cars) is made up of a number of separate parts, then we are in a position to 'fix' any individual part that might break down on our way to our destination. In a car the engine, gearbox and differential are 'integrated' to produce the outcome that we will call locomotion. When reading, the major components of semantics, syntax and graphophonics are 'integrated' to produce the outcome that we call understanding . . . and a malfunction on ANY component has the potential to cause a breakdown whilst reading or whilst 'driving a car'.

Whilst it is certainly true that reading is a group of processes that are integrated, ALL of these processes have to be in FULL working order unless we are going to be satisfied with readers that are LESS than fully competent.

Myth 5: Reading is a psycholinguistic guessing game

Reading does have the POTENTIAL to be a psycholinguistic guessing game in those instances where something MEANINGFUL actually precedes the guesswork. However, earlier in this article and elsewhere I have listed a large number of non-test-aided reading tasks where if you guess you will NOT be right and will therefore FAIL TO READ. And when CHILDREN fail to read, it's no game.

Myth 6: Reading is getting meaning from print

Only the foolhardy would attempt to refute the proposition that the main FUNCTION of reading is to get meaning from print but only the very hasty should try to *define* the *operation* of a whole group of processes by simply stating only its main function.

The main function of a car, for example, is transport but if I define a car as 'transport' I do not in actual fact tell anyone what a car IS, if only because I fail to point out how you can *distinguish* the car from a *camel* which also can be defined as 'transport'. The *definition* of what reading IS, therefore, as 'getting meaning from print' leaves a lot to be desired. Though the definition might be seen to apply quite clearly in some circumstances.

Myth 7: Reading is processing language in meaningful chunks

Again, we have an attempt to define what the essence of reading IS by simply stating what its main FUNCTION is. An advisory experience of mine exemplifies the shortsightedness that is embodied in this type of thinking.

About 12 months ago I was in a school where one child in every THREE in all the grades III and IV did not have the skills embodied in reading three-letter (CVC) words. Nor could these children read the alphabet charts that were up on the walls around the rooms, nor could they read the language experience wall stories, not could they read a large number of items on 'meaningful' shopping lists. Now, what I am trying to say is the following:

1. Competent readers can read words in ANY setting, not just in meaningful chunks.
2. The ability to read words in meaningful chunks to any great extent, necessitates that the child can cope also with the (graphophonic) BITS that go together to make up the CHUNKS. That is, it is categorically *wrong* to think that the child can get to the stage of *mastering* the CHUNKS without a good knowledge of the bits.

Myth 8: Reading represents meaning not sound

Reading represents (in the sense 'entails') both sound as well as meaning. It is pretty hard to imagine what 'soundless' speech would sound like. Whether we like it or not, writing is at least in part a substitute for *speech*, and reading is in part a substitute for *listening*. Sound IS involved in speaking and listening, therefore writing AND reading represent sound *as well as* meaning.

Myth 9: The total reading process

Nobody knows what the TOTAL reading process IS. People who refer to the TOTAL reading process (clearly trying to imply THEY know substantially what it is) are either supremely optimistic or are contaminated with an overdose of mis-skewed reading theory.

Myth 10: Reading is language processing

When you read you are in actual fact processing the language (or words) that somebody has written down for you to process. Therefore reading is PRINT processing that is combined with language RE-PROCESSING. Assertions to the *contrary* would imply both that reading can occur *without* print and that the writer didn't *process* the language as he or she *wrote* it; and either of these contrary propositions is ludicrous. An exercise in clear thinking would really help some promoters of theory.

Myth 11: Reading is learned from whole to part

The truth of this assertion really does depend upon how the child learns or how and when the child is taught. If we are to face the facts of vast and conclusive American and English studies then we will have conclusive evidence as to the clear superiority (for some purposes) of PART TO WHOLE teaching and learning in reading.

Myth 12: Learning to read is developmental and it follows logically from learning to talk

Earlier I referred to a group of grade III and IV children who did not have the skills embodied in reading three-letter (CVC) words. These children had spent up to three and four years with a singularly devoted school staff that had adhered to this (naturalistic) philosophy. The school had been rather avant garde in this respect some years before. Oddly ALL of the children could TALK well before they commenced formal schooling in reading. Fortunately I was able to intercept their 'naturalistic' reading education with a behaviouristic additive called COHESIVE PHONIC DEVELOPMENT. They have all since STARTED to learn to read independently. They are progressing well, many showing signs of self-esteem for the first time and into the bargain showing many fewer examples of anti-social behaviour.

Now that these children are developing SKILLS for coping with print, their READING is starting to catch up with the level of TALK that they possessed well before they started school. Learning to read does NOT in many instances develop *quite* so 'naturally' from learning to talk unless there is also a modicum of finely graded direct instruction.

Myth 13: A phonic programme should develop naturally out of a child's reading

At this date some hundreds of (reputable) studies involving *millions* of children and *billions* of dollars have all served to demonstrate that phonic instruction with a pre-planned, finely graded and COHESIVE sequence, produce better overall results in reading and spelling than ANY OTHER type of reading instructional system for beginning readers. I am NOT wishing to imply that we should all once again climb on the phonic instructional bandwagon for all children. Rather, it is to say that if we ARE going to teach phonics to those children that NEED them, then we would be more responsible to give these children the *type* of phonic instructional programme that a vast pool of research data shows to be the most effective.

Myth 14: *The natural language approach makes reading easier for* all *children*

This has NOT been the case in a number of schools where I have tested a LARGE number of children . . . . In these cases there has been a distinct slip up between this 'naturalistic' slogan and its implementation by (single) teachers who face up to thirty (single) children each day.

Let's face facts, the much extolled 'natural' language approach requires a LOT of work with each INDIVIDUAL child . . . or it CANNOT lay true claim to being a 'natural' language approach. NOW, assuming that the teacher has 30 children to teach reading to on an *individual* basis, and all of this within a 60 minute reading period each day, this (in fairness) amounts to two minutes per child per day each week. And a mere TWO minutes of time in which to find where the child is AT as well as to organise for and *deliver* 'natural language' instruction (in its true form) is just NOT possible. Anyone that asserts that it IS possible is suffering from self delusion.

The 'natural' language approach, however, just MIGHT make things easier for all children if only you had enough TIME to implement it at the 'natural' individualised level. I estimate that anywhere between 15 to 45 minutes PER INDIVIDUAL CHILD PER DAY would make it a 'workable' proposition. All we would need to do then is reduce the pupil to teacher ratio in schools to about one third of its current level. Imagine the COST! Naturalistic approaches are 'nice' when workable but 'nasty' when not.

Myth 15: *Readers process print by sampling, prediction and testing*

A little publicised fact needs to become better known here. The truth is that it takes the competent reader of prose passages MORE TIME TO MAKE A PREDICTION than it does accurately to *read* the word in the first place. This is not to say that prediction doesn't occur. Rather it is to say that its value as a mechanism in normal fluent prose (passage) reading has been overrated by those that overrated the meaning getting side of the reading processes (see Stanovich, 1980).

Additionally, specific semantic and syntactic predictions are NOT usually possible in either:

1. those SURVIVAL literacy tasks listed earlier in this paper

or

2. semantically unhelpful contexts such as JANET SAT ON THE _____ _____ .

Furthermore, we really have no clear idea as to precisely what factors actually put the word into the contextually-aided (or predictable) category. Given that syntactic and semantic prediction is not operative in many situations, let us now look at the notion of graphophonic prediction.

Two internationally acclaimed writers in the field have written a 21-page chapter on the notion of *predicting* graphophonic cues in reading. This is very sad. You see, apart from the situation in which you can predict that a 'U' will follow a 'Q' predictions in reading are *semantically* or *syntactically* initiated. International experts who wish to elaborate upon the notion of predicting graphophonics, need first to revisit the study of the *Structure of English Orthography* with particular reference to the following issues:

1. the graphic determinants of the predictability of the graphophoneme
2. the phonological determinants of the predictability of the graphophoneme
3. how meaning-seeking VARIABLES assist in the *confirmation* but never prediction of the two CONSTANTS above.

I DO APOLOGISE FOR THE VERBIAGE but it is necessary to set such persons RIGHT so that in turn they might correct certain features of their published and widely distributed works.

Myth 16: Guesswork in reading is nearly always goodwork

I will shortly demonstrate that repeatedly encouraging the child to GUESS is no better than a pseudo-benign recipe for child interrogation. I explain exactly why this is the case. As a preliminary, however, it is perhaps advisable to detail the Language Experience technique that is *commonly* recommended for reading interrogation. Do not forget that this procedure should ideally be fitted to occur within the TWO MINUTES ONLY time allotment referred to when I described Myth No. 14.

The child who is experiencing difficulty with a word should be given the following instructions . . .
READ ON TO THE END OF THE SENTENCE and see if you can tell what the word ought to be
READ FROM THE BEGINNING OF THE SENTENCE to see if you can tell what the word ought to be
TELL ME IN YOUR WORDS what this part of the message is about. Now, do you think you know what the word is?
READ OUT AS MUCH OF THE SENTENCE AS YOU CAN. Now, does that sound like language? Do people talk like that? Can you tell me what the word might be?

Finally, the authors of the above FRAMEWORK FOR INTERROGATION do concede that AFTER the interrogation (i.e. above questioning) it is reasonable that the teacher should read for children what they cannot read for themselves

The *technique* above originates of course from the land of extremes. It has potential for benign sadism and this is why.

When children GUESS answers and then GUESS again and then GUESS on top of this, this means that they have THOUGHT once then RE-THOUGHT and then RE-THOUGHT again.

In other words GUESSWORK is the product of THINKWORK and it usually occurs when the thinking processes do not have enough *basic information* to work on. Additionally do not forget that BETWEEN the guesses there is *pausing* time within which the child is thinking more rapidly than usual and thereby *heightening his or her apprehension* about non-learning. When the child is guessing too much he or she is actually thinking too much. He or she needs to be given more basic information.

In reading and writing and phonic work then, children must be 1. TAUGHT to use their brains (i.e. think logically) AND 2. TRAINED to use their eyes (i.e. perceive correctly basic information).

It is therefore perfectly legitimate to say to the habitually guessing child something like the following:

'My goodness, you ARE guessing too much today. This means that you are *trying too hard to remember* or you are *using your brains too much* for the time being. Let me teach you how to use your EYES *before* you use your brains' OR, more simply
'Look kid! Leave your *brains* out of this for the time being. They're just getting in the way! Let me teach you how to use your eyes *first*.'

All of this, of course, is technically imprecise from the standpoint of reading theory. But then again, none of the reading theories that I have read of seem to give much of a damn about the specific detrimental emotional dynamics of the guesswork process!

For goodness sake, if it is your intention to teach rather than to interrogate, make attempts to put the information IN rather than test first to see whether you can get it out!

When, for example, children are clearly confused as to what they are supposed to do or SAY in response to either a reading or sounding-out task, I advise teachers to say something like the following:

'It looks like I haven't TAUGHT you well enough because you are still a bit unsure . . . . So let me teach you again please.'
OR
'If you don't get enough right answers, it's because I haven't given you the right stuff to do. This makes me a poor teacher.
In other words if you make too many mistakes it's MY fault *not* yours. It means simply that I haven't been smart enough to teach you in the right way.'

When teachers say things such as this to children (and mean it) it helps immeasurably to remove the child's *apprehension about NON LEARNING.*

The child AT ease
learns WITH ease . . . well, most of the time anyway.

Teachers must realise that the modern RELENTLESS push to meaning, meaning and meaning has the potential to cause as much damage to children as the relentless push in yesteryear to the TESTING rather than TEACHING of a rigorously predetermined course of phonic instruction.

Myth 17: Readers read for meaning

Please add to this statement a further one to the effect that readers often GET the meaning only AFTER they have correctly READ the materials in the first place. In actual fact the MEANING side of reading can either PRECEDE the reading or FOLLOW IT.

Myth 18: All readers make mistakes . . . the right might be wrong

Right is right
Wrong is wrong
Right might be partly wrong
Wrong is nearly always partly right
      BUT
Right is NEVER wrong

Myth 19: The language experience approach is a structured approach ·

On some occasions and with some teachers this might be correct. But in the largest ever educational experiment conducted in the United States, the language experience approach *ranked* as follows with seven other instructional philosophies.

	RANK							
AREA TESTED	8th	7th	6th	5th	4th	3rd	2nd	1st
Self Concept			*					
Reading				*				
Maths					*			
Spelling			*					
Language					*			

The graph above is really quite a flattering one for language experience because it seems to indicate that as a performer which gets results it hovers around the 'middle' mark when compared with other philosophies. However, even when language experience achieved the dubious distinction of FOURTH place, the winner was ahead by three and four TIMES the necessary degree of statistical difference.

The cost of the experiment cited above was 500 million American dollars with 30 to 50 *million* dollars being allocated to the EVALUATION ALONE. The graph given above was taken from summary information written by Becker and Engelmann whereas the RANKING was determined by TWO independent evaluative bodies (House *et al.* and ABT Associates, 1978). Separate (more CONVENTIONAL) analysis by Bereiter and Kurland (1978) noted that the American version of language experience (code named TEEM) was the MOST UNRELIABLE of all systems studied. Also, the margin of statistical difference between the approaches was very much BIGGER STILL in this still more conventional analysis!

Hence any assertion that 'LANGUAGE EXPERIENCE IS A STRUCTURED APPROACH' needs to be tempered by the FACTS as we know them. Proponents of this view should be required to show *where* the system is and what it *does*.

Please note from the graph, for example, where it rated on a very basic issue such as the SELF CONCEPT of the children that were TAUGHT with it. To date I have been able to discern NO SIGNIFICANT differences between the Australian Brand of Language Experience and the American Brand of Language Experience. (You know, basic philosophy, classroom procedures and all *that* stuff). Has anybody in Great Britain attempted a comparison?

Myth 20: *Hierarchies of symbol sound correspondence in reading should be avoided*

The TWO winners in the conventionally analysed version of the experiment just described were two phonically based ones. These winners won by a huge margin. The plain fact is that if you should happen to decide that children should get the basic literacy skills that accrue from a knowledge of phonics, then the VERY BEST TYPE of way is the one which has finely graded steps, sufficient reinforcement at each step and a COHESIVE sequence. There are some hundreds of other studies that come to similar conclusions. All of these studies are academically reputable. Because in ANY diet stands a better chance of maintaining good health.

Myth 21: *New knowledge of reading does not support sounding out as a major strategy for identifying unknown words*

The proof of the pudding is in the digestion rather than the eating. Vast survey research AS WELL AS recent research into the *reading processes* have demonstrated this particular myth to be incalculably incorrect. Proponents of this view are wrong. Regular reading of at least *Reading Research Quarterly* would provide up to date information.

Come to think of it...down to earth commonsense tells you they are wrong. Have you ever travelled to new places and seen new words? How did you work them out? Have you ever looked down the head words in a dictionary and 'read' many words that you hadn't heard before? How DID you work them out when no guesswork is possible in this setting?

To be kind, assertions that 'sounding' out is NOT a major strategy for working out unknown words can be supported only by those that have NOT looked at a sufficiently COMPREHENSIVE array of DIFFERENT everyday routine reading tasks which ALL competent readers have to cope with.

Myth 22: *You don't need graded reading schemes*

In summary, the dubious qualifications of the language experience approach to reading are as follows:

1. It has classroom managerial problems that are very serious to downright impossible for the teaching of basic information to many children who need to be taught with finely graded steps.
2. The theoretical premises on which it is based are insecure in the extreme being based upon mythmanagement rather than mismanagement.
3. When subjected to trials and scientific comparison with a *comprehensive* array of other teaching of reading methods, it was a DRAMATIC FLOP.

Despite these glaring inadequacies, some of the proponents of language experience suggest that it might substantially replace both CONVENTIONALLY GRADED READING SYSTEMS as well as phonically graded ones. One would have thought that after all the dramatic failures of the language experience approach, its proponents would have had the caution to:

1. Face facts
2. Admit to the faults of the approach
3. Strengthen the approach at its proven weak points
and then
4. Re-launch it.

THE CHILDREN IN OUR SCHOOLS DESERVE NO LESS.

Summary comments . . . the practicalities versus the dimensions of dogma

I am most sensitively aware that this paper has not given due acknowledgement to the benefits of the procedural DIVERSIFICATION which would constitute the hallmark of difference between phonic reading systems and language experience procedures. This omission of mine is excusable only in light of the all-persuasive sway of the slogans that make up the fabric of the anti-phonic banner. These slogans fortunately are much more clearly seen in the modern *literature* than in the 'average' of the *classrooms*. So our saving grace as reading teachers then may well be that our teachers are much more constrained by classroom realities than are our writers, consultants and curriculum designers.

The length of this paper does not permit me to enumerate all of the truly appealing features of the exceptional language experience classroom. I have, however, submitted to U.K.R.A. Journal an article that has been submitted for publication in an Australian journal too. In this article and in others I have written, the theme is predominant that I will support BIAS of any type in reading programming. But I cannot support the slogan assisted BIGOTRY that has been the focus of my analysis in this address. My concern is NOT quite so much that extremes throw the baby out with the bathwater, but more that *hyper*-extremes throw out the plumbing fixtures as well.

I end with a slogan of my own:

BIAS IS SUPPORTABLE
BIGOTRY IS NOT.

References

ABT ASSOCIATES (1977) *Education as Experiment: A Planned Variation Model*, Vol. IV A. Cambridge, Ma.

ANDERSON, R. B. (1978) 'Pardon Us: But What Was That Question Again?' in *Harvard Educational Review*, 48 (2). Cambridge, Ma.

BARMBY, S., LAWRY, F. and POWELL, D. (1982) *Real Reading: A Focus on Meaning*. Ringwood, Victoria: Ringwood Special Education Unit.

BECKER, C., ENGELMANN, S. and CARNINE, D. (1979) *Direct Instruction Technology: Recent Findings*. Oregon University.

BEREITER, C. and KURLAND, M. (1978) *A Constructive Look at Follow-Through Results*. Ontario: Ontario Institute for Studies in Education.

GOODMAN, Y. and BURKE, C. (1980) *Reading Strategies: Focus on Comprehension*. New York: Holt, Rinehart and Winston.

HOPKINS, H. (1977) *From Talkers to Readers the Natural Way*. Ashton Scholastic.

HOUSE, E. *et al.* (1978), in *Harvard Educational Review*, 48(42).

JUEL, C. (1980) 'Comparison of word identification strategies with varying context and reader skill', in *Reading Research Quarterly*, 3.

JORM, A. and SHARE, D. (1982) *Phonological Recoding and Reading Acquisition*. Deakin University, Australia: Psychology Department.

LATHAM, R. and SLOAN, P. (1981) *Teaching Reading Is . . .* London: Nelson.

NUGENT, C. K. (1973) *Interaction Effect Among English Letter Combinations*. Unpublished B.Ed. paper (copy lodged with U.K.R.A. library).

NUGENT, C. K. (1978) 'Reply to the Goodmans. A series of counter arguments'. Paper sent to Victoria Special Education Units. Also in *Australian Journal of Remedial Education*.

NUGENT, C. K. (Submitted for publication) 'Two-way phonics for language experience'.

NUGENT, C. K. (1981) 'In support of language experience and of Johnny getting systematic help from both sides', in *Primary Education Journal*.

NUGENT, C. K. (1982a) 'Pardon me for being adamant but there are different children out there', in *SPELOSA Bulletin*, Glenside, S. Australia.

NUGENT, C. K. (1982b) 'Curriculum induced disablements in reading'. *Victorian Teachers Union Journal*.

NUGENT, C. K. (1983a) 'Language experience and the reading experience crunch'. *Primary Education Journal*.

NUGENT, C. K. (1983b) *Planning Illiteracy?; A Sporting Chance to Reading*. Richmond, Victoria: Primary Education Publishing Co.

PULVERTAFT, A. (1978) *Carry on Reading*. Ashton Scholastic.

SMITH, F. (1978) *Reading*. Cambridge, C.U.P.

STANOVICH, K. (1980) 'Toward an interactive compensatory model of individual differences of reading fluency'. *Reading Research Quarterly*, 16, pp. 32–71.

YELLAND, G. (1981) 'Word recognition processes in skilled and beginning readers'. Unpublished. Monash University, Psychology Department.

Part II

4 The child and the book: exceptions and the rule

Nicholas Tucker

Adults who press books on children very often have little idea whether the particular title in mind is below, at, or well above any individual child's present capacities. When a mistake is made, it can sometimes be an important one. To give a child a book he or she considers as silly can be an insult quite as bad as attempting to resurrect any hated baby-talk they have now proudly grown away from. A book that is too difficult may simply confirm a child in the belief that literature is a lost cause, since children read for pleasure rather than to improve themselves, and books that make them feel inadequate can provoke resentment as well as boredom. No wonder, therefore, that so many parents as well as teachers often ask for specific advice on this score, given they seldom get more from the publishers than a 'suggested reading age' – if that – on a book's inside flap to guide them and this often of a suspiciously elastic nature. ('Suitable for children between 8–14.')

It was largely because of this situation that I eventually decided to write my own study, *The Child and the Book; a Literary and Psychological Exploration* (Cambridge University Press, 1981; paperback edition 1983). In this, I bracketed what was known about children's intellectual and social development at various ages along with the type of literature that would seem most appropriate at any particular time. The fiction I chose to illustrate this last point was not always from great literary masterpieces for children but more from those perennial best-sellers that really did seem to offer something which, at certain stages, a lot of children wanted. Now that my book has been published, there is nothing in it I would radically wish to revise. And yet, I am nagged by the feeling that the developmental norms I described in children and their corollary in children's fiction, still do not explain anything like the whole of a child's responses to any book, nor indeed the whole of any book's appeal to a particular child.

To give an example: smaller children, I pointed out, prefer stories that are not too long told in a language they can understand. I would still defend this view; concentration among the young is limited, and incomprehensible language is a bore for everyone. Yet how does this explain the tendency of truly favourite authors like Beatrix Potter to get away, every now and again, with a fine-sounding word in her stories quite unknown to children? Or the way that nursery rhymes, equally successful with the young, use make-up language (Humpty-dumpty), archaisms ('curds and whey'), remote place-names ('Three wise men of Gotham'), and ancient counting systems ('Eena meena mina mo'). None of this will be already familiar to children, yet it soon becomes so after a few hearings. Does this contradict my previously stated, surely quite unexceptionable developmental norm, that children prefer language they can easily understand, both in books and with people?

The answer, of course, lies in the definition of a norm, and this perhaps is something I could originally have brought out more strongly. As it is, any norm only describes what generally happens; there will always be room for exceptions. In the case of child development, such exceptions take on extreme importance. Childhood, by definition, is never static; within it, children constantly edge forward on some fronts while keeping others relatively unchanged. Seen like this, children's preference for the odd exotic word or phrase among a mass of better-known ones becomes more explicable. While prose that is made up entirely of exciting, unknown words would be of little use to them, prose that always sticks determinedly to words they know well can fail to stimulate that other part of a child anxious for something new.

In fact, the more I look at books for children, the more I am struck by the way that the best authors tend to get this delicate equation between conservatism and innovation more or less right, not just for language but where other reading responses are concerned. Take the whole issue of plot predictability. Smaller children tend to get puzzled by stories with complex plots; accordingly, favourite tales for this stage often revolve around simple stereotyped situations, heavily repetitive but comforting to younger readers in their predictable symmetry. In fairy stories, the 'rule of three' helps accustom readers to the fact that it will generally be three wishes, three tasks or three riddles in such stories, and that the third will always be the most important. Where non-fairy, more domestic tales for this age are concerned, children will soon get to know other patterns true from story to story: how precious lost objects generally turn up by the last page; how naughty, rebellious children are usually put right by events; or how longed for wishes are most often realised, at least in some form. Armed with this type of knowledge, even quite young readers can have a good go at answering rhetorical questions of the 'And who do you think was there?' type that crop up so regularly towards the end of such tales, and in classrooms can sometimes be heard chanting the 'right' answer in concert with the triumphant tones of their reader-teacher.

So far, so good; children after all are newcomers to everything, literary or otherwise, and it will take practice and possibly regular repetition of particular favourite stories before they feel thoroughly at home with the pretty well invariable forms of early fiction for their age group. Yet at the same time, the same children can occasionally relish stories that break such conventions. Children clearly like tall stories, for example, and in the case of a popular author like Dr Seuss they are quite happy to take on his weird monsters and strange culinary inventions such as goose-moose burgers, such a contrast to the cups of tea dispensed by Mrs Tiggywinkle in the more ordered world of Beatrix Potter. Where fairy stories are concerned, selections from the *Arabian Nights* have always been well liked, even though this means that the

Western-style get up and go philosophy already familiar to children from European fairy tales is largely replaced by something much closer to Eastern fatalism. But lack of a happy ending each time, plus the feeling of personal helplessness at the whim of an inscrutable universe, does not necessarily seem to put children off, however different the tone is here from the breezy optimism found in Joseph Jacobs' *English Fairy Tales* or the dogged belief in personal success in tales retold by the brothers Grimm.

Even so, children still do not endlessly enjoy topsy-turvy humour or any other systematic distortion of more predictable expectations in fiction. They will continue to have to learn the norms before they appreciate the abnorms, and too much iconoclasm in any art can eventually lead to shapeless incoherence. But the fact remains: children do seem to enjoy variation as well as theme, as in their reactions to character descriptions in fiction. On the whole, smaller children do not normally respond well to complex literary characters, given that it is much easier for them – and often for us as well – to think in terms of extremes rather than in more indeterminate shades. When they get older, it does become easier for them to accept 'role-drift' in characterisation, where the not so good can occasionally show redeeming features half way through, while the heroic may sometimes reveal an unexpected Achilles' Heel, if not two feet of clay. The classic example of more complex characterisation of this type in children's fiction occurs in *Treasure Island*, where Long John Silver is only half a villain, the potentially tragic figure of Ben Gunn turns rapidly into a comedian (well brought out by Spike Milligan when he acted the part) and the Squire and the Doctor reveal themselves as a little too greedy for their or other people's own good.

Infants cannot usually take on such subtleties, and *Treasure Island* has accordingly never been a favourite story among younger readers. Yet once again, it is quite wrong to insist that infants therefore only like characters who never change, wear their hearts on their sleeves, and can always easily be labelled. No less an authority than Bruno Bettelheim, for example, suggested in *The Uses of Enchantment* that one reason for fairy tale popularity with infants was precisely the way that main characters are presented as either good or bad and stay that way through to the end. A moment's thought would surely reveal a more complex picture. In *Beauty and the Beast*, Beauty grows in understanding while the Beast develops from the horrific to the pitiable. In *King Thrushbeard*, the haughty young bride has to make a similar personal journey from pride to humility.

These are not stock, absolute characters, yet infants seem to like them well enough, just as they can also enjoy more rounded, realistic fictional portraits of children their own age. In Dorothy Edwards' stories about *My Naughty Little Sister*, for example, the young lady mentioned in the title has as her best friend a little boy always referred to as 'Bad Harry'. But it would be inaccurate to imagine that such pejorative adjectives really described anything truly 'bad' to a young audience. Harry and his little girl friend are certainly mischievous, yet they usually try to make it all up by the end and can almost always be won round by superior adult guilt-producing cunning. What emerges from these stories, therefore, is nothing like the continuously disruptive behaviour of Enid Blyton's gollywog characters, or the mayhem caused by the young tear-aways found in the *Beano* and *Dandy* comics. In contrast, the naughty little sister and Bad Harry are subtle, many-sided characters, who do not fit easily into any particular moral pigeon-hole, yet they remain very popular with their young readers.

There are other ways in which children seem to welcome deviations from orthodox, moral norms from time to time. While wild animals usually appear as fearsome objects in fairy tales, for example, the same stories – or modern picture books – will sometimes offer a contrasting view featuring various happy lions, pacific bulls or nurturant wolves, with children quite able to accept such contradictory images from one story to another. While young readers generally like justice to be seen to be done where 'bad' characters step seriously out of moral line, the American psychologist E. Turiel also claims that the same children are willing to discuss more complex moral issues arising from a story, and will not always foreclose on any simple concept of reciprocal justice for the wrong-doer, come what may. Looking at an older age-group, readers here often enjoy stories rich in 'cognitive conceit' – David Elkind's phrase for the common early adolescent fantasy that most of them are really far brighter than those maddening, out of touch adults in their lives who always think they know best. While this fantasy is reflected in legions of stories of the *Emil and the detectives* type, featuring pubescent gangs going it alone, there are also other stories from E. Nesbit onwards revolving around the failure of children to foresee just those snags in certain adventures that adults sharing the same story understand so much better.

All this is not to suggest that most children are constantly ready for a consistently more complex view in their fiction. Adult masterpieces that attempt a really fully rounded description of childhood, as in Henry James' *What Maisie Knew* or L. P. Hartley's *The Shrimp and the Anemone* will always be too hard for younger readers. But while it is valuable to know the type of fictional norms children generally do find it easiest to understand at various ages, we should also remember that another part of them may always want to advance such norms into something a little more complex, not all at once, but every now and again while other familiar fictional attitudes still remain constant. An analogy here would be those fruit machines where punters can 'hold' a line of three symbols intact while remaining free to spin the fourth. In the case of reading, children may sometimes, in the course of an otherwise conventional, predictable story, be led to consider that certain characters or attitudes even so are really a little more complex than they sometimes have appeared so far.

There are, of course, players of fruit machines who dislike any element of choice, just as there are child readers content to stick with a writer like Enid Blyton who never advances any line of thought away from current childish clichés at all. On the other hand, there are also gamblers who find all fruit machines boring and limited; the analogy here could be those precocious child readers who quickly tire of most children's fiction, even those books which do offer an occasionally more sophisticated view of human affairs. Here, such readers generally cannot wait to get on to the complexities of adult fiction, although they may relish meanwhile more difficult writers for children such as Alan Garner, William Mayne and Leon Garfield.

To sum up

If any aspiring children's writer was still kind enough to think they could refer to my *The Child and the Book* for some guidance as to where exactly they should pitch the material for any projected book, I would tell them the following cautionary story. In 1971 the great Swiss psychologist Jean Piaget was aked to help with a book for children by a French artist and author Étienne Delessert. In particular, Delessert wanted Piaget – who at that time knew more about developmental psychology than anyone else in the world – to tell him how infants aged five to six understood and interpreted various natural phenomena such as the sun, the moon, clouds, winds and so on. Piaget was ready to oblige and, with the help of a collaborator, infants of this age were duly questioned, with their answers woven loosely into a text reflecting their most typical ideas in the course of a short, simple story, entitled *Comment la souris reçoit une pierre sur la tête et découvre le monde (How the mouse was hit on the head by a stone and so discovered the world*, translated into English for an American publisher, but so far unpublished in the U.K.).

It would be nice to say that the book was a success, given all this prior preparation. Its illustrations are certainly charming, particularly a collage on the last page consisting of some of the new things the mouse was going to discover in her future travels which includes a charming portrait of Piaget himself. The text, however, is woefully pedestrian, composed chiefly of different explanations as to how exactly this or that originated and what was its present function. The reasoning displayed by the mouse may well follow how infants think about the same things, but when such exact echoes of childish thought are reproduced *in toto* and without development the end result can seem very tedious, both for child and for adult readers.

So while it is essential for an author to know or else feel for a child's typical psychological outlook at any one time, only instinct can tell him or her when a text should go along with an audience and when it should strike out in what may look like a relatively new direction. That is why so many really good books for children are mixtures of the stimulating and the reassuring; that is why they can only be analysed in terms of developmental norms up to a point. What happens between them and their young readers after that, and whether the way the story pushes forward is always the particular way any one child may be ready for at that moment, is something that can only be tackled, if at all, on an individual basis. To that extent, global surveys of the type I attempted in my book only take us so far when it comes to mediating interactions between children and their favourite literature, though I would still argue that even this fairly short journey in understanding is worthwhile. At least, after having completed it, we should know how far we have come as well as how far we still have to go before reaching anything like full understanding of what happens when one child reads one book.

References

BETTELHEIM, B. (1976) *The Uses of Enchantment; the Meaning and Importance of Fairy Tales*. London: Thames and Hudson.

DELESSERT, E. (1980) *Comment la souris reçoit une pierre sur la tête et découvre le monde*. Paris: Éditions Gallimard. (Available in the U.K. from Baker Book Services, Little Mead, Alfold Rd, Cranleigh, Surrey GU6 8NH.)

TUCKER, N. (1981) *The Child and the Book; a Literary and Psychological Exploration*. Cambridge: Cambridge University Press.

5 Improving reading by matching children's books with the reading ability, interests and needs of the students

Dr Richard Bamberger

The basis of the success of our work for children's reading lies in the awareness of the importance of reading for the mental and spiritual development of the child and for our culture in general. We, therefore, cannot emphasise enough the value of good reading in all branches of education.

Thinking of the importance of reading we deplore that so many children grow up without experiencing the benefit of books. They are handicapped in their intellectual and human development. This may be stated almost mathematically in the growth of the vocabulary of the individual child. In interpreting the results of vocabulary tests I came to the following conclusion: children that do not read at all enlarge their vocabulary in one year by about 500 words, with average readers this number rises to about 1000, and children that read one or more books a week will enlarge their vocabulary within one year by 2000 words and even more. Of course, this is not simply a result of reading books; there is an interaction of different causes.

Why do we have so little success in our efforts to build up permanent reading habits? I will provide a few answers to that question.

In our educational work we were (and are) guided by the old slogan: 'The right book for the right child at the right moment'.

However, despite this, we did not have much success in bringing children and books together. It seemed that we did not know enough about children's reading interests. This is why we attached great importance to the study of reading preferences. (Bamberger, 1975)

We now know a great deal about children's likes and dislikes in reading. Theoretically! But in practice we do not always apply this insight to the individual child. The task remains to note the reading development of each child and to consider the great differences in their interests and habits.

In Austria we have developed an instrument that proved quite helpful in this respect: *The reader's passport!* This is a little booklet in which the children write all the stories and books they have read. They add numbers – from 1 to 5 – to each title, denoting whether they liked the story: 1 for 'very much', 5 for 'not at all'.

Interpreting the books with '1' we find out what sort of reader a child is. Does the child prefer fantasy, realistic stories, adventures, non-fiction, problems etc.?

But, alas, many children had nothing to prefer, because they did not read at all. Our insight into the nature of reading interests and needs did not help us.

On examining the question why these children did not read at all, we found the answer in the following paradox:

Many children do not read books, because they cannot read; and they cannot read, because they do not read books.

Our answer to this discovery was: We must improve education in reading! We must not only teach reading skills, but also use books, especially picture books, from the very beginning in the process of learning to read. We advocated the method: Teaching reading with the help of children's books.

The success was a surprise. Not 20 to 30 per cent, but 50 to 60 per cent of all the children read books.

But there were still many children who were not converted to reading books.

And we again found the reason why: the first two or three books with which they were confronted were too difficult for them. The children could not tackle these books and so they did not touch books any more.

Thus we may say: It is good to have a better insight into the general or individual reading interests of children, but it is also important – especially for poor readers – to use reading material that does not discourage them. For these children we must match reading material with their limited reading ability.

In this task we got the necessary help by reading research. We had to find out:

1. the degree of reading ability of each child,
2. a text with a level of difficulty that matched the reading ability.

To discover the degree of reading ability we used – for the first time in Austria – two kinds of tests: multiple choice tests and Cloze tests. In Austria even experienced teachers were surprised at the great differences in reading speed and comprehension, and they admitted that something ought to be done to improve the situation.

This is what aroused our interest in readability research. At the beginning we adapted American formulae for use in German language. But our teachers found the formulae, based on regression equations, somewhat odd. It was easier to interest them through additive methods. The forerunner of these is the Swedish Lix (*Lesbarkeitsindex*). This method simply involves adding average sentence length and the percentage of long words (these are words with more than six letters).

The result is a scale of difficulty ranging from about 20 (very easy) to about 75 (very difficult). We converted this scale into grade levels with the following results:

Lix scale:	20	25	28	30	32	34	36	38	40	42
Grade level:	1	2	3	4	5	6	7	8	9	10

This is for literature, and also holds good for English (with non-fiction the scale is a little different).

Continuing our research project we tried out a combination of other language factors and developed the so-called *language profile* by analysing about 500 books, whereby we separated fiction and non-fiction. We ascertained the relation of language factors by pooled assessment.

In this way we found out the different values of the language factors for each grade of:

    average sentence length
    word length
    the percentage of one-syllable words
            of polysyllables,
            of long words
            of hard words,
            of verbs
            different words and
            abstract nouns.

(Hard words are those, which are not on a list of the thousand most common words in the written language of ten-year-old children. We developed this list especially for our readability project).

This language profile proved very convincing. We found that the values of the language factors rose systematically in concordance with the rising difficulty of the books. This fact is the base of readability research.

In practice we now only use the language factors that can be counted with the help of a small computer: sentence length, word length (multiplied by ten), percentage of polysyllables and percentage of long words give very good results. If somebody works by hand, we recommend the use of Lix only. Teachers prefer this method to abstract formulae because it is so clear and convincing.

But as in the U.S.A. and Great Britain, many critics in Austria pointed out the limitations of readability measurements, i.e. they do not take into account difficulty of content, organisation of the material, print, style, the reader's background (e.g. prior knowledge, experience background, interest, motivation etc.). This criticism led to a research project in which we tried to combine measurement and judgement. The method of judgement is called *readability analysis*. Subjective judgements of the mentioned features (content difficulty, organisation, print, style and reader relationship) are translated into figures that give the grade level for which the respective feature is suitable. To help us, we use a checklist with about 20 points. A detailed introduction furthermore gives guidance on how to get the best results when assessing the five features of the readability analysis – using the knowledge of reader's psychology, of psycholinguistics, memory research and so on.

The application of this readability analysis resulted in some surprises. Certainly, in some cases we were convinced that the results of language measurement were improved by the analysis. But in most cases the average of the points of the reading analysis more or less corresponded to the language difficulty.

Language difficulty, therefore, is not only a factor *per se,* but also an indicator of the difficulty overall.

Readability analysis may thus be regarded as a contribution towards restoring faith in the usefulness of readability measurement by formulae or additive methods.

But we do not believe that the confirmation of the reliability of the traditional readability procedures (which can nevertheless still be improved) by the readability analysis makes this analysis irrelevant. No, because only the average of the different features corresponds to the grade level of the language difficulty. The single features – as a rule – differ. Let us give a practical example:

Language difficulty	5
Difficulty of content	7
Organisation difficulties	4·5
Print	4
Style	5
Reader relationship	4·5
Average grade level	5

Now the teacher knows *where* the difficulty lies, and she or he can do something to help the poor reader – in this case by imparting prior knowledge or background experience. This – perhaps – by some sort of advance organisers or by a book that gives an introduction to this field of knowledge.

And now I come to the main task of our topic: 'Improving reading by matching children's books with reading ability, interests and needs of the student'. The readability analysis may be regarded as a method or guideline in this task.

First we assess language difficulty. Then we develop methods – and apply them – for getting a better insight:

into the extent of prior knowledge;
into the impact of organisation;
into the impact of print;
into the impact of style;
into the interaction between reader and text

(motivating qualities of the text, and what we can do to motivate the reader).

In short, what can we do with the help of these guidelines to improve our reading instruction, and to bring children and books together. For the purposes of this paper I will discuss only one point a little more extensively, but I think it is the most important one: reader relationship, especially interest, motivation and needs.

Research has proved that when pupils are really interested in a topic, they will tackle a book with a difficulty grade that is two years above their reading grade level. A more important consideration is that the pupils' motivation to read will or may result in developing lifelong reading interests and lifelong habits.

What can we do to reach this aim? More than ten years ago I wrote an article on the subject 'Opportunities for Reading'. I advanced the opinion that it was sufficient to teach the mechanics of reading properly, and then utilise every possible opportunity for providing books: within the family, in the classroom, in the school library, in the public library, in persuading children to use some of their pocket money to buy paperbacks, and so on. However, I have since collected new experience in the course of further work in this field.

'Persuasions' and 'allurements' of all kinds have become so omnipresent and powerful that many children and teenagers do not find their way to books, despite the best intentions in the world.

It is of little help to tell the child how fine and important books are, and that they should make use of the school and public library. What children are really interested in is the story, the plot, and the identification with characters they admire.

So we stopped talking *about* the book, but tried to find a way to lure the child into the story by making the reading rask easier and more interesting and captivating.

We tried different ways and compared the results. Thus we developed a method which we called 'Lure Into Reading'. The idea was to supply a class with paperbacks containing an equal number of the same books as there were children in the class. Then the teacher, or one or two good story-tellers among the children, told parts of the book – up to 30 or 40 per cent – to the class. So the children were drawn into the plot in the manner that was most easy for them: they had only to listen to a good story-teller. Then the teacher read a few pages to them, and they got some feeling for the language of the book, especially for its rhythm.

Next the teacher distributed the books, and the children quietly continued reading at their own speed. Some minutes before the end of the lesson the class stopped reading and played a guessing game: how could the story end? And the pupils discussed different possibilities.

What were the pupils interested in now? Of course, in the real end of the story! So the children were motivated in four ways to carry on reading at home: by listening to story telling, by being read to, by reading themselves and by finding an ending to the story! Thereafter they usually finished the story at home within a few days.

After some days a short discussion took place in class – according to the motto: impression leads to expression!

This method 'Lure Into Reading' proved so successful that more and more teachers in all parts of Austria wanted to borrow the 'boxes' (as we called the sets) with 30 books with the same title. The non-profit-making association 'Austrian Bookclub for Children and Young People' had to buy – in the course of time – about 500,000 paperbacks, with the publishers granting a discount of 50 per cent. Neighbourhood centres for the distribution of the books – where the teachers could collect them for a few weeks – were established all over Austria.

The results of this method are manifold. First of all, reading ability is improved considerably. This is due to the 'practice effect'. If children read a few pages from a reader at school and repeat them – perhaps – at home, they experience the practice effect (one could also speak of a storage effect) of a few hundred words. The interesting book entices them to read about 50 times more. Thus many words and phrases are repeated dozens and hundreds of times. Reading grouped phrases becomes an automatic process. The children read better. And who reads better reads more.

It is now easier to interest children in group reading or individual reading, which is – in the end – the most important of all.

In short, a good teacher tries to promote reading habits in many ways. His or her chief aim is that children experience joy when they are reading. This aim is easier to reach when the teacher knows as much as possible about books, about reading and about children. These are fields of interesting studies and experiments.

In my opinion the chief task is not to improve the different reading skills. Let us teach reading by reading, by the joy of reading. If we succeed in promoting lifelong reading habits we come nearer to all the other educational aims.

What needs are there which cannot be fulfilled by the right book at the right time for the right child?

Good children's authors know the children. This is why their books meet their needs best. The need for security, for having friends (even in the characters of books), for success, for adventure, for challenges, for being able to see things from different aspects, for enriching their lives.

Thus children's books not only give the teacher more success in reading instruction, but also play a major role in helping the teacher in reaching most of his or her educational objectives. To lead to the joy of reading is one of the best of them.

Reference

BAMBERGER, R. (1975) *Promoting the Reading Habit*. Paris: U.N.E.S.C.O.

6 Nurturing every child's literacy development: a four-pronged teaching strategy

L. John Chapman

This paper has two purposes and is in two parts. Firstly, it aims to give teachers of pupils of all ages and abilities some idea of what it is about literacy that is developing during the years of compulsory schooling. Secondly, in an extended second section, it attempts to give all teachers strategies for teaching reading based on this knowledge.

Part 1 Theory and practice

One of the obvious starting points for the first of these purposes is to try to specify what it is about language acquisition and development that is taking place in the pre-school years that is pertinent to later success in school.

The first statement that has to be made, a statement that must be accorded primacy for an understanding of children's motivation to use language, is that children are *learning how to mean*, that is, they are grappling with the functions of language. (Halliday, 1975). Learning how to use language to make meaning is one, an important one, of a number of meaning potentials available to the child. Associated with this statement is another, that is, learning how to mean does not occur in a vacuum. It is developed alongside and together with particular social and cultural aspects in the child's environment (Halliday, 1975). In Western civilisation it is important to note that a large part of the totality of the meaning systems of that culture is language and literacy.

Research in the pre-school period has recently begun to yield more specific information for teachers as a recent review by Snow (1983) shows. This gives some clear indications of the characteristics of parent-child language interactions that matter in our culture. Firstly, Snow distinguishes between the use of the terms language and literacy, retaining the former to cover oral language and the latter for reading and writing. Secondly, she pinpoints, as have others, social aspects of language development as well as the quality of the language interaction that takes place between parent and child in *some* home situations.

But what is important about this work is the specification of the characteristics of the interactions that lead to the successful acquisition of literacy. These are: semantic contingency, scaffolding, accountability procedures and the use of routines and conventions. It is very important to note the setting of the interactions. These often take place in parent-child *literacy* encounters so that questions about books, the stories in books and other text characteristics are raised and answered. But it is more than a haphazard encounter for in these 'successful homes' the equivalent of positive literacy teaching, for example, the attention paid to letters and words, takes place and other demands are made, e.g. for tasks to be completed.

Perhaps the most important outcome of these literacy interactions is the encouragement of the ability to decontextualise. This has also been one of the main contentions of Margaret Donaldson (1978) in her work. She emphasises that written text requires the ability to move away from the here-and-now situation of speech to the remote and abstract, the implicit context of print. A point also made by Chapman (1983a).

Many factors now begin to fall neatly into place. Some of these have been known for some time but what is becoming clear from the findings of research into textual cohesion (see Chapman, 1983b), is that children's cultural and social development is one of the main factors associated with reading development. In another recent article (Durkin, 1983) attention is drawn to this phenomenon outlining its scope from a social psychology perspective. Durkin notes that 'Language is a distinctive and integral component of the range of complex social processes that characterize human interaction, education and development. These processes, including language acquisition, continue well beyond infancy'. But note its importance, for unless teachers realise the extent of language variety and the need to construct programmes to cater for it, they will eventually produce reading casualties. Unfortunately some of these will not appear until some time, perhaps years, later. A little of the detail of this was given in Chapman (1983b).

Summarising the points made so far it could be said that the child from its early beginnings is learning how to mean. This learning takes place at the same time as the child is absorbing his or her culture. The twin process of culturalisation and language acquisition are interactive, the one relying on the other. One of the dominant characteristics of Western culture is literacy, the acquisition of which depends largely on the ability to decontextualise. Also children's growing awareness of the need to match social situation with appropriate language is one of the other bases of their language, and hence reading, development.

A model of language for reading development

The model of language that involves these features and that gives them support can be found in the works of Halliday (1978) and Halliday and Hasan (1976). Their model can be illustrated by a diagram as in Fig. 1. In this the text-forming component of the semantic system is seen to comprise three subcomponents. These are theme-rheme, the information structure and cohesion. The text-forming component is always embedded in register. Although registers have basic language similarities, as register changes so do the language patterns in the sub-components. For working purposes theme-rheme is to do with the structure of the sentence, the information system with 'given-new' aspects and is realised through intonation in oral text and in some way, as yet unresearched, in written text. The other component is cohesion which is a global property of texts. It is also realised locally by the inter-

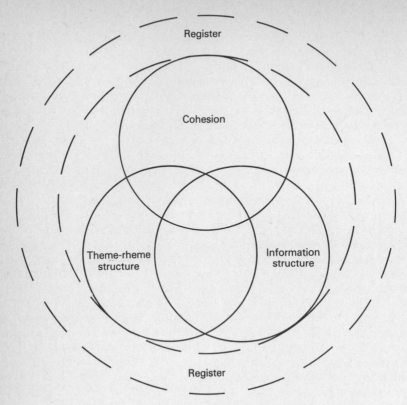

Fig. 1. The text-forming component of the semantic system

sentence linkages provided by a system of cohesive ties. The text-forming component and register will be further discussed as the recommended teaching strategy is described.

Part 2 A teaching strategy for reading development

The second purpose of this paper was to provide a teaching strategy for teachers of reading; a strategy that would take into account the findings from research into both early and later development. At the same time the language model will be further specified as it provides theoretical unity for teaching reading throughout schooling.

The first prong of a four-pronged strategy is to teach reading and writing together.

1. TEACH READING AND WRITING TOGETHER

Firstly, children should be encouraged to write for different audiences. In the first instance the teacher (or parent) is the first audience, but teacher knows most of the situation of the snippet of language being recorded by the child and will supply some of the meaning. Yet the child, because he or she has already begun to acquire the rudiments of register, is already becoming sensitive to language variation and is capable of learning how to mean at an early age in different social situations. For instance, most children learn, on entry to school, how to speak to adults or teachers. They know that they should not use the same language as they use in the playground or at home. Teachers convey the status dimension of the head teacher for example, in subtle ways; similarly the policeman, the upholder of the law, is addressed with diffidence. Children's language begins to show an appreciation of these situation factors at a very early age.

These are the foundations for the later intricacies of register and in this area special needs soon become apparent. For example, second language learners have begun to acquire the culture within which their first language is embedded so when they begin to make meaning in a second language, this requires a new set of cultural situations. Some will coincide with their first language but others will indeed be foreign. They will have very special needs.

When writing has begun and the first meaningful sentences have been written it is important to move ahead using the basic concept of cohesion. It is important to teach aspects of cohesion in text situations, and not just isolated sentences. Almost every sentence, unless it is a citation, carries within it the *presupposing* mechanism that links it to other sentences. Any teaching limited to single sentences inhibits the text forming process.

For example, when children are struggling to make meaning, they are more often than not using text to express themselves. They can make the connections orally by using simple cohesive ties like 'and' or other repetitions and indeed Garber (1979) has shown that cohesive ties are already active in the speech of young children. Often the teacher, keen to get a simple sentence down picks only one statement from the child's text. This may be an appropriate stragegy for a while but should not be pursued for any length of time.

As the child moves, still at an early age into text (i.e. communications of more than one sentence), it is of vital importance to point out the connections or between sentence relationships, for *every child should have good connections*. The emphasis from writing is towards making meaning by using the textual function and now the drive in reading teaching needs to be on prediction.

The second prong of the four-pronged strategy is:

2. TEACH PREDICTION IN READING AND WRITING

Here the dual function of the cohesive tie words ought to be shown in a simple way. In any small story passage it is often clear that a pronoun, e.g. 'he' signals the actor or subject of a sentence, the rest of which tells us what 'he' is doing. (Theme and rheme.) But it also carries the reference load simultaneously. Reading then involves horizontal left to right processing across the page, and vertically down the page as actors and events are tracked. (See Anderson, 1983.) Unfortunately attention to this two-dimensional process hardly ever occurs in reading and writing lessons. It is nearly always left to right – with book marker under the words preventing the vertical progression – left to right reading involves prediction from syntax or structure but does not help the child to predict so as to remake the author's textual meaning.

This brings a new dimension, or a hitherto unused one, to the fore helping children who may be struggling with reading. It is noticeable, and other research has shown, that children who are below average often do not move about the text to discover the clues that are there that will enable them to read more efficiently. This may be due to reliance on the horizontal attack only, the children not having been taught the predictability or presupposing nature of the cohesion system. The process has been seen at a macro-level but the concentration in this work has been largely on content words. Potter (1983) shows some useful ways of tackling this by providing passages that are written so as to encourage reading on into the context when an unfamiliar word is holding up progress.

Next, and as important for these teaching strategies for literacy, should be to aim at a teaching goal that is one step ahead (at least) of where the beginning reader is at present. That is, in order to progress, the teacher should be preparing and teaching to the next step.

3. WHEREVER THE CHILD IS IN HIS/HER READING DEVELOPMENT, THE TEACHER SHOULD BE AIMING TO BE AT LEAST ONE STEP AHEAD

And here there is an enormous draw-back, or has been until very recently. We haven't had enough knowledge to give to teachers about what it is that is developing as children become mature readers. In the main all that has been advocated when reading has begun is to read more, to practise or to read more difficult material. To find what is ahead it is necessary to turn to what is to be read. This, in turn, is dependent upon the school's curriculum and the demands of modern living.

For educational purposes children are faced with an ever-increasing reading load. The range of tests is staggering. You would appreciate this if you brought all your school books together in one place. And remember the range outside the school that all our youngsters will have to meet later as adults, is enormous. Merrit (1978) has given a list of different types of text. These ranged from books, fiction and non-fiction, periodicals, newspapers, regulations, forms, reference materials and correspondence through to notices. And the demands are increasing. Never be led to think that reading teachers will become redundant. To make them so will not be because they are not needed. To do so will be to sacrifice the nation's literacy. For, if our schools aim to produce independent learners able to conduct their own affairs as they go through life and who can have access to their own and other cultures, then the key person is the reading teacher. But note – not just the beginning reading teacher but the primary, secondary, college and university reading teacher. To be one step ahead requires knowledge of these text types and the textual demands of the curriculum.

4. TEACH TEXTURE

Each and every text has a quality that makes it recognisable as a text. When confronted with two pages of print, one, a haphazard collection of words and sentences and the other a page from a book or magazine, any skilled adult reader, in a matter of seconds will be able to tell which is the genuine text. This is so even if the print and layout of the page of the haphazard collection of words and sentences is identical to the page from the book. From this undoubted fact it can be said that there must be a quality or qualities about a text that enables us to single it out from a non-text. To describe this quality, Halliday's term 'texture' has been used: a text has the quality of texture. But what does this texture consist of? It has two main features, one is COHESION and the other is REGISTER. And it is the development of the perception of texture that is the corner stone of reading development or reading growth. However, as indicated above, foundations have to be laid early. Cohesion is the text's internal unity and register is the text's unity with its contextual situation.

Register

As children mature and their horizons are extended, the curriculum chosen for them widens and deepens. This, together with the literacy demands outside the school, means that they are meeting texts of ever-increasing variety. But each of those texts has its *own* individual quality of texture. So not only can adult skilled readers tell a text from a non-text, they can also easily distinguish different types of text. Again a quick test would convince the most sceptical. If faced with a number of different texts, after reading a few lines most would be able to say 'That's a maths text', 'That's a sermon', 'That's a novel' and so on. For instance:

1. And it came to pass, as Jesus went down to Galilee . . . .
2. Using the formulae provided, calculate the area and volume of the following:
3. Once upon a time in a far-off land, there lived a King and five beautiful princesses . . . .
4. In the reign of King . . . .
5. Draw an outline map of Great Britain and mark the position of these ports . . . .

Children have to acquire this expertise so as to develop full understanding. Sometimes the register shock is so great on entering secondary school, their reading progress halts or even regresses. (See Lunzer and Gardner, 1979.)

To begin an appreciation of register it is useful for children to begin quite early to develop the sense of audience. This is already apparent in rudimentary ways but there is a need to refine the choice of text to match the situation. Below are a few 'special kinds of writing' given by Raleigh (1981).

a) John was not the only boy involved but it seems to me that since his was the leading role in this unfortunate incident I must . . . .

b) It came slowly towards the crowd, its eyes glaring, its teeth bared. The people in the crowd stood stock-still, frozen with fear while . . . .

c) And so it came to pass that on the fourth day the men, women and children came out from the city into the valley below and . . . .

d) Just can't help myself –
It's you, it's you, it's you –
You're the one oooh I need . . . .

e) I am 16 years of age and just about to leave school after taking CSE examinations. I am interested . . . .

f) To release the cylinder block, first slacken off the camshaft chain tensioner. Then unscrew and remove the single bolt at the rear . . . .

g) Lovely Eleanor, 18, is training to be an air hostess and tells us that she can't wait to fly . . . .

h) Didn't do much today. A. came round in the afternoon and we just sat around and talked . . . .

i) Pinchas Zukerman began his mastery of the violin when he was eight. Two years later he won a scholarship . . . .

j) Now when the little Dwarf heard that he was to dance a second time before the Queen he was so proud that . . . .

k) With their album already flying high, the band are planning a number of gigs . . . .

l) I know how difficult it must be for you – but be patient because in just a few weeks' time we'll be together . . . .

m) Stir in the sugar with a swift motion and simmer over a very low heat, adding more milk if necessary . . . .

n) After last month's fun and games you're due for a slow down. Watch out for some odd events next week . . . .

o) And what's more your cat will simply love the juicy flavour of . . . .

p) In case of emergency press the red button and wait until the machine stops. Do not . . . .

q) Your postal order is enclosed herewith. We regret any inconvenience caused by our inability to send the goods you require . . . .

Primary children soon appreciate that there are many different kinds of language and find that attempting to write them, e.g. teacher's horoscope, can be fun. In this way the preparation for the later much more drastic change to the registers of the different disciplines has begun.

Cohesion

We recognise a text first by the way its parts hang together because it is cohesive. An adult skilled reader can quickly discover how this global quality is built up. This is done by a series of cohesive ties that act together in such a way as to chain the author's threads of meaning. And here is the fundamental point made earlier – cohesive ties work on the principle of presupposition.

And presupposition enables the reader to predict. Having named a person or persons at the outset of a story, thereafter it is usual in English to refer to them by a pronoun. The reader then anticipates a pronoun to provide the linkage. But pronouns, although extremely common, are not the only cohesive ties. There are substitutes, for instance:

I bought a new car last week.
I like the old *one* better.

Here 'one' is substituting for car (note not the identical car by the way), and this relationship also contributes to the cohesion of the passage.

Then there are the conjunctions, the 'and', 'but', 'so', 'then' type of words. These too have a cohesive effect. Finally there is the association between words that provide a further cohesive dimension. Word pairs like 'war and peace' used in a text have an attraction (the attraction of opposites) that draws the text together. Having mentioned the first, the second is more likely to be found in the same text environment rather than any other word that has not this relationship.

The chaining of ties is most important for here we can discern the author's thread of meaning running through the text. To pick out the author's main chain from subsidiary chains needs discrimination and practice or the reader will be in a similar comprehension position to the discussant who is told 'But that's not the point of what I'm saying'.

The operation of the cohesive tie system is such that it enables the reader to integrate the text and recover its unity. As the ties are chained it provides the reader with the author's thread of meaning. So the first part of the fourth prong is:

4a.   TEACH TOWARDS INTERNAL TEXT UNITY: COHESION

But how may this be taught? In broad terms, there are three ways:

A. Writing
B. Group Discussion
C. The GAP technique

A. Writing

In school all our apprentice readers are also apprentice writers. They are learning a craft. You will already know of the importance of preparation for writing and for not expecting perfection first time round. Just as the craftsman spends time refining his work so it is with literacy teaching. It should become quite acceptable classroom practice for children to expect to work at a piece of writing, polishing it through several drafts or, if it is not worthwhile, abandoning it. By this is not meant that teachers should inhibit the creative urge, it is part of the skill of the teacher to so encourage writing creativity as not to dampen the desire for authorship. However, there is a crucial stage in writing production that allows discussion of a piece of writing as to its internal unity or cohesion. It is here that the teacher can alert the young writer to the action of cohesive ties, to show how they can pull the text together more effectively. That is, give them some tools for better writing. It has been found that children often lose the thread of meaning themselves as they write and need to have their attention drawn to the links. The teacher can therefore scan a piece of writing looking for three problems:

1) Have the ties been tied securely?
2) Have the ties been chained adequately?
3) Does the main chain have sufficient prominence for the reader to follow the main thrust of the piece?

These are the basics. There are, of course, more sophisticated areas that can be followed, e.g. those indicating the development of style. (See Gutwinski, 1976.) Further guidance can be had from the Ohio State University writing project. This showed how children's sense of texture grew between the ages of six and eight years. Two things stood out in this work. Firstly, children approached writing as though talking. That is, in early writing quite often children expect the reader to 'know' who and what they are talking about, the pronouns have few, if any, referents. They point to factors outside the text so the text they have composed has little internal unity. As noted earlier they need to develop the ability to decontextualise.

Other relations like the associations of lexical cohesion need time to build-up as they are dependent upon both actual real-life experiences as well as reading. To foster this the language experience approach in teaching is recommended.

B. Group discussion

It is necessary to ensure that this teaching, which is perhaps more effective during writing, is reinforced during reading. This again needs a sensitive approach and knowledge of individual progress in both reading and writing. So that reading may grow it is necessary to build up the children's knowledge of texts and how they work. They need not only to read the lines, but also to perceive the ties that link the author's meanings between the lines.

Alerting children to text unity can be achieved by discussion of how authors use cohesion to achieve their intended meanings. Discussion groups, particularly as children get older, are particularly useful. So is the other method to be recommended, the GAP technique.

C. The GAP technique

This is a type of selective Cloze procedure but so as not to confuse it with Cloze and to fit the way of measuring performance, the procedure here is called GAP filling. This is done by first identifying the cohesive ties in a passage, then deleting one end of the tie. The reader is asked to then fill in the tie. This involves the perception of the pre-supposing nature of that particular tie. The advantage of this method is that the rest of the text is kept intact so that other cues are not disturbed thus keeping the situation as near to that of normal reading as possible.

With the GAP technique it is possible to invent many different ways of alerting children to the construction of a text. Different groups of ties can be deleted, different combinations as in chains, and different distances between the onset and completion of the tie can be chosen for examination. Training in reading using these features can follow. And, most advantageous, the method is applicable to silent reading.

Register dimensions

The other important textual feature is register. This, as has been shown, is the relationship between the text and its situational context. You will remember that earlier (p. 59) a few sentences were given to illustrate how readily an adult can detect register. It is only necessary to mention a few words from a text – e.g. formulae, calculate, area, volume – and the hearer is alerted, without even putting the words into sentences let alone texts, to the topic or subject. Again, 'Once upon a time, far-off land, beautiful princesses', establishes a story, whilst 'map, ports,' etc. geography.

Field

These words help us to predict what the topic is about, that is, establish the field of the discourse.

A quote from Woody Allen shows mismatch in field:

'Yeats and Hygiene. A Comparative Study. The poetry of William Butler Yeats is analyzed against a background of proper dental care.
(Course open to a limited number of students'.)
(from Benson and Greaves, 1981)

Here the formality of the university announcement of a course is clearly established but the mismatch lies in the field. Dental care and literary criticism are not usually associated with each other!

This is important in reading, for establishment of field helps us to predict what the topic of the text is likely to be. There are two other important characteristics of register and it is these that play a large part in the development of reading. These are known as *tenor* and *mode*.

Tenor

'Don't speak to me like that – I'm your mother!'

Obviously something has been said that is ill-fitting to the relationship between mother and child. The mother expects respect and language carries that respect as well as content. Teachers can tell when children are being insolent, one doesn't address superiors in a very familiar way. It is a characteristic of register that it is easier to detect when there is a register clash than to say what its constituents are. So,

'Ta-ta your holiness, see you soon luv.'

breaks tenor that is along the status dimension. There are other facets that are much more subtle. Woody Allen makes a great deal of them and it is the essence of some of his humour. The speaker is led along as the field is established, associated with this goes the tenor, the kind of language used in that particular situation. A maths text with the title of 'solving algebraic equations', for example, does not start off 'Once upon a time there was this little algebraic equation. It lived in a far-off page and its family was made up of x's and y's . . .'. Somehow there is a mismatch, and more particularly our predictions are not realised.

Because it is to do with various social relationships, status and so on, it is a feature that only begins to be appreciated as children gain social experience of the world and what is acceptable behaviour and appropriate language in social situations. This also applies in a very real way to scholastic subjects where the language of many school texts is so unfamiliar to the child as to be impenetrable.

Mode

The third facet of register is mode. And this has to do mostly with differences between spoken and written language. There is a language of books which has developed over the years and the characteristics of that mode are different from that of speech. Here is an important point, for the children bring their oral language with them to school and it is this facility that they use to begin and develop reading. And that spoken mode, in which children are undoubtedly fluent, is with them as they continue through schooling, intruding often into written work and reading.

The research that has been undertaken has yielded five main findings in the area of register (see Chapman and Louw, forthcoming).

1. A reading register clash as children move from primary to secondary education. This inter-register situation, which involves full sensitivity to text register, may only be complete when students reach the tertiary level and even then some have problems.
2. Register clash is mostly mode-lag or lack of familiarity with written text registers.
3. There is considerable evidence that children are motivated to 'be in register'. That is, there is drive to make meaning in all the language situations that confront them.
4. Equally, there is much evidence to show that early reading exposure is to literary texts only, i.e. stories.
5. There is little evidence up to 15 years of any great improvement over the years.

The final advice is to teach using similar methods as with cohesion but with the focus on register.

4b. ALWAYS MAKE READERS AWARE OF A TEXT'S UNITY WITH ITS SITUATION: REGISTER

See Sylvia Winchester's article, pp 186–200.

Concluding summary

There is much agreement among reading teachers particularly that the basic goal of reading instruction is to help the child understand or comprehend what he or she reads; that is, to help the child make meaning.

For reading progress or growth, two other important new elements are involved: *cohesion*, the way in which the author signals what is to be integrated, and *register*, the relationship between the text and its contextual situation.

References

ANDERSON, J. (1983) 'The writer, the reader and the text', in B. Gillham (ed.) *Reading Through the Curriculum*. London: Heinemann.

BENSON, J. D. and GREAVES, W. S. (1981) 'Field of discourse: Theory and application'. *Applied Linguistics,* 11(1).

CHAPMAN, L. J. (1983a) *Reading Development and Cohesion*. London: Heinemann.

CHAPMAN, L. J. (1983b) 'A study in reading development. A comparison of the ability of 8-, 10- and 13-year-old children to perceive cohesion in their school texts', in B. Gillham (ed.) *Reading Through the Curriculum*. London: Heinemann.

CHAPMAN, L. J. and LOUW, W. (forthcoming) '*Register shock in the secondary school*', in B. Gillham (ed.) *The Language of School Subjects*. London: Heinemann.

DURKIN, K. (1983) 'Language development past, present and later'. *Bulletin of the British Psychological Society,* 36, pp. 193–6.

GARBER, M. D. (1979) *An Examination and Comparison of Selected Features in Child-produced Texts and Beginning Reading Materials*. Unpublished Ph.D. dissertation, Georgia State University, Atlanta, Georgia, U.S.A.

HALLIDAY, M. A. K. (1975) *Learning How to Mean*. London: Edward Arnold.

HALLIDAY, M. A. K. (1978) *Language as a Social Semiotic*. London: Edward Arnold.

HALLIDAY, M. A. K. and HASAN, R. (1976) *Cohesion in English*. London: Longman.

LUNZER, E. and GARDNER, K. (1979) *The Effective Use of Reading*. London: Heinemann.

MERRITT, J. E. M. (1978) 'Learning to read and reading to learn: developing effective reading', in E. Hunter-Grundin and H. V. Grundin (eds) *Reading: Implementing the Bullock Report*. London: Ward Lock Educational.

POTTER, F. (1983) 'Teaching children to use the linguistic context more effectively'. *Reading,* 17 (2), pp. 95–104.

RALEIGH, M. (1981) 'Special kinds of writing'. *The Languages Book*. London: I.L.E.A. English Centre.

SNOW, C. E. (1983) 'Literacy and Language: Relationships during the pre-school years'. *Harvard Educational Review,* 53(2), pp. 165–89.

7 Conveying the message that reading is necessary, valuable and pleasant

Nigel Hall

Evidence from recent studies demonstrates clearly that there are many children who, even before they have begun school, have started to understand some important facts about literacy. They have realised that there is some purpose to literacy, that it is a valuable skill to possess, that the possession of that skill has a certain status, and that the exercise of the skill can be a pleasant activity (Goodman, 1980; Ferreiro and Teberosky, 1983; Harste, Burke and Woodward, 1982; Teale, 1982). It is, however, equally clear that not all children have developed this knowledge. As Downing (1978) put it, 'the conclusion that young children's understanding of the function and features of written language cannot be taken for granted seems inescapable' (see also Johns, 1976/7; and Tovey, 1976). Even in some cases where children have developed knowledge about contextualised print, the shift from the contextualised print of the environment to the decontextualised print of reading schemes and other books can result in confusion.

Children who have failed to develop understandings about literacy or children who are confused about the nature and purpose of literacy clearly have a special need. They need to understand why they are being asked to perform certain classroom tasks. For these children the content of the need relates to literacy but the general nature of that need is one that is relevant to all learners. Everyone likes to feel that they know why they are doing something. No-one likes to engage in activities that do not appear to have any purpose.

This need for the world to make sense lies at the heart of all cognitive functioning. This 'effort after meaning' is a feature of almost all learning and adults, as well as children, strive to reorder bits of experience into compartments which make sense. In pre-school lives the relative absence of dictation allows children to create categories which for them have significance. The creation of such categories is influenced by observation of those things 'significant others' consider of importance. This 'importance' can be measured by the child according to criteria like the frequency of adult engagement in behaviour, the interest and enjoyment of the engagement, and the consequences of such engagement. Language and literacy are inextricably social. Such is the claim of Goodman and Goodman (1979) and Teale (1982a). The child gives significance to literacy events because important people in that child's life act towards those events in purposeful and meaningful ways.

Children who have the fortune to grow up in an environment where the primary caretakers are fully literate and engage frequently in literate acts, will constantly see behaviours which reflect the assignment of high status to the state of being literate. For those children literacy begins to have meaning not because of the ultimate consequences of being literate, but because it is important to those that the child cares about. As those children interact with literate adults and begin to engage in simple literacy behaviours (looking at books, noticing signs, copying their name etc.) so the general functions and purposes of print become more evident.

When those children begin school and are exposed to the less contextualised activities of classroom instruction, the lessening of context is unlikely to be a problem. They know that the purpose of the activity is to learn to read and write. They know already that literacy is necessary, valuable and pleasant. Even relatively boring activities can be tolerated if it is understood that a useful consequence follows. Such children are the advantaged ones. They are probably children who arrive at school knowing some words, anticipating starting a reading scheme and keen to begin to sort out the mysteries involved in becoming literate.

It is unfortunately the case that large numbers of children are not approaching schooling with the same advantages and awareness. Many children still come from homes where the parents are semi-literate, choose not to exercise their literacy, or have difficulty when dealing with their children's involvement with literacy skills (Anderson, Teale and Estrada, 1980). Children from such homes may not have been exposed to stories in books, may not have observed their parents reading and writing, and may not have had the opportunity to talk with their parents about books, words, signs and letters.

The purpose of literacy and the nature of literacy will be virtually unknown to that group of children because they are largely unaware that literacy exists. In all probability the number of pre-school children who have no knowledge of literacy is very small; it is, after all, almost impossible in our literate society to avoid exposure to print and it would be an extreme situation where no literacy events were experienced. However, there will be a group of children who, although having a dawning awareness of the print in their environment, have not begun to appreciate just how useful or interesting decontextualised print can be. Some of these children will be among those who, arriving in school having been told they are going to learn to read, are dismayed when the skill is not achieved on the first day.

The need of children who do not have an adequate literacy background to understand the purpose and nature of the new activities of school is a fundamental one. It does not matter how caring a teacher is, nor how carefully constructed the syllabus. If the learner does not know why learning is taking place then the learning becomes more difficult. When learning becomes more difficult the teaching becomes more demanding. Thus it is not simply in the interests of the child that the purpose of a learning activity is understood.

All children when they start school can be under no illusion that reading and writing are important. Why else should so much time be spent on these activities. In the selection of activities, and in the amount of an activity, teachers convey the message that the school attaches great significance to becoming literate. However, the combination of signals received by the child can convey an ambiguous message. On the one hand there is evidence that literacy is important; on the other hand that the importance is to the school rather than to the personal needs, interests and enjoyment of individuals. The evidence of recent studies shows clearly that the books children are asked to read do not always convey the message that reading is necessary, valuable and pleasant, and reflection will reveal that the personal literacy behaviour of teachers in classrooms also frequently fails to support that message.

Books and teacher behaviour are, of course, only two ways of indicating to children the value of literacy. They are, however, potentially very powerful ways of giving children positive messages about literacy. Gibson and Levin (1975) point out that 'if a child can identify himself with a model who commands his respect, he may adopt as his own the motives of the model'. They say, 'the teacher reads, presumably likes to, and encourages the child to. But if one considers this idea seriously for a few minutes, it seems obvious that in many cases – perhaps even most of them – the teacher as a model for the child is a mismatch'. Where books are conerned Zimet (1976) points out 'We have substantial proof, therefore, that access to many ideas and values from the printed media can have a positive influence on attitudes and values of children growing up in a democratic society'.

At an earlier U.K.R.A. conference Tonjes (1982) said 'Teaching, among many other things, involves modelling'. Much early learning involves forms of modelling and while it is not necessarily a way of teaching actual strategies it is of vital importance in conveying information about the status of an activity. Literacy, as has been already stated, is no exception. Pre-school children can receive messages about literacy by observing literacy-role models. Once children start school other individuals, in particular teachers, begin to enjoy the status of 'significant others', and certain items like reading schemes become endowed with the merit of 'significant objects'.

Clearly the potential for positively influencing children's beliefs about the purpose and nature of literacy, by providing appropriate literacy-role models, is considerable. Such models offer the chance to go beyond simply telling children the messages about literacy; they offer a chance to demonstrate the truth of the message that literacy is necessary, valuable and pleasant.

Regrettably such demonstrations are unusual, indeed in many situations they are completely lacking. The rest of this paper will look in more detail at two aspects of literacy-role modelling: firstly the provision of literacy-role models in the books to which children are exposed, and secondly the nature of the literacy-role models inherent in teachers' classroom behaviour.

Literacy-role models in books

The majority of teachers in infant schools use a reading scheme to help initiate children into the world of literacy (Grundin, 1980), and thus the responsibility becomes, in part, that of the reading scheme. Reading schemes provide a magnificent opportunity to show people using a wide variety of print in a purposeful, positive and happy manner. Such modes of presentation provide numerous opportunities for teachers to help children see the value of literacy. Teachers can use those opportunities to help children see the non-arbitrary nature of literacy as well as the fact that it can be enjoyable and fascinating. How well do reading schemes help children perceive the range of purposes for reading and how well do reading schemes promote reading as an enjoyable experience? If one had to rely on the content of the books in reading schemes then the answer would, too often, be – hardly at all. Joyce Morris in a paper given at this conference (see pp. 16–28) lamented the impoverished reading-role models provided by television, and the media generally. How much more important it is that the provision of good reading-role models should be available when children most need them – when they begin to read.

Both in the United States and in England reading schemes seem to fail to provide good literacy-role models. Snyder (1979) reviewed and analysed ten representative sets of basal readers. She wrote, 'the relatively limited incidence of reading materials is rivalled only by the paucity of other aspects of communication'. She found that in general few characters read, and she commented, 'while many reading series are generous in providing reading-role models, other series have such a dearth that teachers would be wise to revise the texts used in their classrooms to see whether or not their children are receiving the message that reading is necessary, valuable and pleasant'.

In another study in the United States, Burris (1978) examined two common basal series, and the reaction of first-graders to literacy incidents in those series. She was able to find reading incidents in only 18 per cent of the pages of both series and she decided that only around 3 per cent of the pages had explicit models of book or magazine reading. The most significant part of her study was her claim that the first-grade students she examined were significantly able to recall reading incidents. If she is right then the provision of good literacy-role models becomes of considerable importance.

In an attempt to see how British reading schemes compared with their American counterparts the author examined six schemes in common use in England. The six schemes and their ranking in popularity are given in figure one. *Reading 360* (U.K.) appeared after the Grundin (1980) data had been collected. It was, however, included in this study as it has proved to be very popular.

	Position overall	Position among recently purchased schemes
Through the rainbow	2	1
Ladybird	1	4
One, two, three and away	7	2
Language in action	16	9 =
Link-up	12	5 =
Reading 360 (U.K.)	–	–

Fig. 1. Position of reading schemes in order of frequency of use according to Grundin (1980)

A more extensive presentation of the results is given in Hall (1983) but, in brief, the results were very similar to those studies of American schemes. The range was from *One, two, three and away* where there were no incidents of characters reading and only one of a character writing, to *Link-up*, where there were almost as many literacy incidents as in the other five schemes put together. Too often literacy events were scarce, characters did not look happy engaging in them, or the situations were restricted to schools. It appears that only men read newspapers and then usually in the kitchen while mother makes the breakfast. On occasions the only characters reading as if they were enjoying it were animals. Sometimes the 'message' was depressing. What should a child make of an illustration of dad asleep in bed, with a book in his hand? Frequently the incidents were utterly decontextualised, particularly in the Ladybird books; the characters did not seem to be reading or writing for any reason. Writing was far less common than reading and was usually restricted to children in school or children 'playing' school.

The three more recent schemes were manifestly better than *Through the rainbow, One, two, three and away,* and *Ladybird.* But even *Reading 360 (U.K.)* and *Language in action* presented, in relation to the total number of pages in each series, a very small number of literacy incidents.

As a result of examining these six schemes Hall (1983b) drew up a set of questions for evaluating the literacy-role content and the explicit presentation of literacy incidents. This set of criteria could (with the exception of 1, 2 and 3) be used for any books. Those questions are:

1. Does the manual contain an explicit aim to foster awareness of the meaningfulness of print and the value and pleasure of reading and writing?
2. Does the manual help the teacher develop activities and materials to advance such awareness?
3. Is the emphasis on the meaningfulness of print at the beginning of the series when children need most help?
4. Do the story characters show interest in, and enjoyment of, reading and writing?
5. Do the characters read and write frequently and to some purpose?
6. Do the characters read and write in a wide variety of situations, and for a wide range of purposes?
7. Are the characters interacting with print in a positive manner?
8. Do the illustrations feature a wide range of instances of environment print?
9. Do all the characters read and write, and in particular, do both male and female engage equally in a wide range of literacy activities?

Such a set of criteria should not be used to reject the use of a particular reading scheme; a whole range of criteria should be used in making such choices. They may, however, help a teacher identify those areas for which some kind of compensatory activity might be necessary.

The absence of literacy-role models is not only a feature of reading schemes; it seems to be a feature of books in general. D'Angelo (1982) coined the term 'biblio-power' to mean the 'invisible influence of books'. She examined 106 Caldecott and Newbery medal-winning books to see the extent to which they would 'invisibly' influence the attitude towards books and literacy of the children reading them. She found that in the majority of these distinguished and popular books that reading and writing occur either incidentally or not at all. Reading occurred as a theme in 18 of the books and writing in only seven. Parker (1979) reviewed a range of books that focused on the excitement of learning to read. There were not many of them and few of them were aimed at beginning readers.

This situation seems typical of the fiction books available in British schools. A list of books for infant schools that contain literacy-role models or literacy incidents has been produced by Hall (1983c). It is a short list!

The message that reading is 'necessary, valuable and pleasant' is evidently not being conveyed by many of the books to which children are exposed. The message actually being conveyed more usually seems to be, 'that reading is a marginal activity, certainly not very functional, highly school based, and not particularly pleasurable; all the attributes of a low status activity' (Hall 1983a).

It is a very unfortunate situation that reading schemes, which have as their intent the facilitation of reading development, should actually fail to give demonstrations of the value and purpose of developing literacy ability.

Literacy role models in classrooms

It is difficult, if not impossible, for a teacher to avoid being a model for all kinds of learning. It is therefore particularly important that teachers give consideration to the nature of the roles that they exhibit. Where literacy is concerned there would appear to be some cause for anxiety.

There is evidence that some teachers do little reading either for personal pleasure or for professional reasons (Mangieri and Corboy, 1981; George and Ray, 1979; Rogers, 1978; and Hughes and Johnston-Doyle, 1978). That some teachers hardly ever read is a depressing state of affairs. Can teachers who do not read really hope to engender interest in, and a passion towards, reading? If teachers do not like reading can they ever convey positive messages about reading to the children they teach? Hopefully the number of teachers to whom such questions apply is small. If teachers recognise, in themselves, a passivity or ambivalence towards reading and writing then it behoves them to take particular care about the images they project.

Teachers, on the whole, do little reading in classrooms except for their professional functions relating to reading children's work and reading stories. This is rather unfortunate. Teachers are, to young children, very 'significant others'. They tell children to read and write, they set reading and writing tasks, provide books and read stories. They frequently reprimand children if they do not learn to read. Sometimes teachers write on blackboards, in children's books, or under paintings. The teacher may place labels on objects and fill in a register. Sometimes the teacher may be seen to read a note from a parent (although those kinds of activities are often private affairs and completed before the school day begins). Clearly, literacy-based activities are going on, but equally clearly those activities are part of the school's instructional function rather than being for general communicative purposes. As a result the range of literacy acts witnessed by children is severely restricted. It seems that it is relatively rare for teachers to demonstrate a wide range of reading and writing acts occurring naturally, yet in a school setting. In other words providing broad reading role models. Too many such incidents are hidden from children and thus cannot be perceived as meaningful and relevant. From a child's perspective a teacher's literacy experience can appear decidedly impoverished.

The general scenario being outlined is one in which young children are constantly being told by teachers that literacy is important and that they must learn to read, yet the observations that the children make tell them consistently that teachers often do not behave as if literacy is of personal significance. The difficulty is compounded by the fact that when teachers do read, they often do so silently, thus disguising their involvement with literacy processes.

For those children who have the advantaged backgrounds described earlier this lack of appropriate role models is relatively unimportant. They may well assume that teachers, as adults, behave like their parents. However, for children with limited early experience, teachers' behaviour may reinforce any view they might have that literacy is simply something one is forced to do in school. These children need to see that teachers themselves care about literacy. They need to see that teachers themselves believe that literacy is necessary, valuable and pleasant.

It therefore seems incumbent upon teachers, and especially on those teachers who make claims about wanting to make literacy meaningful, to examine their personal literacy practices in the classroom. Are they maximising the opportunity to provide a wide and meaningful set of literacy-role models.

It is certainly not an easy task. Teachers already have considerable demands made upon them. Southgate, Arnold and Johnson (1981) comment on the results of their observations: 'What comes out very clearly is how hard teachers work'. However, the rider is, 'Even so the records indicate that the teacher does not always do what she thinks she is doing'.

What can teachers do to ensure that their children perceive a broad-based set of literacy-role models? One possibility is a shared reading time. During these sessions all the children and the teacher read self-selected material for a specified period of time. Such an activity can help children see that teachers do read for pleasure. The disadvantage of shared reading is that it derives not from a natural context but from the dictates of a timetable. Nevertheless, its widespread use in the United States indicates a considerable belief in its purpose and value.

In connection with this teachers could have and, when time allows, use personal books in the classroom. Too often personal reading items are left in staffrooms or hidden in bags. Why shouldn't a school library have shelves of books for teachers. Perhaps, most important of all, teachers could discuss their own reading with children. There are, inevitably, limitations to the ways in which it is possible to discuss adult literature with children but it can be very rewarding when children indicate they want to know what the teacher has read.

Teachers could bring work into their classrooms. In one nursery school known to the author the head teacher takes a lot of her work into the classrooms. She opens letters, answers them, orders material and equipment, and sometimes reads professional literature. It is not always easy; the difficulty is caused by the very reason she is there. The children always want to know what she is doing. She takes the time to answer their questions. Such opportunities are rarer for the infant class teacher but there will undoubtedly be possibilities that can be exploited. The important thing is to be aware of such opportunities and to maximise their benefits.

Teachers can create better opportunities for written communication. To some extent this is done already; children do see teachers send notes to other teachers. Such activities can be easily extended. As in the previous example, it is remembering to respond to all potential incidents that is important.

Teachers write in front of children but it is usually on the blackboard or in an exercise book. They seldom write in creative or interesting ways. However, even teachers who disclaim any literary ability can write simple rhymes, poems and stories. They do not have to be 'good' in any conventional literary sense. The mere fact that they have been written by the teachers endows them with respect. When children realise that teachers can write, they may begin to understand that books are actually written by people. If they see teachers writing stories then they will begin to appreciate that all books begin like that and perhaps, more importantly, they will begin to realise that their own writing may eventually allow them to create more 'polished' literary writing like that of the 'significant other', the teacher.

No doubt there are many more examples to be found of situations where teachers can demonstrate their own commitment to literacy. The wider the range the more likely it is that children will begin to perceive the relationship between their own limited literacy experiences and the developed literacy behaviour which is the aim of education. If teachers engage more visibly in a diversity of literacy experience then their children are more likely to view literacy as having meaning, value and purpose.

Conclusion

There are, of course, many other ways of helping children learn about the nature and purpose of literacy. Many of these other strategies are in common use in classrooms. However, the existence and frequency of these other strategies does not diminish, in any way, the value and necessity of providing appropriate role models both in the books children read and in the behaviour of the adults who teach them. This is especially true for children who have not yet learnt anything about literacy or children who have confusion about the nature and purpose of literacy. Those children are the ones who need to understand that literacy is meaningful, that literacy is purposeful, and that literacy is worthwhile. It is not sufficient just to broadcast that message; it must be seen to be true. The available models of literate behaviour can help determine whether literacy is seen as simply an instructional activity, or whether it is perceived and understood to be one of the most significant, powerful and enjoyable experiences available to people. Let those models be positive ones and let the message be clearly conveyed – literacy is necessary, it is valuable, and it is most certainly pleasant.

References

ANDERSON, A., TEALE, W. and ESTRADA, E. (1980) 'Low-income children's pre-school literacy experiences: some naturalistic observations'. *Quarterly Newsletter of Laboratory of Comparative Human Cognition*, 2, pp. 59–65.

BURRIS, N. A. P. (1978) *The portrayal of readers in selected elementary reading text books and trade books, and an exploration of student inferred identification with those story characters.* Ph.D. Thesis. Texas Woman's University.

D'ANGELO, K. (1983) 'Biblio-power: promoting reading and writing with books'. *Reading Psychology*, 3(4), pp. 347–54.

DOWNING, J., AYERS, D. and SCHAEFER, B. (1978) 'Concept and perceptual factors in learning to read'. *Education Research*, 21(1), pp. 11–17.

FERREIRO, E. and TEBEROSKY, A. (1983) *Literacy before schooling*. London: Heinemann Educational Books.

GEORGE, T. and RAY, S. (1979) 'Professional reading – A neglected resource – Why?' *Elementary School Journal*, 80, pp. 29–33.

GIBSON, E. and LEVIN, H. (1975) *The psychology of reading*. Cambridge, Ma.: MIT Press.

GOODMAN, K. and GOODMAN, Y. (1979) 'Learning to read is natural', in L. Resnick and P. Weaver (eds) *Theory and practice of early reading, Vol. 1*. Hillsdale, New Jersey: Lawrence Erlbaum Associates.

GOODMAN, Y. (1980) 'The roots of literacy', in M. P. Douglass (ed.), *Reading: a humanising experience*. Claremont: Claremont Graduate School.

GRUNDIN, H. (1980) 'Reading schemes in infant schools'. *Reading*, 14(1), pp. 5–13.

HALL, N. (1983a) 'The status of reading in reading schemes'. *Education* 3–13 (in press).

HALL, N. (1983b) 'Characters in British basal series don't read either'. *The Reading Teacher* (in press).

HALL, N. (1983c) A list of books, suitable for infant schools, that promote literacy. Manchester: Centre for the Teaching of Language and Literacy, Manchester Polytechnic School of Education.

HARSTE, J., BURKE, C. and WOODWARD, V. (1982) 'Children's language and world: initial encounters with print', in J. Langer and M. Smith-Burke (eds), *Reader meets author: Bridging the gap*. Newark, Delaware: International Reading Association.

HUGHES, A. and JOHNSTON-DOYLE, K. (1978) 'What do teachers read? Professional reading and professorial development'. *Education Canada*, 18, pp. 42–5.

JOHNS, J. (1976/7) 'Reading is "stand up – sit down".' *New England Reading Association State Journal*, 12, pp. 10–14.

MANGIERI, J. and CORBOY, M. (1981) 'Recreational reading: do we practise what we preach?' *The Reading Teacher*, 34, pp. 923–5.

PARKER, L. (1979) 'Reading as an activity and theme in children's books', in J. E. Shapiro (ed.). *Using literature and poetry affectively*. Newark, Delaware: International Reading Association.

ROGERS, J. (1978) 'Media competence of teachers: a review of measurement research'. *Educational Technology*, 18, pp. 16–22.

SNYDER, G. (1979) 'Do basal characters read in their daily lives?' *The Reading Teacher*, 33, pp. 303–6.

SOUTHGATE-BOOTH, V., ARNOLD, H. and JOHNSON, S. (1981) *Extending Beginning Reading*. London: Heinemann Educational Books.

TEALE, W. (1982a) 'Pre-schoolers and literacy: some insights from the research'. *Australian Journal of Reading*, 5, pp. 152–62.

TEALE, W. (1982b) 'Towards a theory of how children learn to read and write naturally'. *Language Arts*, 59, pp. 555–70.

TONJES, M. (1982) 'Selected instructional strategies for promoting content reading and study skills', in A. Hendry (ed.), *Teaching reading: the key issues*. London: Heinemann Educational Books.

TOVEY, D. (1976) 'Children's perceptions of reading'. *The Reading Teacher*, 29, pp. 536–40.

ZIMET, S. (1976) *Print and Prejudice*. London: Hodder and Stoughton.

8 Meeting students' need to understand structure in expository text

Christian Gerhard

Introduction

To think a certain way is also to 'see' a certain way. Since each person is unique both genetically and in terms of experience, uniformity of perception in a group of people is hardly possible. For example, if four people from different backgrounds walk into a beautiful garden, they see four different gardens. The artist perhaps sees the vivid colours and structural arrangement of trees, plants and flower beds. The botanist pounces on a rare species discovered in a corner full of flowers. The interior decorator sees the possibility of dramatic arrangements of cut flowers. The tenant of a city flat sees a nice sunny corner with a bench. In each case, the inclination and prior knowledge of the viewer determines what is seen.

Reading comprehension is very similar. Four people reading an article about political elections can come up with four different versions of its meaning. It is not surprising, then, that students also interpret differently. Nevertheless, to insure reasonably convergent interpretation, the intended significance of conventions of text must be made clear. At present, while conventions of symbolic representation in the form of letters and whole words are stressed in beginning reading, little attention is paid to visual aspects of the process at later stages of instruction. It is as though this form of perception were a thing of the past, not worthy of notice from those who have been initiated into the mystery of sentences and paragraphs. This paper will address itself to the point that all ways of addressing the structure of ideas on a page of expository text are valid and that visual perception of the page is one of these.

Perception of the code system needs to be stressed and stressed differently as children progress in reading. Just as even kindergarten children's perceptions of the nature and purpose of reading can be enhanced by stressing familiar code elements such as signs, logos, and symbols (Mayfield, 1983), so older students can learn to make use of what they already know and can do. Elements common to all stages, such as looking for similarities and differences between symbolic forms and noting the divisions between them, can serve as a foundation for consistently calling attention to new visual aspects, such as headings. The visual elements act as signals to the inner structure of the text (Brooks *et al.*, 1983; Loman and Mayer, 1983).

Teaching students the skill of looking for structural or code systems as they progress in reading might be compared to the process of teaching someone first to ride a tricycle, then a small bicycle, next a ten-speed racer, and finally perhaps a pediplane. Instruction has to be geared to providing a conceptual model of the act of reading certain kinds of text since it has been found that if no model is provided by the teacher, the students will create their own (Norman, 1980).

Mindful of the great volume of recent research on text processing and of the present key words in educational research – interaction, particular context, and ecological validity – no claim is being made that understanding of the visual aspects of text processing is the only way of achieving a conceptual model of structure. There is, however, a need to go a step 'behind' verbal processing and its metacognitive aspects to the perceptual and biologically adaptive (Lenneberg, 1967) aspect of learning. All students with normal vision can *see* what is on a page besides words, given a little guidance. If structural cues or signals are seen, then the words are chunked, or grouped, into units with particular inner relationships. Each inner relationship can then be more minutely processed by syntactic, semantic, or cohesion methods (Halliday and Hasan, 1976; Chapman, in press). If the cues are *not* seen, hundreds of separate pieces of information must be processed.

The meaning of structure

What do we mean by structure? According to the dictionary, a structure is a complex system looked at from the point of view of the whole rather than any single part; it is a manner of construction. In text, structure is not only the hierarchy of categories, but also the logical relationships between elements of content, such as comparison, cause and effect, or statement and supporting detail. Not only is there an outline to follow in expository text, but many paragraphs are constructed around a category, elaborating on the category label, or generalisation, to form a topic sentence and on the category items to support this sentence (Gerhard, 1975). Students trained to see the structure of ideas in this way can use the category format, or reduction, to list a group of items which do *not* have a generalisation in order to provide one by abstracting the common characteristic.

The particular difficulty of discovering structure in text is that more is required than perception of one page. Higher level structure may cover a whole chapter. Memory of what has been read and prediction of what is likely to be read are necessary at the same time that the eye is busy conveying symbols to the brain. If readers are not looking for structure, they cannot remember what they did not perceive (Neisser, 1976, 1982), nor have a plan about what is likely to be perceived.

The outline, the most visible form of structure in expository text, is faithfully taught to most older students. However, the emphasis is usually on the production of writing and the stress is on Roman numerals, capital letters and so forth. If the underlying *meaning* of these is not understood, the significance of outline form is lost. The meaning needs to be addressed first in terms of single categories. There is a fundamental difference between the items in a set and the category label. The items may be concrete and may differ considerably while they are perceived as equivalent in some way (Olver and Hornsby, 1966). The category label, on the other hand, is an abstraction in every case, just as is any naming word.

Categories in expository text have labels which state a relationship between the items of a set. However, this relationship may be transitory so that individual members of this set may be combined with other items to form different sets. Herein lies a processing problem. The shifts may be confusing unless the structure of the whole is understood. In an article on Albert Schweitzer's many accomplishments, for example, he can be included with other people in several different sets: theologians, musicians, Bach scholars, missionaries, and doctors of tropical medicine.

The complexities of expository text comprehension

Expository text comprehension consists of integrating at least three systems or structures. There is the structure of the written text, the structure of the concepts which undergird the text, and the structure of concepts already in the mind of the reader to which unfamiliar ideas can be related.

The structures cannot be pictured as three points on a triangle, or even a circle, with arrows going back and forth, because within each structure the language elements both represent actual feelings and experiences and affect the way in which these are perceived and coded in memory (Britton, 1972; Copple *et al.*, 1979; Sigel, 1981). There is, therefore, not only a necessary interaction between the three structures for reading comprehension to take place, but also interaction within each structure of all the elements: cultural values, feelings, actual experiences, and language. Language is only the visible part of this interaction. An artist might be able to conceive of a way to represent all this inner activity, but a tidy model will prove inadequate. A tidy representation will distort the picture of reading comprehension and therefore frustrate instructional attempts.

Text structure will depend in part on conventions of written language, in part on the particular structure of the content being discussed (Binkley, 1983), and in part on the writer's manner of structuring information and subjecting it to a particular bias. However, all three elements combine to form a pattern of categories arranged in a hierarchy.

At the base of this hierarchy are individual paragraphs. A great number of these are based on a category. The label, or generalisation, is elaborated to form a topic sentence, or else it is implied. The items are elaborated within the relationship of the whole category to complete the paragraph (Gerhard, 1975). Several paragraphs are related in sections with headings, so that, in a sense, the items under a heading are the contents of the topic sentences. Several headings may in turn be 'demoted' to the status of items under the general title. If all goes well, every word is related in some way to this title.

Particular subjects, or content, will also require particular structures of ideas. For example, a textbook on history will emphasise time sequences and cause and effect relationships.

The writer's cultural and professional bias will determine the prominence of some information over others, the divisions of information, and additional illustrative material included. It is only fair to say that the publisher and demands of the market place also play a part.

The structures underlying the text consist of cultural values, assumptions, shared historical experiences, and shared metaphors (Lakoff and Johnson, 1980). In essense, the writer anticipates that using certain language forms will trigger mental representations and feelings similar to his or her own and essential to meaningful reading (Paivio and Begg, 1981).

The structures, concepts, or schemata in the mind of the reader have been the subject of so much discussion that they will only be touched upon here. Human beings employ the biologically adaptive tool of categorising (Lenneberg, 1967) as a system for filtering the myriad bits of information available at any moment in the environment so that only those bits which are significant or meaningful are fully processed. As people look for similarities and differences in groups of experiences and form generalisations about relationships, such as naming words, these in turn influence the way in which new experiences are coded. Forming category labels allows distancing (Sigel, 1981) from immediate perceptual experience and provides the means for gradual development of more abstract, symbolic, and formal ways of processing information such as expository text. However, the same basic conditions of learning will apply to the processing of abstract information as in the early years of development. That which is not significant and meaningful to the learner will be filtered out and only information which is considered relevant will be processed. Therefore, if the reader is unaware of structure in text or considers it irrelevant, it will be glossed over or not seen at all.

The structures in the mind of the reader and the structures in a passage of expository text are at least theoretically related through the categorising process. It may be possible to indicate ways that have been found to harmonise the two structures.

Harmonising the text and the reader will depend on an understanding of concepts underlying the text as well as the reader's culture and stage of development. Here again the categorising process is relevant, even when cultural metaphors are considered. Just as children categorise by different systems as they grow up (Vygotsky, 1962; Piaget and Inhelder, 1969), so also cultures in different environments and in different stages of development categorise differently (Bruner, 1966; Rosch, 1973; Luria, 1976; Scribner and Cole, 1981). While people schooled in western industrialised societies may naturally categorise first by function, other groups see experiences as related by colour or other attributes. This natural way of relating perceived information affects whole patterns of thinking. In a similar way, devout and total adherence to particular religions appears to affect perception of events.

Instructional implications of seeing comprehension as the harmonising of structures

If the foregoing exposition is true, instruction in comprehension must take the structures of the text itself, its underlying concepts, and the reader's prior knowledge into account. The three structures are related through the categorising process. While there are different forms of categories, in expository text the classical form (Smith and Medin, 1981) is used. This form establishes relationships by defining attributes and sees items in a group as equivalent in some way. In a history textbook, for example, kings are likely to be grouped by their accomplishments or horrendous mistakes rather than by being related in ever-widening circles to a prototype king, or lumped together because the writer happens to like them personally.

Making use of existing categorising skills

A fundamental aspect, then, of teaching comprehension of expository text must be an understanding of the process of forming classical categories. This implies the need to bring into the conscious range of students their own strengths as categorisers in daily life, then relating this ability to the eventually desired goal of perceiving categories in text (Gerhard, 1975). The very great differences between the category label, a general abstraction about the way in which items are related, and the category items needs to be approached first in concrete situations which every student can understand. The concrete activities clearly have to include the learning and use of appropriate language for discussing the relationships being studied (Beilin, 1981).

Seeing process as an entity

A related aspect of this approach to instruction of comprehension concerns reaching an understanding of process, or procedures for thinking about information, as, in a sense 'concrete entities' (Papert, 1980). That is to say, they exist independently of the particular content at hand and therefore provide transfer of advances in comprehension. Papert compares this concept of process to that of object permanence in early childhood since it gives children a tool for moving towards abstract thinking. The concept can perhaps best be approached through metaphor and analogy, or correlating a known system with one little known. For instance, students might be asked how they handle any problem at home, such as getting permission from parents which they anticipate is likely to be withheld. Do they just blurt out the request, or do they work out a plan of action which perhaps includes specially good behaviour and careful choosing of the timing and particular parent? In the abstract this plan is one of problem-solving, requiring identification of the problem, analysis of various approaches, making a decision, carrying it out and so on. If a student can be shown that the schema for problem-solving is already in hand, then the instructional task is one of learning to apply it (Underwood, 1982). Plans must become operational (Flower and Hayes, 1981).

Providing a specific knowledge framework

This emphasis on process is not meant to detract from the importance of having knowledge of content also available. There can be no such thing as comprehension without domain-specific knowledge (Simon, 1980; Greeno, 1980; Mayer, 1983). Providing a framework of requisite knowledge before approaching a text is an honoured tradition. This often includes collecting information from all the students. What is not often done is then to apply the categorising process to the list of items provided, having the students group and label them, and carefully reviewing the language generated for appropriateness and precision. This act of categorising information prior to reading offers opportunities to become familiar with the structure of the material and to consciously act upon it (Brooks *et al.*, 1983).

Having briefly considered the instruction of the categorising process, of process as an entity, and of building a scaffolding (Ausubel, 1960) of domain-specific knowledge prior to reading, the task is now to approach the structure of text as found on the page.

Seeing structure on a page of text

Expository text as a hierarchy of categories has already been mentioned. This hierarchy is visually signalled by such devices as headings, different types of print, and spacing on the page. Other types of structure are signalled by relational words like *and, if,* or *because,* and by endings such as *-er* or *-est.* Other comparisons are expressed through analogies signalled by words such as *like* or by metaphors (Torangeau and Sternberg, 1982). Thus, once students are made aware of different structures of ideas, they can be trained to interpret the visual signals for them correctly and mentally act upon them, or follow a plan. A word like *but* can trigger a search for juxtaposition of positive and negative statements in a manner not unlike pressure being applied to the brake pedal on seeing a red traffic light. The difficulty in the past has been the 'beguiling fiction' (Zalusky, 1981) that purely visual and verbal representations were completely separate: this in spite of the efforts of figures such as Arnheim, Kolers, and Feuerstein.

In speaking of the structure of expository text there is an intention of indicating that it is very different from that, for example, of story grammars, although developmentally one leads into the other. The differences have recently been pointed out in studies of detecting and remembering main ideas. Children who could do this well in stories often could not do it in expository text (Goetz and Armbruster, 1980; Baumann, 1983).

1. Setting the stage

This author suggested (1981) that students might find it easier to discover main ideas if they were made aware of visual cues to the structure of ideas. A page of text was translated into large and small X's with the format retained. Since that time a variety of ways of using this instructional method with particular subject textbooks has been tried. It was found that presenting a page with nothing but X's without introduction is counter-productive because it strays too far from traditional ways of thinking about reading. However, if a picture incorporating desired features such as vertical, horizontal, and diagonal lines, significant spaces, a frame, light and dark features, and symmetry or asymmetry, is used first to collect the necessary vocabulary and focus on the purely visual processing act, the technique serves to make structure a vivid concept. Once the features of the picture have been fully discussed and the appropriate words written, it is still necessary to explain the point of the exercise, knowing that people filter out information that is not meaningful to them. The point is to capitalise on visual ability in the interests of looking for the structure of ideas in the particular book being studied so as to save time and increase the chances of both understanding and remembering what is read.

While one could quote percentages of students who found the approach helpful, a significant study would have to include a large and varied sample and extensive follow-up exercises. Such a study has not yet been done. Nevertheless, because the approach shows real promise in making the structure of ideas vivid and emphasising the search for structural cues, an example follows (Figure 1).

Lines

1.	xxxxxx xxxxx. Xxx xxxx xx xxxxxxxxxxxxxxxx xxxxx xxxxx
2.	xxx xxxxxxxxxx xxxxxxx xxxx xx xxxx xxx "xxxxxxxxxx" xx
3.	xxxxxx xx xxxxxx xx xxx xxxxxxx xxxxx xxxx xxxxxxxxxx
4.	xxxxxxxx. Xxxxx xxx Xxxxx (1981) xxxxxxx xxxx
5.	xxxxx xxxx xxxxx xx xx xxxxxxx xxxxxxx
6.	xxxx xxxxxxxx xxx xxxx xx xxxxx (xxxxxxxx)
7.	xxx xxxxxxx xxxxxxxxxxx (x. 182).
8.	Xxxxxxxxxx Xxxxxxxxx Xxxxxxx xxx Xxxxx
9.	Xxxxxxxxxxx
10.	Xxxxxxxxxxxx xx xxx xxxx xx xxxxxxxxxxxxx xxxxxxxxx
11.	xxxxxxxx xxxxx xx xxxxxxxxx xxxxxxxxx xxx xx xxx xxxxxx
12.	xx xxx xxxxxx/xxxxxxx xxxxxxxxxxxxxx. Xx xxxx xxxxx xx
13.	xxxxxxxxxxxxx xxxxxxx, xxx xxx xxxxx xxx xx xxxxx xxxxxx
14.	xxx xxxxxx xxxxx xxxxx xxx xxxxxxxx xxx xxxxxxxx xxxxx
15.	xxxxxxxxxx xxx xxx xxxxx xx xxxxxxxxx xxxxxxx xx xxxxxx
16.	xx xxxxxxxxx.
17.	Xxx xxxxxxxx xx xxxx xxxxxx xxxxxxxx xxx xxxxxxxxx
18.	xxxxxx xxxxxxxxxx xxx xx xxxxxxxx xxxxx xx xx xxx xxxxx
19.	xxxxxxxx xxx; xxxx xx xxxxxxxxxx; xxxxx, xxxxxxxxxxx,
20.	xxx xxxxxxxxx; xxx xxxxxx xx xxxxxxxxxx xxx xxxxxxxxx;
21.	xxx xxx xxxx xx xxxxxx.
22.	Xxxxxxxx xx Xxxxxxxxxxx Xxx
23.	Xxxxxxxxxxx
24.	Xxxxx xxxxxxxx xx xx xxxxx xxxxxxxx xxxxxxxxxxxxx,

Fig. 1. Transformed text

(*Note*. No attempt is made to reproduce the exact number of letters of the original page because this cannot be done on an ordinary typewriter.)

In looking at Figure 1 as a *picture* and speaking in strictly visual terms, it is possible to discern two main divisions of uneven extent, the bottom part being again subdivided by dark lines. There are two different examples of the use of symmetry, one made up of small shapes in three lines and the other with large and small shapes emphasised by a dark line. The divisions on the page are not only created by dark lines, but also by spaces between horizontal lines of shapes and in relation to the frame. Besides the predominant shape in large and small versions with an emphasis on horizontal lines, there are a number of other shapes presented, such as ( ), /, a number of dots and 1, 2, 8, and 9 in different combinations. This will suffice for the following discussion of the significance of the visual signals when thought of as cues to the structure of ideas.

2. *Interpreting visual cues*

Looking at Figure 1 now as a page of text, a few salient features can be mentioned. The symmetrically placed heading (line 8) which divides the page is apparently a main heading. Below it are two subheadings (lines 9 and 22) and a sub-subheading (line 23). Interpreting these divisions of the text and predicting likely structural features might lead to the conclusion that the lines above the main heading (1–7) are the end of another main portion of the text, or an introduction to what follows. Clearly, the three closely spaced lines are a quotation from a recent book which contains at least 182 pages. The presence (line 23) of a sub-subheading indicates that on the following pages where will be at least one more such heading and that, when the page is turned, all three layers of headings need to be kept in mind, but especially the third layer, until the next heading is encountered.

The punctuation on the page reveals further structural aspects. The conspicuous slash mark (line 12) might indicate contrasting terms. The one comma in the following line (13) probably indicates a clause. This is in contrast to the commas (line 19) coming close together almost certainly indicating items in a previously named category. These commas occur within a passage divided by four semicolons which indicate complex items within a higher level category. There is, then, a good example of a hierarchy of categories, one embedded in the other.

By looking at this page in purely visual terms and then relating these to what is known about conventions of expository text, it has been possible to determine a number of structural aspects without reading a word. Eliminating the words appears to force a stress on structure. Interestingly, in a parallel development, Michael Twyman of Reading University has been using the same technique for several years in order to teach typography. A mental representation of structure as an entity, to return to Papert's expression, is provided and there is therefore a possibility of having an operational plan of looking for specific visual cues which are likely to reveal elements of structure.

3. *Predicting from headings*

The next step in encouraging readers to use pattern recognition as a projective tool is to reveal the topics being discussed by providing the headings. These are:

Cognitive Intervention Through the Categorizing Process (line 8)
Introduction (line 9)
Deficit or Developmental Lag (line 22)
Introduction (line 23)

It appears likely that the first introduction places (1) cognitive intervention, and (2) the categorising process in a particular context. The second paragraph is indeed likely to list the five forthcoming sections, followed by the first topic as a heading. This topic will be covered at least by the introduction and a section on (1) deficit, and (2) developmental lag. The subsequent heading on a following page is highly likely to be about deficit.

Predicting from headings is certainly not a new technique in teaching reading comprehension. However, having puzzled over the 'X' page, students may be curious about identifying the topics. In other words, now that

---

formal terms. The kind of information being processed may well affect the categorizing approach used so that more "natural" information, such as colors, is related to a prototype while textbooks require classical categorizing. Smith and Medin (1981) conclude that
there will likely be no crucial experiments or analyses that will establish one view of concepts (categories) and rule out all others irrevocably (p. 182).

Cognitive Intervention Through the Categorizing Process
Introduction
Intervention in the rate of developmental change or the ultimately attained level of cognitive processing goes to the heart of the nature/nurture controversy. In this brief review studies are presented not as conclusive evidence, but for the way in which they add small pieces to the immense jigsaw puzzle and indicate how teacher knowledge about categorizing and its place in organized thought might be a useful aspect of intervention.

The discussion in this section includes the question of whether student difficulties can be accounted for by a deficit theory or one of developmental lag; ways of looking at intelligence; memory, metacognition, and prediction; the question of consciousness and automatic operations; and the role of language.
Deficit or Developmental Lag
Introduction
Those subscribing to a deficit theory of poor student performance,

---

Fig. 2.   Original text

Source: Gerhard (1983) p. 46.

they have concentrated on structure and have a mental representation of the structure of this particular page, they are no longer filtering it out as being meaningless. If the 'X' page is indeed a translation of a page of text they need to read for a class, it will perhaps be of interest to find out something about it. There is also an element of playing detectives involved. Famous detectives often find solutions to crimes in fiction by shifting the way in which they perceive events. In order to accomplish this shift, they use plans of listing everything that is known about a problem and then categorising the items on the list in novel ways. The plan for solving the problem of readers seeing only *words* on pages of text has consisted of promoting a visual mind set with the picture, analysing visual aspects of the 'X' page, relating these aspects to known conventions of expository text, and predicting content from headings. Actual reading of the page (Figure 2) should result in students being surprised at how much they can anticipate.

This plan, if frequently referred to or used several times, may provide a way of encouraging an automatic search for structure when reading. Certainly, it will not be effective as a one-shot lesson plan.

Understanding different conceptual systems

Harmonising the structure of text and the schemata of prior knowledge in the reader's mind will be incomplete without including the accompaniment of underlying concepts: assumptions, inferences, metaphors and cultural bias. No area of comprehension is more difficult to approach in instructional terms. The underlying concepts are not broadly stated, but rather implied by the use of particular language.

In any given culture or subculture there is a likelihood that members of that group will expect all people to think as they do. In fact, as already noted, people even categorise events in their environment by different attributes. There can also be differences in orientation. Lakoff and Johnson (1980) provide a telling example. In Western countries, a writer might refer to a cloud as being *in front* of a mountain if it is between the person and the mountain. The orientation is away from the body. In other cultures, the identical spatial situation could be described as 'the cloud behind the mountain' because the orientation is towards the body. These authors list other aspects of conceptual systems which can vary greatly. They include dimensions of experience such as participants in an action, the prototypes developed individually through experience, and interactional properties. As one example of conceptual systems leading to different interpretations, any text related to the role of women nowadays would surely evoke very different reactions around the world.

It is not possible here to pursue the many ways in which fundamental relational concepts can differ from culture to culture. The only certainty is that they do. Instruction must therefore include a careful look at the language of an expository passage for clues as to personal and cultural bias. Equally important, however, is knowledge about student ways of processing information which can only be obtained by providing opportunities for groups of students to work on problems and then observing and listening very carefully. This type of observation has been an important part of instruction and research in the early school years (Cocking, 1983) and should be promoted on the secondary level.

Secondary teachers also have to remain open to the idea that there may be more than one way of *logically* relating items of information, even though one or the other is more appropriate at a given juncture. If the reader is to become independent and feel competent to comprehend the ideas of others, then his or her own ideas must be considered seriously. If there is an error, the reasoning behind the error needs to be addressed. In other words, the Piagetian framework needs to be extended in order to understand self-directed learning within the ecological setting of the school (Ginsburg, 1981). At the same time, readability needs to be looked at in terms of structure and the learning strategies of the reader (Admiran and Jones, 1982; Garner and Anderson, 1982; Wagoner, 1983).

Secondary teacher thinking about categorising

Secondary teachers' own thinking processes must play a significant role in helping students comprehend the content of texts used in their classrooms. The same learning conditions apply to them as to their students: they categorise information in daily life and they process the information which appears meaningful to them. Fully understanding the categorising process and applying that understanding to instruction of comprehension should logically lead to certain kinds of teaching behaviours, as demonstrated in the Taba studies (1966, 1969). Clear, unambiguous examples of information which was important for comprehension would initially be provided (Bruner, 1956). Opportunities for students to participate in making decisions about grouping the information would be given. Cues to particular relationships would be studied and the interpretation of these practised (Lysakowski and Walberg, 1981, 1982). Opportunities for creating category labels in appropriate language would be created and new examples of items for these categories sought. The reasoning behind incorrect categorising would be looked for.

There has been a recent revival of interest in teacher thinking (Mandl and Huber, 1982; Bamberger, 1983). One study investigated teacher knowledge about categorising and ability to create category labels (Gerhard, 1983). Science teachers were significantly better in both areas than the English and sixth grade teachers in the sample. It is probably easier to understand the significance of categorising in science classes, but opportunities for learning about language should be greater in the other areas.

Conclusion

Approaching reading comprehension as the harmonising of three structural systems, that of the text itself, the underlying concepts, and the reader's prior knowledge, may seem to make it even less tractable. However, using techniques to improve comprehension of expository text which address only superficial aspects of the problem is not likely to produce independent readers who feel competent and therefore are able to enjoy reading. Equally, crash, short-term projects, while initially stimulating, will have to give way to long-term instruction in thinking processes.

There are two basic tools with which to work, although one might be considered a part of the other. Students are capable of being trained to perceive information in different ways and they are capable of seeing other aspects of a page of text besides words. This perceptual aptitude is part of the adaptive tool of categorising experiences in order to note them, remember them, and predict from known patterns to unknown events.

The basic categorising process includes looking for similarities and differences and forming general statements, or category labels, to express relationships between groups of items. While this is initially done with very little language, language becomes more and more important in organising ideas.

These human potentials point the way to the instructional implications of looking at comprehension as reconciling the three structures. These are related by the categorising process which would therefore appear to be central to comprehension. Consequently, ways of encouraging accurate perception of similarities and differences in items of information and of making the seeking of them an automatic part of the learning process would seem to be called for. The early grades are the place to start this emphasis, but the information there would not, of course, be presented in the form of expository text.

A second implication of making the categorising process central in comprehension instruction is that it would require numerous opportunities for students to not only find common characteristics in information presented, but to create for themselves generalisations about these characteristics in language which is both appropriate and precise. While the productive use of language may be different from the act of reading, learning how to form generalisations should enhance the ability to recognise those of others. In both the seeking of common characteristics and their description in suitable language, the emphasis has to be on student decisions. Memorising the categories of others may have many uses, including perhaps improving the amount of domain-specific knowledge available, but it will not lead to the active seeking of relationships essential to comprehension of expository text. When language remains connected to perceptual decisions about concrete or abstract information it is more likely to serve the user well.

The third implication of attempting to harmonise the three structures of text, underlying concepts, and reader schemata is that the reading of expository text and the seeking after relationships be made in some way meaningful to the students. The inborn capacity to create categories functions by filtering out information which is not at the moment meaningful. Returning to the opening figure of the four people seeing four different gardens, it might be said that if all four are to see the structure of the garden, like the artist, they must have a convincing reason for changing their natural information-processing system. Perhaps there is to be a prize for drawing the most accurate plan of the garden or the group is planning an entertainment in the garden. No matter what the reason, it must make sense. The complexities of expository text comprehension are givens. Fortunately, the human mind possesses the tools of perception, of categorising, and of identifying and solving problems. It remains for instruction to bring these existing tools out into the open and show how to apply them consciously to reading.

References

ADMIRAN, M. R. and JONES, B. F. (1982) 'Toward a new definition of readability'. *Educational Psychologist*, 17, pp. 13–30.

AUSUBEL, D. P. (1960) 'Use of advance organizers in the learning and retention of meaningful verbal material'. *Journal of Educational Psychology*, 51, pp. 267–72.

BAMBERGER, J., DUCKWORTH, E. and LAPERT, M. (1983) *An Experiment in Teacher Development. Final Report*. National Institute of Education Grant G-78-0219.

BAUMANN, J. F. (1983) 'Research on children's main idea comprehension: A problem of ecological validity'. *Reading Psychology*, 3, pp. 167–77.

BEACH, R. and PEARSON, P. D. (eds) (1979) *Perspectives on Literacy:* Proceedings of 1977 Perspectives on Literacy Conference, College of Education, University of Minnesota.

BEILIN, H. (1981) 'Language and thought: Thistles among the sedums', in I. E. Sigel, D. M. Brodzinsky and R. M. Golinkiff (eds) *New Directions in Piagetian Theory and Practise*. Hillsdale, N.J.: Erlbaum.

BINKLEY, M. (1983) *A Descriptive and Comparative Study of Cohesive Structure in Differing Academic Disciplines*. Unpublished doctoral dissertation, George Washington University.

BRITTON, J. (1972) *Language and Learning*. London: Pelican.

BROOKS, L. W., DANSEREAU, D. F., HOLLEY, C. D. and SPURLIN, J. E. (1983) 'Generation of descriptive text headings'. *Contemporary Educational Psychology*, 8, pp. 103–8.

BROOKS, L. W., DANSEREAU, D. F., HOLLEY, C. D. and SPURLIN, J. E. (1983) 'Effects of headings on text processing'. *Journal of Educational Psychology*, 75, pp. 292–302.

BRUNER, J. S., GOODNOW, J. J. and AUSTIN, G. A. (1956) *A Study of Thinking*. New York: Wiley.

BRUNER, J. S., OLVER, R. R. and GREENFIELD, P. M. (1966) *Studies in Cognitive Growth*. New York: Wiley.

CHAPMAN, L. J. (in press) 'Register development and secondary tests', in B. Gillham (ed.) *The Language of School Subjects*. London: Heinemann.

COCKING, R. R. (1983) 'Structure and function in constructivism: Examples from children's play and language'. Paper given at AERA, Montreal.

COPPLE, C., SIGEL, I. E. and SAUNDERS, R. (1979) *Educating the Young Thinker: Classroom Strategies for Cognitive Growth*. New York: van Nostrand.

FLOWER, L. and HAYES, J. R. (1981) 'Plans that guide the composing process', in C. H. Frederiksen and J. R. Dominic *Writing: The Nature, Development, and Teaching of Written Communication*, Vol. 2, Hillsdale, N.J.: Erlbaum.

GARNER, R. and ANDERSON, J. (1982) 'Monitoring-of-understanding-research: Inquiry directions, methodological dilemmas'. *Journal of Experimental Education*, 50, pp. 70–6.

GERHARD, C. (1975) *Making Sense: Reading Comprehension Improved Through Categorizing*. Newark, Delaware: International Reading Association.

GERHARD, C. (1983) *Teacher Knowledge about Selected Aspects of Categorizing and their Use in the Instruction of Sixth, Seventh and Eighth Grade Students*. Unpublished doctoral dissertation, George Washington University.

GINSBURG, H. P. (1981) 'Piaget and education'. In I. E. Sigel, D. M. Brodzinsky and R. M. Golinkoff (eds) *New Directions in Piagetian Theory and Practice*. Hillsdale, N.J.: Erlbaum.

GOETZ, E. T. and ARMBRUSTER, B. B. (1980) 'Psychological correlates of text structure', in R. J. Spiro, B. C. Bruce and W. F. Brewer (eds) *Theoretical Issues in Reading Comprehension*. Hillsdale, N.J.: Erlbaum.

GREENO, J. G. (1980) 'Trends in the theory of knowledge for problem solving', in D. T. Tuma and F. Reif (eds) *Problem Solving and Education*. Hillsdale, N.J.: Earlbaum.

HALLIDAY, M. A. K. and HASAN, R. (1976) *Cohesion in English*. London: Longman.

LAKOFF, G. and JOHNSON, M. (1980) *Metaphors We Live By*. University of Chicago.

LENNEBERG, E. H. (1967) *Biological Foundations of Language*. New York: Wiley.

LOMAN, N. L. and MAYER, R. E. (1983) 'Signalling techniques that increase the understanding ability of expository prose'. *Journal of Educational Psychology*, 3, pp. 401–12.

LURIA, A. R. (1976) *Cognitive Development, its Cultural and Social Foundation*. Cambridge, Ma.: Harvard.

LYSAKOWSKI, R. S. and WALBERG, H. J. (1981) 'Classroom reinforcement and learning: A quantitative synthesis'. *Journal of Education Research*, 75, pp. 69–77.

LYSAKOWSKI, R. S. and WALBERG, H. J. (1982) 'Instructional effects of cues, participation, and corrective feedback: A quantitative synthesis'. *AER Journal*, 19, pp. 559–78.

MANDL, H. and HUBER, G. L. (1982) 'On teachers' subjective theories. A review of research in West Germany'. Paper presented at AERA, New York.

MAYER, R. E. (1983) *Thinking, Problem Solving, Cognition*. San Francisco: Freeman.

MAYFIELD, M. I. (1983) 'Code systems instruction and kindergarten children's perceptions of the nature and purpose of reading'. *Journal of Educational Research*, 76, pp. 161–8.

NEISSER, U. (1976) *Cognition and Reality: Principles and Implications of Cognitive Psychology*. San Francisco: W. H. Freeman.

NEISSER, U. (1982) *Memory Observed: Remembering in Natural Contexts*. San Francisco: Freeman.

NORMAN, D. A. (1980) 'Cognitive engineering and education', in D. Tuma and F. Reif (eds) *Problem Solving and Education: Issues in Teaching and Research*. Hillsdale, N.J.: Erlbaum.

OLVER, R. R. and HORNSBY, J. R. (1966) 'On equivalence', in J. S. Bruner, R. R. Olver and F. M. Greenfield (eds) *Studies in Cognitive Growth*. New York: Wiley.

PAIVIO, A. and BEGG, I. (1981) *Psychology of Language*. Englewood Cliffs, N.J.: Prentice-Hall.

PIAGET, J. and INHELDER, B. (1969) *The Psychology of the Child*. New York: Basic Books.

PAPERT, S. (1980) *Mindstorms: Children, Computers, and Powerful Ideas*. New York: Basic Books.

ROSCH, E. (1973) 'Natural Categories'. *Cognitive Psychology*, 4, pp. 328–50.

SCRIBNER, S. and COLE, M. (1981) *The Psychology of Literacy*. Cambridge, Ma.: Harvard.

SIGEL, 1. E. (1981) 'Social experience in the development of representational thought: Distancing theory', in *New Directions in Piagetian Theory and Practice.* Hillsdale, N.J.: Erlbaum.

SIMON, H. A. (1980) 'Problem solving and education', in D. Tuma and F. Reif (eds) *Problem Solving and Education.* Hillsdale, N.J.: Erlbaum.

SMITH, E. E. and MEDIN, D. L. (1981) *Categories and Concepts.* Cambridge, Ma.: Harvard.

SZWED, J. F. (1981) 'The ethnography of literacy', in M. F. Whiteman (ed.) *Writing: The Nature, Development, and Teaching of Written Communication,* Vol. 1. Hillsdale, N.J.: Erlbaum.

TABA, H. (1966) *Teaching Strategies and Cognitive Functioning in Elementary Children.* USOE Cooperative Research Project No. 2404. San Francisco State College.

TABA, H. (1969) 'Learning by discovery: Psychological and educational rationale', in E. P. Torrance and W. F. White *Issues and Advances in Educational Psychology.* University of Georgia: Peacock.

TOURANGEAU, R. and STERNBERG, R. J. (1982) 'Understanding and appreciating metaphors'. *Cognition,* 11, pp. 203–44.

UNDERWOOD, G. (ed.) (1982) *Aspects of Consciousness, Vol. 3: Awareness and Self-Awareness.* London: Academic Press.

VYGOTSKY, L. S. (1962) *Thought and Language.* Cambridge, Ma.: MIT.

WAGONER, S. A. (1983) 'Comprehension monitoring: What it is and what we know about it'. *Reading Research Quarterly,* 18, pp. 328–46.

ZALUSKY, V. L. (1982) 'Relationships: What did I write? What did I draw?, in W. Frawley (ed.) *Linguistics and Literacy,* New York: Plenum.

9 Direct instruction reading for children with special needs

Roger Cocks

Introduction

In 1978 the Warnock report recommended that existing categorisation of handicapped children be abolished. Causes of handicap were recognised to be extremely complex making classification problematic. Research on aptitude treatment interactions suggests that the ideal of reliably measuring hypothetical abilities (said to underlie learning) in order to tailor instruction to individual differences is some way from being achieved. As a result some psychologists and teachers suggest a shift in emphasis away from studying individual differences (i.e., what it is about children that causes learning difficulties) to a much neglected complement to learning, namely task structure and teaching methods. This paper examines (1) the changing concept of special needs, and (2) three major models of remediation, focusing on the prescriptive implications of each, and then (3) describes the rationale behind one reportedly successful task analytic scheme.

1. The Concept 'Special Needs'

The concept of special educational needs is one that has evolved over a number of years. A brief examination of Figure 1 (page 92) reveals changes in emphasis that have occurred.

Prior to 1944 the main aim of diagnosis of children with special needs was focused on the discovery of children who deviated from the norm developmentally, or in their educational achievements. Psychometricians developed new tools with the explicit purpose of predicting likely failures. One major consequence of such an investigation was the process of categorisation. Using a criterion such as a score obtained on an I.Q. test the lucky individuals could find themselves (should they score below 70) being described as mentally defective. As if that weren't enough, the individuals could find themselves pigeon-holed into sub-categories with delightful names like moron, imbecile, or idiot. The dividing lines for such categorisation were purely arbitrary. There is no doubt that the use of psychometric instruments made classification more objective: but the consequences of classification, the stigma associated with being labelled, and the non-prescriptive nature of such diagnoses, were issues of which diagnosticians were relatively ignorant.

1944 brought the introduction of the term 'educationally subnormal' and was a welcome move from the derogatory connotations of previous classification. It was all the same a far cry from Warnock's 'education is a good to which all are entitled' since arbitrary cut-off points were established which

Model 1: Diagram showing the distribution of I.Q. scores

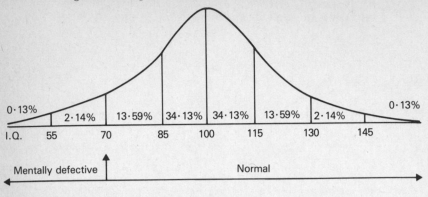

Model 2: Categorisation in terms of intelligence

I.Q.	Prior to 1944		Post 1944		1971	1978
70–80	Borderline deficiency		Borderline educationally subnormal		Borderline moderately educationally subnormal 'remedial'	Warnock recommends abolition of statutory categories of handicap and states that children should be described as having learning difficulties the extent of which could be described as mild, moderate or severe.
50–70	Moron Feeble minded	Mentally defective	Educationally subnormal	educable (50–70)	Educationally subnormal moderate ESN(M)	
20–50 below 20	Imbecile Idiot			Ineducable Trainable (below 50)	Educationally subnormal severe ESN(S)	

Figure 1

allowed dividing lines to be drawn between the educable and the ineducable. In addition, although children were described as educationally subnormal, the legal basis of special education and provision for children's needs was seen in the context of 'disability of mind or body'. Special education was organised on the assumption of there being ten official categories of handicap of which educational sub-normality was but one. A rather simple medical model of causation was implied; the obvious person, therefore, to carry out the assessment of children suffering such disabilities was thought to be the medical officer. The gradual emergence of greater numbers of Educational Psychologists, and the recognition of their contribution to assessment, meant that the educational aspects of assessment received greater attention.

Peter Mittler (1970) noted that as multiple handicap was the rule rather than the exception this made the classification of children into one of the ten official categories problematic. The concern for the practical problems and the consequences of labelling, the arbitrariness of the line drawn between normality and subnormality, led Peter Mittler to declare in his book *Assessment of Mental Handicap* that in respect of the official categories, diagnosis should concern itself with the educational and developmental aspects of the problem (as opposed to administrative considerations). This, he claimed, would help reduce the confusion between the child's 'disability' and the form of education he or she needs. Handicapped children, Mittler concludes, have educational needs that are not fundamentally different from other children. They need an environment in which their skills can be developed and in which their learning problems, regardless of cause, can be expertly identified and dealt with.

The realisation slowly emerged that the causes of special educational needs were complex. Warnock, like Mittler, suggested that such causes and their manifestations did not necessarily fall within the boundaries defined by the ten statutory categories. The emphasis shifted towards discussion of educational needs. It was suggested that the major focus of intervention should be via education. Indeed the 1970 Education Act gave a lead here by transferring responsibility for severely handicapped children from local health departments to local education authorities.

Warnock concluded, as did Mittler many years earlier, that no clear line could be drawn between handicapped and non-handicapped. 'The distinction between remedial education and special education should be dropped.' 'The statutory categorisation of children should be abolished.' What emerged was a broader concept of special needs including up to 20 per cent of the population. More importantly categorisation was de-emphasised and the focus turned to *intervention*. 'The help to be given to a child to allow him to overcome his educational handicap.' (Warnock, 1978.)

2. Assessment in relation to three major models of remediation

It is in the context of the present focus on educational intervention that I wish to examine assessment. For the Warnock committee and the 1981 Education Act assessment and educational intervention are major concerns. Important too is the fact that teachers and officers will have to show that their children are not simply part of an environment in which education takes place around them, yet is not of benefit to them. The argument in this paper leans very heavily on evaluating the models of remediation in terms of the way in which they benefit children. The models can be evaluated in terms of their prescriptive implications. It isn't the case that one model is more accurate than another in its description of causes of difficulty, rather it is simply that some models have clear prescriptive implications for teacher action and the specific help needed to be given to assist the child in overcoming his or her handicap.

Table 1.

| | Indirect approach | | Direct approach |
	1	2	3
	Etiological	Diagnostic Remedial	Task Analytic
Example of stated cause	Minimal brain dysfunction Dyslexia Chromosomal aberrations *Sensory Deficits Maladjustment	Perceptual difficulties Psycholinguistic difficulties Low I.Q.	Task deficiency *or* Teaching difficulty
Major focus	Factors within the child	Lack of crucial ability related to or underlying learning	Task construction and teaching methods
Diagnostic instrument	Bender Gestalt Health screening E.E.G.	Frostig test of visual perception Illinois test of psycho-linguistic abilities Aston index W.I.S.C.	1. Instructional sequence placement test 2. Noting what class of error has been made in performing a task and providing appropriate meaningful feedback in order to correct. Check correction on delayed test.
Classifying causation	Biological usually	Mismatch of learner and his/her ability to the instruction	1. Teaching: Placing a child at the incorrect entry point in a programmed sequence. 2. Task: Failure to master the component skills required to master the task.

Relevance to teaching and implications of diagnosis	Biological factors are not under the control of the teacher and are quite often used as labels to avoid responsibility for the problem.	The child's strengths and weaknesses are assessed and programmes devised to build on them	'Specific statements of what the child has not been taught represent a sufficient diagnosis in the educational setting. If such statements are not presented the teacher is not told specifically what to do. Statements about the child's brain injury do not alter one fact about what the child must be taught to achieve specific criteria of educational performance. A diagnosis expressed in terms of the child's perceptual deficiency or immaturity do not guide instruction. The only facts that are really helpful are facts about performance. Why does a child fail a complex task? Because he hasn't been taught certain skills required by that task.' (Engelmann, S., 1969)
Research	No-one has shown how programmes should be designed to cater specifically for different etiologies	1. The tests have not been shown to be reliable or valid. 2. The child after training becomes better at the test but this does not transfer to the academic task.	See Bibliography for research in U.S.A. and U.K. including teacher effectiveness research (Reith *et al.* and Stalling)

An inspection of the table on pages 94 and 95 provides a means of comparing models. Of the three models described two suggest indirect approaches to remediation (the Etiological and Diagnostic-Remedial models) while the third, the Task Analytic model offers a direct approach (hence the term direct instruction).

After inspecting Table 1 it soon becomes apparent that there are a number of ways of describing causes of learning difficulty, and this fact accounts for the confusion and complexity of etiology that Mittler (1974) and Warnock (1978) refer to. Causes, however, are the focus of most teachers' concerns. Referrals by teachers seeking causes often elicit confusing and wide-ranging replies. Doctors, psychiatrists, and even some psychologists, might describe children with special needs as being 'brain damaged' or suffering from 'minimal brain dysfunction' (see Table 1). On the other hand teachers might receive reports from the school's psychological service or remedial service in which mention of the above causes may be made, in addition to weaknesses or deficits in abilities said to be crucial for learning, i.e. perceptual and psycholinguistic abilities (see Table 1, model 2). The plea in this paper is not to suggest that there are more correct or less correct ways of describing children with special needs but simply to argue that some models go further than description; and that we should support the approaches that focus on causes that are relevant to teaching, and which thus have implications for educational intervention.

2.1. THE ETIOLOGICAL MODEL

As far as pinpointing etiology is concerned little can be found in this diagnostic strategy which is of help to the teacher. Those parents and teachers who are relieved to hear that the reason for the child's failure is, for example, dyslexia fail to stop and think how the information can possibly help the child overcome his or her problem. In many instances when the 'cause' is found, responsibility for the child's education gets shelved. The fact of the matter is that no-one has yet devised programmes which have been shown to be etiology specific. That this is the case can be seen by the fact that those who claim they have developed programmes specifically for brain-damaged children, for example, have failed to explain why their programmes work equally well on children with similar learning difficulties but who have an absence of any underlying pathology. There may be a correlation between severity of condition (listed in Figure 1, model 1) and academic failure but correlations do *not* imply causality. As Bateman (1977) says

. . . some brain damaged children do learn to read as do children with:

malnutrition	thyroid deficiencies	inadequate lateralization
double hair swirls	poor vision	low IQs
disinterested parents	oedipal conflicts	chromosomal aberrations
jagged ITPA profile	older sisters who achieve well at school	

speech defects	hyperactivity	finger agnosia
lefthandedness	undescended	
	testicles	

and every other alleged etiological factor!

2.2. THE DIAGNOSTIC-REMEDIAL MODEL

The model in column 2 offers an approach for the teacher which goes further than simple categorisation. The teacher can, with the help of experts, diagnose deficiencies in, for example, perception and psycholinguistic abilities. She or he can also follow training programmes designed to remedy deficiencies in these areas. Before selecting this apparently useful approach there are a number of questions that need answering.

2.2.1. Are these abilities as defined by the test designers prerequisites for learning?

As with the etiological model it must be pointed out that simply because scores on tests correlate with academic achievement, it does not mean that one can infer causes or that such abilities are therefore prerequisites for learning. Carnine (1981) pointed out in a survey of hundreds of children that many who had not been taught the difference, and therefore could not discriminate, between a triangle and a square (a typical exercise in a perceptual training programme) could nevertheless read fluently.

2.2.2. Can one match children to programmes based on assessment of strengths and weaknesses in the domains described by the test designers?

Ysseldyke (1973), in a review of research on aptitude treatment interaction, concluded that there was little empirical support for the claims that instruction can be differentiated on the basis of diagnostic strengths and weaknesses of the sort referred to in Table 1.

2.2.3. Are the subtests on which the children's ability profiles are based reliable?

Ysseldyke (et al., 1974) points out that the diagnostic instruments described in Table 1, model 2 are not sufficiently reliable. Where important education decisions are concerned it is usual to accept as reasonable reliability coefficients of ·95 and higher, with ·90 as the absolute minimum. Table 2 (page 98) gives the reported test retest reliability figures quoted by Ysseldyke. None of the subtests on these widely used diagnostic instruments reaches that level.

2.2.4. Does the remedial programme transfer to the academic task?

Many studies described by Ysseldyke (1973, 1974) of the sort carried out and reviewed by Sabatino and Dorfman (1973) suggest that (a) children following a programme of remedial education based on assessment of strengths and weaknesses in perceptual or psycholinguistic abilities improve in those areas as measured by the original diagnostic instrument, but that (b) the transfer to the academic task (i.e. the effects of the programme on reading) is negligible. Engelmann (1969) points out, therefore, that some practitioners are questioning the relevance of remedial bead stringing and puzzle assembly!

Table 2: Frequently used ability measures – their reliability and forecasting efficiency. (From Ysseldyke, 1974.)

Measure	Reported test–retest reliability	Percentage increase over chance
Developmental test of visual perception	·69	27·62
Eye motor coordination	·29–·39	4·3–7·9
Figure ground	·33–·39	5·6–7·9
Form constancy	·67–·74	25·1–32·7
Position in space	·35–·70	6·3–28·6
Special relations	·52–·67	14·6–25·8
Bender visual motor Gestalt test	·39–·66	7·2–24·9
Chicago test of visual discrimination	·35–·68	6·3–26·7
Revised visual retention test	·85	47·3
Memory for designs test (Graham-Kendall)	·72–·90	30·6–56·4
Primary visual motor test	·82	42·8
Development test of visual motor integration	·80–·87	40·0–50·7
Illinois test of psycholinguistic abilities	·66–·91	24·9–58·5
Auditory reception	·36–·79	6·7–38·7
Visual reception	·21–·69	2·2–27·6
Auditory association	·62–·90	21·5–56·4
Visual association	·32–·75	5·3–33·7
Verbal expression	·45–·74	10·7–32·7
Manual expression	·40–·87	8·4–28·6
Gramatic closure	·49–·87	12·8–50·7
Visual closure	·57–·82	17·8–42·8
Auditory sequential memory	·61–·89	20·8–54·4
Visual sequential memory	·12–·71	0·7–29·6

2.2.5. Why is there no transfer?

Bateman (1977) suggests that recommending activities like remedial bead stringing, are attempts to fulfil prescriptions for the development of visual memory or visual closure. But she points out that the diagnosticians may have neglected to ask questions about the task on which the child was failing. If the end product of the intervention, the educational outcome (e.g. reading) was in the mind of the remedial designer different recommendations for intervention would have emerged, and the remedial programme would more nearly resemble the desired outcome. The child would have his or her 'perceptual abilities' developed with letters rather than beads or puzzles. By analogy the suggestion is this. If you want to teach a child to ride a bike then teach him or her to ride a bike and not to master a whole set of balancing skills said to be related to and 'crucial' for bike riding. If a child confuses b's and d's teach him or her the discrimination directly not indirectly by playing with triangles and squares.

2.3. THE TASK ANALYTIC MODEL

The task analytic approach goes further than simply describing causes. In focusing on causes that the teacher can do something about the task analyst suggests that it is necessary to see the cause of a learning difficulty as a function of the task design and/or teaching difficulty. This means that the focus of enquiry will be the task structure and the teaching methods. Diagnosis, instead of being a very general process of categorising, becomes highly task specific.

In mathematics, for example, diagnosis could consist of deciding whether a child's error was a 'strategy' error or 'fact' error. The intervention would consist of providing the appropriate meaningful feedback for the class of error. Diagnosis would also reveal whether the child was appropriately placed in a sequence of instruction. In any event, though, the relevance to teaching of such an approach is abundantly clear. Why does a child fail? 'Because he hasn't been taught the component skills required to master the task.' (Engelmann, 1969.)

Evaluating the models in terms of 'the help given to a child to overcome his handicap' seems to lead us to suggest that the direct approach, the task analytic approach, holds out the greatest promise. My position is clear. I am not suggesting other causes listed in models 1 and 2 of Table 1 do not exist. For those pursuing the task analytic approach the often quoted statement 'task and teaching methods are the only cause of failure' isn't necessarily true, but it is *necessary* because such a position has implications for successful teacher intervention in a way that the other approaches do not.

3. Corrective reading and DISTAR: A direct instruction task-analytic approach

After many years' successful teaching of disadvantaged learners Siegfried Engelmann came to the conclusion that there was no magic in learning. If disadvantaged learners were to catch up with their middle-class peers, then ways would have to be found which would enable them to learn *more* in *less* time. The way in which he has achieved this has been to control teaching methods and task design.

3.1. TEACHING METHODS

3.1.1. Scripts

Scripted lessons are one of the unusual features of the programmes. The reason for having scripted lessons is apparent when one observes teachers operating without scripts. Firstly the potential sources of confusion (the teacher's use of language, task presentation and organisation) are all too apparent even amongst the best of teachers. Secondly, the intellectual indigestion and failure that the child often suffers and which results from, amongst other things,

1. The presentation of too much information
2. The failure accurately to assess 'entry behaviour'
3. The lack of appreciation of the component prerequisite skills required for mastery of a specific task
4. The lack of adequate review

are common avoidable errors frequently found in the teaching of children described as learning disabled.

Since those adopting the task-analytic approach fail to entertain the idea of 'children with learning difficulties' and would rather describe such children as difficult to teach it is clear that the focus of intervention for them are the many variables in the process of teaching which are seen to be, effectively, the cause of learning difficulties. Engelmann's approach has been to control such variables in order to minimise the chance of learning failure. His research at the University of Illinois showed that when scripts were not in use (unless teachers had substantial training) teachers had great difficulty coping with the amount of information which needed their attention during the course of a lesson. The solution to this problem was sought in the form of scripted lessons. The idea was to control some of the many variables not with the aim of removing the teacher from the process of teaching but to free her or him so that full attention could be devoted to *presenting* fluid and dynamic lessons and *monitoring* the children's performance, two important aspects of successful teaching. The scripts remove from the teacher the daunting if not impossible task of presenting tasks and monitoring pupil performance while simultaneously devoting attention to the design of such tasks and the means of getting the information across. Unless all the details of instruction are carefully controlled successful teaching, and therefore learning, may not take place.

3.1.2. Group instruction

The children are selected for a group on the basis of a placement test. The test shows (1) what skills the child has acquired in the past and (2) allows for placement in the programme at the appropriate level of difficulty. The programmes are designed to teach small groups because this is in keeping with the guiding principle of teaching MORE in LESS time.

An examination of the script in Figure 6 (p. 107) shows that the children are told something and then a series of prompts (questions) follow ('is the last letter *e*?' etc.). The children all respond in *unison* under the control of a 'point then touch the board' signal. If the children all respond on cue then no child will be in the position of simply following! Extracting information all at once by closely observing all in the group is extremely efficient. The teacher has to have a high degree of skill to monitor the pupils, who are prompted and reinforced in a highly individualised way. Attention and feedback is given according to need and is based on observations of children's performances. The children need never fear being 'put on the spot'. Corrections for errors are modelled by the teacher for the whole group without focusing on the child who errs. Later, when the teacher is sure that the child has mastered the skill, he or she will be given an 'individual turn' which tests his or her knowledge.

The presentation is paced rapidly so that attention is continuously secured, and the high number of responses per minute demanded by the programme increases academic engaged time – a *crucial variable* in *achievement* (see Reith *et al*. and Stalling).

3.2. TASK DESIGN

Tasks are designed with the principle of teaching more in less time and this is achieved by teaching general case strategies. Skills must be taught so that they can be generalised. By this we mean that, wherever possible, children must be provided with an educational experience in which they acquire a strategy for attacking different but related problems, not specifically taught. (See Figure 2.)

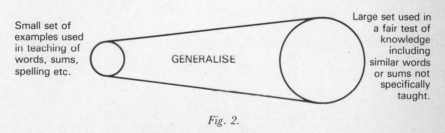

Small set of examples used in teaching of words, sums, spelling etc.

GENERALISE

Large set used in a fair test of knowledge including similar words or sums not specifically taught.

Fig. 2.

Slow learners are often described as being unable to generalise. We have seen that if we describe a problem as being a property of the learner there are no implications for interventions. It is unhelpful to describe generalisation as something that magically happens to some people and not others. Rather, generalisation should be seen as a function of task design and tasks must be designed so that children acquire strategies for dealing with previously unseen words.

In teaching a child a sight vocabulary using the whole word approach the words taught are the words known. Once a child has been taught to read *tip, tap, top*, a fair test of his or her sight vocabulary would consist of those same three words. The teaching set and test set are the same size (see Figure 3).

This may seem entirely reasonable where initial reading is concerned. Many schemes employ such an approach. By controlling vocabulary, grading the readers and providing the opportunity for a great deal of repetition even the most disadvantaged learners learn. However, an inspection of such graded readers will show that after three years the vocabulary jump is

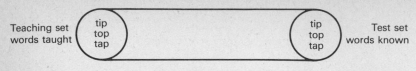

| Teaching set words taught | tip top tap | | tip top tap | Test set words known |

Fig. 3.

enormous. The subsequent memory load imposed on children with special needs is too great. The major strength of the phonics approach, on the other hand, is the potential it has to provide children with general case word-attack strategies which greatly reduce the amount of information needed to be retained.

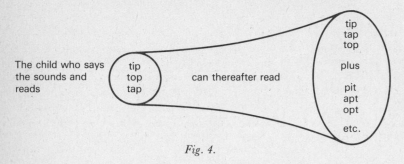

| The child who says the sounds and reads | tip top tap | can thereafter read | tip tap top plus pit apt opt etc. |

Fig. 4.

Although the teaching of strategies to children is important there are a number of questions that are often asked about the direct instruction programmes. Most relate to the problem of teaching reading in this particular way and the replies illustrate some of the design features built into the programmes.

3.2.1. Isn't English too irregular to teach with phonic rules?

Many of the high frequency words required for beginning reading are irregular. Words like *said, the, off, what, where, were,* are impossible to sound out using the sum of the most common sounds such letters usually represent. Controlling sentences so that the sounds for letters remain stable does not provide a useful solution to the problem. While such a strategy may be appropriate for some simple sentences like 'Jan had the jam.' (all *a*'s the same), progress towards sentences of interest such as 'He and she like to go and bake the cakes.' present obvious difficulties. The letter *e* in 'he' and 'she' has the same function but is different in the word 'the' and in the words like 'bake' and 'cakes'. The *h* takes on various sounds as does the *o* in 'go' and 'to'.

Engelmann has sought a solution to the problem because he realises the importance of phonics in teaching general case strategies. For this reason he has developed an alphabet (Figure 4a). This has two functions: it allows for variations of some symbols so that a larger set of words can be sounded out while not violating the spelling conventions. For example, in 'hē and shē went to the lāke', notice the variations for the letter *a* and *e*. This makes the words a ā b c ch d e ē f g h i II j k l m n

o ō oo p qu r s sh t th u ū v w wh x y ȳ z

Fig. 4a

'he' and 'went' regular and they are taught as 'hē' and 'went'. The words are the sum of their letters. The joining of '**sh**', '**wh**' and '**th**' makes '**sh**ē' and '**the**' regular as well as the potentially difficult words such as '**wh**ere' and 'were'; 'lāke' is also regular with the unsounded *e* written in miniature. The ā with a macron signifies a long vowel.

The initial research showed that it was inefficient to keep all the words regular because of the problems encountered when transition to normal print was made. It was discovered that the introduction of some irregular words early in the programme facilitated the transition because the child had been given practice in the kind of strategy required for decoding irregularly spelled words like 'to', 'was' and 'said'.

The alphabet does not provide for all possible sounds but the goal of the programme is simply to offer a variation of orthographies to facilitate initial instruction. Once the child has achieved a high level of skill at the transition stage the communications controlled by the scripted formats do not have to be as careful as those used in initial acquisition.

The modifications described above increase greatly the generality of word attack strategies which otherwise do not lend themselves to English.

3.2.2. *How are the sounds taught so that the child acquires general case strategies?*

In DISTAR, through minor modifications just mentioned, Engelmann has reduced the task of decoding to a manageable 40 sounds. In *Reading I* the sounds and the application of the skills required by sounding out and reading with accuracy and comprehension are taught so that even the most disadvantaged can profit. Sounds are introduced cumulatively and reviewed regularly over a period of 160 lessons. For children with less of a problem the 'fast cycle' teaches the same sounds in 70 lessons. Teachers may, alternatively, avail themselves of the opportunity to use skipping procedures. The strategy for decoding is arrived at through an analysis of the skills needed to attack words. The component skills are taught separately so that early success is achieved. These are then 'chained' together so that the whole sounding out and reading operation can be applied to almost any word.

The component skills referred to are:

1. Symbol identification (is this 'a'?)
2. Saying the sounds (what sound? or say the sound)
3. Knowing where to start (put your finger on the ball) (see Figure 5)
4. Saying sounds in sequence (what's the first sound, what's the next sound, etc.)

5. Sounding out (saying the sounds in sequence without pauses between sounds)
6. Saying it fast (blending)

When these component skills are assembled into a word attack strategy the child can say the sounds in and read words. The 'attack' can be applied to similar but previously unseen words.

An example of part of lesson 57 in DISTAR appears below in Figure 5.

3.2.3. Don't children have great difficulty blending?

When sounds are sounded out as discrete elements in a word, e.g. kuh – aa – tuh (cat), it takes a great deal of imagination to recognise the whole word when read normally. The sounding out operations in DISTAR and Corrective Reading Decoding 'A' require the child to produce a sound as close as possible to the word read normally. There are no pauses between the sounds. Sounding out is effectively saying the word extremely slowly. Children have no difficulty recognising the whole word and blend it by simply saying the word fast.

3.2.4. What about allophones?

Sounds for the same letter vary in the different words in which they appear. The initial consonants in 'dip', 'dup', 'dap', 'dop' are all slightly different because the 'dee' sound has to be formed in a way that accommodates the following sounds. The strategy for 'stop sound first' words in DISTAR involves a variation in the teaching procedure which overcomes the problem. To decode 'tip' the teacher first points to the last part of the word and sounds out 'ip'; she then points to the beginning of the word 'tip' and says 'this word rhymes with *ip*. What word?', 'tip'. The children respond and the allophone problem disappears. Rhyming is a component skill previously taught and is an important skill which shows the child the relationship between similar words. This understanding promotes generalisations about word families (which are based on common endings).

3.2.5. Don't most programmes teach phonic rules?

Many programmes make the mistake of teaching a rule and providing a few applications. Children don't learn to read the word 'have' by applying the final *e* rule. Nor is the word 'gave' read this way. The child learns by categorising the words to which the rule applies. The word 'go' has a final vowel, the word 'to' has the same, but both o's are pronounced differently.

The words 'same', 'hive', 'tape', have final e's as do 'some', 'come', 'give'. For three of these the final *e* rule applies and for three it does not. The child learns to categorise the exceptions and classify them as consistent with a particular form (a family of irregular words). The emphasis in Corrective Reading Decoding B is on form not on the rule. The way such discriminations take place is through seeing in many repeated examples what controls the behaviour of saying 'have' and 'gave'. The child must learn what *is* systematic

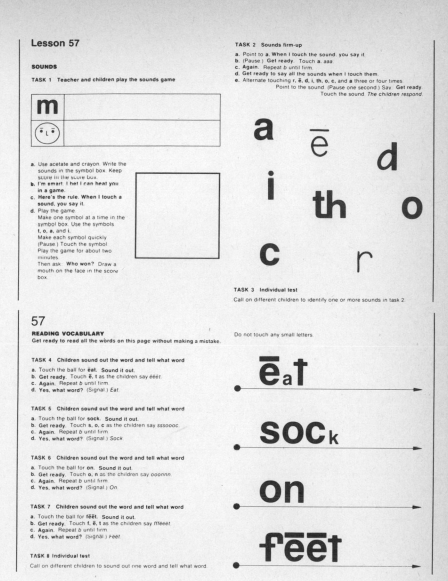

Fig. 5.

Note 1.　Even No. 4 has component skills. The words 'first' and 'next' will have been specifically taught.

Note 2.　Unlike ITA, spellings are not changed.

and what *isn't*, not from rules but from *words*. Decoding 'B' is based on cumulative family control where the emphasis is on form.

Of the many problems associated with teaching decoding skills it can readily be seen that in each case Engelmann has always looked for the task design implications of each. He does not seek to locate the cause of a problem in the child since this would be counter-productive.

3.2.6. What is the theoretical basis of the formatted decoding programmes?

Concise communication is at the heart of Engelmann's approach. Engelmann's programmes and the theory of instruction on which it is based have at their core empathy with the learner. Such empathy has proved instrumental in the development of principles of communicating with the learner in ways that make learning accurate, efficient and remembered. Communication principles are complex and beyond the scope of this paper (see Theory of Direct Instruction for a more elaborate exposition). Central, however, to the effort is the fact that the learner is actively trying to make sense of his or her environment. In so doing the learner makes interpretations which are consistent with the set of examples presented. If the set of examples conveys more than one possible generalisation different learners will learn different things. Carnine *et al.* point out that the implications are to do with identifiable 'sameness' and 'differences' of examples. 'A sameness shared by all examples treated the same way describes a potential generalisation'. A rather simple example in decoding follows. In the words 'robe', 'time', 'came', 'fine', the words contain different letters. The format in Figure 6 shows how they would be taught.

The teacher points to *e* and says: 'Is the last letter "e"?'
She or he then points to the vowel: 'So are you going to hear a letter name?'
The sameness is communicated by providing the learner with a series of greatly differing examples but which are labelled or responded to in the same way. (They are the same because they end in 'e' and the vowel says its name.)

Communicating differences is also important. 'A structural difference is implied if two examples are treated differently. Here the communication is more efficient if there are small differences between positive and negative examples.' (See Figure 6.)

e.g. fine-fin   rode-rod   robe-rob

There is only one structural difference between the juxtaposed examples – the final 'e'. The examples are treated differently so the difference must be attributable to the disappearance of the 'e'.

The scripts control the presentation of examples in keeping with the communication principles which are the heart of efficient instruction.

3.2.7. Won't the children become too dependent on the teacher?

The scripts also control the progression of skill development with independent reading as the goal. The amount of help the child receives is dependent on his or her skill acquisition. Note in Figure 6, the rule about the 'e' is quoted by the teacher. A prescribed number of lessons further on sees the rule not fully stated, and finally the vowel is no longer underlined. The rate at which the learner is progressively weaned from dependence is determined by the results of 16 years continuous feedback on the use of the programmes and thousands

EXERCISE 3 Vowel conversions
1. Print in a column on the board: r<u>o</u>de, r<u>o</u>d, f<u>i</u>n, f<u>i</u>ne, r<u>o</u>be, r<u>o</u>b.
Underline as indicated.
2. **Here's a rule about these words:**
If the last letter is e, you'll hear a letter
name in the word. You'll hear the name of the
letter that is underlined.
3. Point to rode.
Is the last letter e? Signal. *Yes.*
So are you going to hear a letter name?
Signal. *Yes.*
What letter name? Signal. *o.*
Point to rode.
Get ready to read the word. Pause.
What word? Signal. *Rode.*
To correct:
a. Say the correct response.
b. Repeat the step.
4. Point to rod.
Is the last letter e? Signal. *No.*
So are you going to hear a letter name?
Signal. *No.*
Point to rod.
Get ready to read the word. Pause.
What word? Signal. *Rod.*
5. Point to fin.
Is the last letter e? Signal. *No.*
So are you going to hear a letter name?
Signal. *No.*
Point to fin.
Get ready to read the word. Pause.
What word? Signal. *Fin.*
6. Point to fine.
Is the last letter e? Signal. *Yes.*
So are you going to hear a letter name?
Signal. *Yes.*
What letter name? Signal. *i.*
Point to fine.
Get ready to read the word. Pause.
What word? Signal. *Fine.*
7. Point to robe.
Is the last letter e? Signal. *Yes.*
So are you going to hear a letter name?
Signal. *Yes.*
What letter name? Signal. *o.*
Point to robe.
Get ready to read the word. Pause.
What word? Signal. *Robe.*
8. Point to rob.
Is the last letter e? Signal. *No.*
So are you going to hear a letter name?
Signal. *No.*
Point to rob.
Get ready to read the word. Pause.
What word? Signal. *Rob.*
9. Repeat steps 3–8 until firm.

EXERCISE 7 Vowel conversions
1. Print on the board: **ride, made, mitt, cone.**
2. **You're going to read these words.**
Remember the rule about words that have e
for the last letter.
3. Point to ride. Pause.
What word? Signal. *Ride.*
4. Repeat step 3 for each remaining word.
5. Repeat the list until firm.

EXERCISE 6 Vowel conversions
Task A
1. Print on the board: **fated, fatted, caped,**
capper, pins, pines.
2. **You hear a letter name in the first part**
of some of these words, but the first part
is not underlined. So be careful.
3. Point to fated. Pause.
What word? Signal. *Fated.*
To correct:
a. Underline the first four letters.
b. **Is the last letter of the underlined**
part e? Signal.
So are you going to hear a letter name?
Signal.
c. **Get ready to read the word.** Pause.
What word? Signal.
d. Change the word to the word the students
said in error. Point to the word. **What word**
now?
e. Change the word back to the original word.
Point to the word. **What word now?**
f. Return to the first word in the column.
4. For each remaining word:
Point to the word. Pause. **What word?** Signal.

EXERCISE 6 Vowel conversions
1. Print on the board: **h<u>a</u>ting, m<u>o</u>ping, m<u>o</u>pping,**
r<u>a</u>ting, r<u>a</u>tting.
Underline as indicated.
2. **The same rule you learned for word parts that**
end with the letter e works for word parts
that end with the letter i. If the last
letter of the underlined part is i, you hear a
letter name.
3. Point to hating. **Look at the underlined part.**
Is the last letter i? Signal. *Yes.*
So are you going to hear a letter name?
Signal. *Yes.*
What letter name? Signal. *a.*
Get ready to read the word. Pause.
What word? Signal. *Hating.*

Fig. 6.

of field tests. It is the careful attention to detail, backed by rigorous research, which is the hallmark of the Direct Instruction programmes.

3.2.8. Doesn't independent reading also mean reading with comprehension?

The programmes include specific techniques for teaching comprehension but do not treat reading intially as a comprehension process. The reason for this ordering of priorities is that a child must be able to 'say' the word before the meaning can be considered. A child may be able to comprehend and know what is meant by the words 'boat' and 'moat' but if he or she cannot distinguish them in print, comprehension will be greatly impaired.

In emphasising phonics and decoding skills the impression is given that comprehension, and reading for meaning, are not goals of the programme. This is a common and incorrect assumption. Engelmann and Carnine agree with Caroll, who suggests that an emphasis on phonics does not mean that attention to meaning must inevitably decrease. 'Of course you can teach meaning while teaching phonics and doing otherwise is counter-productive and absurd.' (Carnine, 1979.)

3.2.9. What then is the difference between code emphasis and meaning emphasis programmes?

Carnine (1979) describes the essential difference between code emphasis and meaning emphasis approaches by focusing on the way that they are taught.

In meaning emphasis approaches little account is taken of letter sound regularity. Words like 'not', 'book', 'done', etc. are commonly found in beginning readers. The assumption is that familiar words will be easy to read.

In the process of teaching, children are encouraged to use a wide variety of sources, pictures, context clues, word configuration and initial letters to 'decode' words. While this may be entirely appropriate in most cases, a multifaceted approach proves confusing to many disadvantaged learners. The Direct Instruction programmes can be taught with simpler teaching presentations which are less confusing and less open to interpretation than the lengthy explanations involved in meaning emphasis programmes. (See Figure 6.)

The example that Carnine and Silbert (1979) describe is taken from the Scott Foresman Teacher's Guide.

'if the child reads "duck" for "bird". Draw attention to the fact that "duck" cannot be "bird" because the word begins with a "d" and ends with a "k". The word does not begin with a "b" and end with a "d".'

Anyone who has taught children with special needs will recognise that this information is not only confusing but is unlikely to be retained. As Silbert *et al.* point out, beginning readers and children with special needs have difficulty with learning and applying strategies that require them to use multiple sources of information. Many children master and focus on only one or two sources and consequently accumulate bad reading habits.

3.2.10. What about diagnosis-assessment?

The reason for suggesting structured code emphasis programmes with children with special needs returns us to one of our original concerns – diagnosis and assessment. Diagnosis in the task-analytic sense is *not* assessment of global abilities but is task specific.

As Silbert and Carnine (1979) suggest when the child makes the mistake of reading 'sit' for 'sat', 'run' for 'ran', the teacher can diagnose the faulty sound letter correspondences and remedy the confusion. The multifaceted meaning emphasis approach is not as efficient. In Carnine's example, if the child read 'the boy saw the bird' as 'the boy said the bird' the teacher would prompt the child with a number of clues 'saw' can't be 'said' because (1) it doesn't end in 'd'; (2) it doesn't make sense. The child is told why the word can't be 'said' but this does not provide him with a strategy for working out 'saw'. On the next occasion he reads 'sees'!

Conclusion

Finally there are those who in the face of an ever increasing accumulation of evidence in favour of Direct Instruction programmes (that are so carefully designed) retreat to the argument that in the wholist (meaningful) vs. subskills (decoding) debate, the goals of the wholist approach are more laudable. Some comments, however, are worthy of attention. Carnine (1982) *et al.* point out that an obvious goal of reading is meaningful reading of narrative and expository material for the purpose of enjoyment and gaining information. Clearly it is the belief of task analysts that such goals can be attained via a different route to that proposed by Goodman and Smith (1970).

In this respect Bereiter's (1982) constructive look at *Project Follow Through* (one of the largest educational experiments ever carried out) is worthy of examination. The goals of the Responsive education and Open education (the models which fared so badly with enhancing the skills of children with special needs by comparison with the Task-Analytic Direct Instruction) are goals that Direct Instruction proponents share. A good example of this, says Bereiter, is reading comprehension. There is, as yet, no adequate how-to-do-it scheme for comprehension. Pupils are engated in 'relevant activities', i.e. reading passages and answering questions, but they are not taught comprehension. Child-centred approaches use the relevant activity mode of instruction for all teaching objectives. In an open classroom, child-centred activities appear to engage children in planning and studying, but a close inspection of the learning activities themselves shows 'a hodge-podge of the promising and the pointless, of the excessively repetitive and the excessively varied – of tasks that require more thinking than children are capable of, and of tasks that have been cleverly designed to require no mental effort at all. There is a little bit of phonics here and a bit of phonics there but never a coherent sequence to enable a kid to learn how to use this valuable tool. Materials have been chosen for seasonal appeal. There is a predilection for cute ideas. The conceptual analysis of learning problems, however, tends to be vague and irrelevant, big on name-dropping, low on incisiveness.'

Instructional designers, it is true, aim at teaching specific basic skills in a highly structured way. However, their methods are not intended as a substitute for the child-centred approach but rather as a means of underpinning it by providing the skills needed to undertake more sophisticated tasks. This is especially true in the education of children with special needs.

The child-centred educators, in espousing the virtues of attempting to attain higher order objectives, seek refuge in the knowledge that their programmes are no less effective than anyone else's. However, as Bareiter points out, even this argument may crumble because instructional designers having achieved remarkable success in decoding, maths concepts, spelling and written English, are now turning their attention to the higher order goals emphasised by the child-centred educators. Unless the latter become more sophisticated about instructional design they are in danger of being discredited. This, of course, would not be good for education, as such educators have developed teacher styles which have much in their favour. Unless they also develop an effective pedagogy to underpin their approach it will not bear fruit in the problematic area of teaching children with special needs.

References

ANDERSON, R. B. (1973) 'Pardon us but what was the question? A response to the critique (House *et al.*) of the Follow Through evaluation.' *Harvard Education Review*, 48, (2).

BATEMAN, B. and HARING, N. (1977) *Teaching the learning disabled child.* Engelwood Cliffs (N.J.): Prentice-Hall.

BEREITER, C. and KURLAND, M. (1981–2) 'A constructive look at Follow Through.' *Interchange*, 12, (1).

BRANWHITE, A. B. (1983) 'Boosting Reading by Direct Instruction'. *British Journal of Educational Psychology*, 53, pp. 291–8.

BECKER, W. and CARNINE, D. (1980) 'Direct Instruction: An effective approach to educational intervention with the disadvantaged and low performers'. *Advances in Clinical Child Psychology*, 3.

BECKER, W. and GUSTEN, R. (1982) 'A follow-up of Follow Through: the later effects of the D.I. Model on children in fifth and sixth grades'. *American Educational Research Journal*, 19(1), pp. 75–92.

CARNINE, D. (1977) 'Phonics Vs. Look-say: Transfer to new words'. *Reading Teacher*, 24, pp. 332–42.

CARNINE, D., BECKER, W., ENGELMAN, S. and KAMEERIN, E. (1982) 'A Direct Instruction analysis of reading'. Unpublished paper.

CARNINE, D. and SILBERT, J. (1979) *Direct Instruction Reading.* Weston, Ontario: Charles E. Merrill.

ENGELMANN, S. (1980) 'Toward the design of faultless instruction: the theoretical basis of concept analysis'. *Educational Technology*.

ENGELMANN, S. (1978) *SRA Corrective Reading Programme.* Chicago: Science Research Associates.

ENGELMANN, S. (1974) *DISTAR Reading Level I and II*. Chicago: Science Research Associates.

ENGELMANN, S. (1969) *Preventing Classroom Failure in the Primary Grades*. Chicago: Science Research Associates.

ENGELMANN, S. and CARNINE, D. (1982) *Theory of Instruction: Principles and Applications*. Irvington Publishers.

GOODMAN, Y. M. (1970) 'Using children's reading miscues for teaching stragegies'. *The Reading Teacher*, 23, pp. 455–9.

GREGORY, P., HACKNEY, C. and GREGORY, N. M. (1982) 'Corrective Reading Programme: an evaluation'. *British Journal of Educational Psychology*, 52, pp. 33–50.

HOUSE, E., *et al*. (1978) 'No simple answer: Critique of Follow Through evaluation'. *Harvard Education Review*, 48, pp. 125–60.

LEWIS, A. (1982) 'An experimental evaluation of a D.I. programme 'corrective reading) with remedial readers in comprehensive schools'. *Educational Psychology*, 2(2), pp. 121–35.

MITTLER, P. (1970) *The Psychological Assessment of Physical and Mental Handicap*. London: Methuen.

REITH, H. *et al*. (1981) 'Instructional variables that make a difference: attention to task and beyond'. *Exceptional Educational Quarterly*.

SABATINO, D. A. and DORFMAN, N. (1974) 'Matching learner aptitude to two commercial reading programmes'. *Exceptional Children*, 41, pp. 85–90.

SMITH, F. (1973) *Psycholinguistics and Reading*. New York: Holt Rinehart and Winston.

STALLING, J. (1980) 'Allocated academic learning time revisited, or Beyond Time On Task'. *Educational Researcher*.

YSSELDYKE, J. E. (1973) 'Diagnostic-prescriptive teaching: the search for aptitude treatment interactions', in L. Mann and D. Sabatino (Eds), *The First Review of Special Education*.

YSSELDYKE, J. E. and SALVIA, A. (1974) 'A critical analysis of the assumptions underlying diagnostic-prescriptive teaching'. *Exceptional Children*, 41, pp. 181–95.

D.E.S. (1978) *Special Educational Needs* (The Warnock Report). London: HMSO.

10 Literacy and children's needs in the television age

Valerie Yule

Since so much educational time and money goes into teaching reading and writing over a long period in the life of every child, other forms of visual literacy may seem more attractive in the television age. Even teachers faced with non-readers and obstinate anti-readers may be tempted to hope that Neil Postman was right when he wrote in the Harvard Educational Review (1970) that literacy in the printed word was no longer needed except for an élite.

However, books and screen may be complementary to each other. There are some things that books and writing can still do better than the visual media which surpass them in other respects. There are some ways in which electronic communication threatens book literacy today, and other ways in which they are superb carriers of the printed word. And as books serve a function in teaching computer and video skills, so they too have great potential for radical new methods of learning to read and write.

The video screen can surpass books and periodicals

i) Video and computer graphics are now a near perfect means for visual demonstration of complex operations and events. There was a 'Handyman' series in *Punch* hilariously demonstrating the confusion that can be caused by the limitations of text-and-diagram manuals, and in many shops and training courses textbooks and handbooks are supplementary to the greater efficiency of video demonstration.

ii) Books are inferior to television and film to show the surface manifestations of life and the visual appearance of the world, going far beyond what the eye can normally see, unlimited by distance and up-to-the-minute in time.

iii) Television gives instant entertainment at the touch of a button; at the touch of another button, information can be summoned up and analysed from distant computer data-bases.

However, children still need to learn to read, and it can be extremely dangerous to let them assume that they need not. *Society needs the printed word still.*

Minimum literacy is needed to find one's way around a world of labels and signs, directions and forms, to cope with complex rules and rights in our society, and even to get beyond *Star Wars* level in the new 'computer literacy'.

Literacy gives *access to knowledge,* whether it is stored electronically or on paper, and power still lies with those who have knowledge and access to knowledge – it is a bad day when the power-base relies more on armed force and ignorance.

Maximum literacy for the whole population is needed not just to continue 'civilisation as we know it' but also as it could become for assured life and liberty. B.O.O.K.S., that amazing invention and acronym for 'Bodies of Organized Knowledge' in another famous *Punch* feature, form permanent records that are not dependent on machines in good working order. Electronic media can rewrite history undetectably and obliterate philosophy, with tapes that can be invisibly edited and pictures that can be invisibly re-arranged, but as long as old books survive somewhere, Orwell's nightmare of *1984* cannot be complete.

Television and radio have a major limitation, in that they have become too fast, and operate within time sequences. The world of the mind and of understanding, and communication with other minds far in time and space, is permanently conveyed in books, in forms not transient, but which can be reflected upon. Their world of imagination can resonate in the readers' minds, which supply what the words elicit but do not explicitly determine. The myth and symbol within books survives across time and generations, and provide a common core for culture as a basis for the language of thinking and imagination.

Children who do not become good readers miss out on a world of thought and ideas, and a literary heritage, a source of wisdom and consolation.

Book literacy is needed to complement and even counter-balance what children learn from television

Exposure to electronic media without real experience of the world or the wider world of good books can limit views of life to a tunnel vision at a point in time. Television and film have their own inbuilt risks of developing their own canons of what is thought to be 'realism', what is presentable, and how briefly any sequence of thought can be permitted to run – often no more than four-and-a-half minutes. Book-fashions can reflect these trends too, of course, and it is worth introducing children to the back-stacks in children's libraries too, to help them realise what spectacles we put on and could take off too.

There are some risks in television that have not yet been estimated. Are there limens or appetites for stimulation that keep edging higher, so that more intense and stronger impact stimuli are increasingly required for viewers sated and bombarded – particularly children with tastes set early! There are hypnotic aspects to electronic sound and visual effects that can encourage prolonged passivity of mind and body, with possible consequent risks of impulsivity and failure of self-control when there is action – and again for children, possibly a taste for hypnagogics in other forms as well, to also blur mental faculties in a way that has become for them pleasurable. And when criteria of instant entertainment value become paramount, the presentation of information and opinion is often distorted and cut to snippets.

Speed has a fascination on television, and some child-watched programmes have become too fast in action for events to be comprehensible, and it can seem to adults that in fact meaning is sometimes secondary – the action impact is all. The quickest and visually most dramatic events on television are

113

destruction rather than construction, (count the balance yourself of what is made and what is destroyed and what is cleared up or repaired), criminal rather than responsible behaviour in business and industry, conflict rather than harmony in human relations, and violence rather than wit or humour in comedy. There is some evidence that children make less compassionate identification with realistic rather than superheroes on television, whereas in books the readers supply part of each character for themselves in imagination. Good things, including real-life fun, can seem dull on television, and it is not uncommon to hear adults who are now the first 'television-reared' generation assert that goodness and harmony in real life must be dull too. Books can use the magic of words to evoke happiness, love of the beautiful, and pleasure in peaceful activities or contemplation.

It is, of course, possible that the electronic media are only in their infancy and have not yet discovered a full potential to transmit the less destructive aspects of life. And it is no doubt true that children from happy and caring home environments may seem little affected (but what about sources for adult depression, and morbid tastes?).

The risks of television dependency and maladaptive learning seem to be higher for children whose home circumstances make them most vulnerable through neglect or rejection. They cannot find meaning in their own disturbed early relationships, nor in the television that is their babysitter from infancy, watched with no adult interpreter. A great deal of the television that they watch nowadays consists, if you stop to time it, of fast moving montages that convey visual sensation rather than meaning or information, and of fast cars, fast planes, sudden explosions, inexplicable hostilities – or causation only comprehensible at an adult level.

So there are many children that the teacher is expected to teach to read, who have come to school trained by both home and television not to expect to find meaning in what they do, and without intellectual curiosity because all the answers they expect to find would be unpleasant. How can 'comprehension exercises' teach them to process their school-work with any expectation of purpose or understanding?

And when we speak of 'starting where the children are' and basing new learning only on their own experiences, we should remember that even the most fortunate children today experience at an early age the sight of all the world's troubles in their living rooms.

Learning to love books is therefore extremely important for children, to give a wider source of entertainment and knowledge, consolation and inspiration, and models of real human beings for living.

Children today have often only short periods of time available for reading, away from television. Bombarding them with books regardless of quality can be a mistaken policy, as they cannot sort them out easily and can become disaffected by the chaff. Tastes develop early, and whether lowbrow, middlebrow or highbrow, everything provided for them at every mental age level should be the best that can be found for children, and found with their cooperation. They often have an appetite for 'civilising influences' that teachers would not credit who select more whimsical, dismal or antisocial moral content. It is a shame for teachers to go to such trouble to teach literacy, without regard for tastes, and find they have produced a reading public that has learnt a bias for nasty pot-boiler paperbacks and tabloids, because their other potential has been undeveloped.

Because of television, therefore, there is a greater need for children to be able to read, and to read well and avidly.

But television can also make it harder for children to learn to read

Motivation

You do not have to work to get the immediate reward of entertainment from television. Children need to have some awareness of the rewards of reading in order to work to learn it – to please the teacher cannot be relied upon as a magic carrot. Pictures in books do not necessarily make the print look interesting, particularly if they carry the story better than the text, as they often do in beginners' books. It is also more intellectually stimulating to learn with some understanding of why you are set to learn any subject.

Time for reading

A good reader has usually read over a quarter of a million words before the age of eight, it has been estimated. Television, including television in schools, can take away the time available for this enterprise.

Learning habits

So far there has been more speculation than research on whether early television-watching unmatched by early book-watching may train habits that could interfere with easy acquisition of reading skills, through establishing different styles for attention and concentration, selective memory, attention to language, and in perceptual strategies of eye-movements and scanning, and integration of visual and auditory modalities. Many poor readers can be observed to sample books by flicking through them – almost as if they expected the pictures to move – without a second glance at any page, in contrast to the good readers whose sampling methods include momentary pausing to taste the text or examine a picture.

Tuning out to language

It has been shown that children's language and vocabulary benefit from audio-visual media such as television when they have been accustomed to conversation with adults at home, but children lacking that adult catalyst can learn to watch without attending to the words at all except as noises, and fail to try to get the meaning of events from the spoken word. Despite work showing that language inadequate for school learning may be effective in everyday life (e.g. Labov, 1972) 'restricted' language may be a problem when children come to school with speaking vocabularies of under 500 words, and comprehension of speech limited even in their own dialect.

Educational expedients may also be maladaptive responses to these problems

They make the children's situation worse in the long run.

When children have poor language development for school learning, the limited-vocabulary reading books intended to help them learn to read can also limit further language development. Reading in primary school is known to be a major source of new vocabulary, concepts and ideas.

Much current work is going into efforts to reduce and simplify text and vocabulary in first, infant reading books, then at junior level, and now in secondary-school textbooks and even college books. At each level, simplification passes the problem on to the next level. Simpler text in science books risks oversimplifying the content; in English books, the writing style can be turned into stodge.

Indexes of 'readability' can be used to count the length of words and sentences, and encourage shortening them further, even at the risk of reducing connected thought and argument. Intrinsic 'readability' depends not only on the reader's interest, but also on style and clarity of writing. A book with a pleasing style can be read and read again without wearying, helping the learner to become more fluent through this repeated practice, and a better writer through absorption of many good literary models as a 'compost' for her or his own writing style.

The influence of other visual media also appears in current tendencies not limited to educational books, to turn the printed page into a visual rather than a communicating experience, and to be concerned with immediate attractiveness and 'sales appeal' rather than comfort of actual reading and 'user appeal'.

Even learned journals may now use larger print, with less of it on the page. Economy apart, such trends may handicap very fast, efficient readers whose strategy is to absorb a great deal with each sweep of the eye, so that compact text is an advantage. And it becomes more difficult for other readers to develop faster reading too.

Design schools are emphasising striking, fashionable appearance, with words crammed so close together, barely spaced, that print can look like pretty border patterns with the illusion of a message – the layout artist may not even expect it to be read. The overall effect is pleasing, like a carpet pattern or abstract picture. Many action comics today are looked at, not read – the script may be almost illegible. In school books, a few lines on each picture page may be seen as less 'frightening' for children, as if print was to be feared – but the practice can prevent learners grasping the full sequential meaning of what is presented in such snippets, particularly for poor readers with short-term memory problems even in turning a page.

A third development is to take advantage of children's enthusiastic response and facility with the new electronic media, and simply put all the old boring paper-and-pencil exercises on to computer screens. The motivational assets are novelty, that it is easier to press buttons than to make handwritten responses, and there can be an addictive fascination in the moving lights on the screen. However, education has never got very far on bandwagons, and children will become tired of the screen too if micro programs are merely the old exercises jazzed up, with the same boring lack of meaningful content or continuity or effective transfer into real reading and writing.

There can be a limit to the amount of time young children should spend facing a screen, even an educational one. We do not know enough of the long-term effects on their developing vision, or whether the element of passivity needs much more counterbalance in schools with manual labour and practical mechanics and participation in school maintenance. Even too much exposure to electronic squeaks and blips needs to be ruled out as a long-term risk.

Could modern information technology revolutionise the teaching of literacy?

Although the television age sets new problems and new needs for children, it also has the potential to revolutionise the way literacy is taught – not merely providing faster or different means to learn by the same familiar routes.

The Bullock report affirmed (1975) that 'most children learn to read, whatever the method used'. If this remains true, then improvement in teaching methods should be aimed at preventing reading failure in that rather large minority group of children who are not learning to read, whatever the current method, or are learning so reluctantly that the estimated two million adults functionally illiterate (Adult Literacy Unit, 1983) is partly made up of 'ex-literates' who 'forgot' as soon as they could.

A second major need is to expedite the learning of the first basic steps in literacy for all learners. Then they could be rewarded from the outset by independent reading for personal interest, and in regular school subjects. Although some gap between good and poor readers is inevitable given the variable distribution of human abilities, the width of the present gap is socially intolerable, and largely, perhaps, made up by qualitative differences in reading strategies. The fortunate few 'cotton on to how to do it', as many textbooks on reading admit; how can their more efficient strategies be communicated to all?

Video and computers now make 'Teach Yourself to Read' a real possibility – hire the programs and the books of your choice from the local video library, and learn in the privacy of your own home. It was impossible to teach yourself in the past 'without a little help from your friends', for how could you read the instructions? Now this is possible. Teachers can have more satisfying roles as *educators* undistracted by setting exercises and crowd-controlling, and because learning to read will be challenging and interesting, not traumatic and wearying, everyone capable of learning may not only read, but like reading, and so publishers will have vast new markets of adult and child readers.

One step in this direction is the 'Writing to Read' project of J. H. Martin in the United States, funded by IBM and being evaluated by the U.S. Educational Testing Service. Personal computers, typewriters, taperecorders, cassettes and accessories including voice output and colour graphics for the computers are incorporated for beginners, with typewriting rather than handwriting, and a phonemic spelling that merges into conventional spelling. It is still possible that for all its array of technology, its step-by-step single path learning track may not take sufficient advantage of what research and development in information technology can offer education today.

If knowledge is to be more than an explosion – an incomprehensible barrage – the best key to it is through 'schemata' (Piaget's term) in your own head, a ready-organised mental data-base that can accommodate and change to new knowledge as it assimilates it. Computer graphics with auditory mnemonics could establish a cognitive base for understanding reading through visual spatial 'maps', particularly valuable for socially-disadvantaged children who today come to school without the makings of any schema for reading through previous experience, and for the 'specific learning disability' children who are so easily confused. Video visuals could be used as maps are used, to find your way around, not to learn by heart, and they would act as 'advance organisers' and also as instantly available revision-summaries – a particular boon for learners whose experience of life to date has been that each day's work disappears, usually in the bin. A complete set of learning can be presented in a spatial framework that 'chunks' information, and this information can be visibly presented, taken apart, and as the learner watches, put together again. The basic principle is 'a single way to learn a hundred connected things' that can then be elaborated further, rather than 'a hundred ways to learn one thing', which the average student may profit from, but which bewilders the vulnerable, who can often remember the games and the 'activities' but not the 'words' they were supposed to teach. As the maps fill in – for letters, sounds, spelling, grammar, punctuation, semantics – students discover that what appeared complex has 'jelled' to become simple, as it does in all learning that is mastered. And it is a worthwhile learning experience for life to have the discovery of mastering something that had on first presentation looked so impressively difficult.

A video-cassette can present information in a systematic way, that the user can run through quickly for an overall view, then rattle backwards and forwards at will, to find out where it is all going, revise where it has been, fill in gaps, practise what individual learners find they need to practise. Then quick learners need not be bored, over-eager learners can retrace steps impetuously jumped, slow learners need not be confused or suffer 'How many times have you been told!' while the average learner can study in an independent way that stimulates intellect and reasoning, rather than merely docilely rote-learning. Colour, animation and lively presentation can make a package attractive enough for enjoyable re-running to the point of mastery and beyond.

Animated colour visuals can demonstrate in minutes the main features of how to remember the shape of letters, their flexible relation to sounds, how letters make words, the nature of vowels and consonants, basic grammar, and arrangement and rearrangement of word and sentence order, linked from the very beginning with books that the student can enjoy reading for their content – not snippety 'sentences' or isolated strings of words. Currently available techniques include scrolling vertically and horizontally, running cursors, lighting up key points, zooming and panning so that detail can be related to a complete systematic setting out of information in a pictorial chart form, plus immediate feedback, branching according to learner response, and the prospective option of input by writing or drawing on a pad as well as tapping on keys. 'Language Experience' can be both using one's own language in expression and developing it through good reading.

This idea of 'network' learning of a complex structure through video demonstration is the extension of use of pictorial charts that have been tried out successfully on a small scale. And video can also be used to demonstrate learning methods like these. An example is *Preparing to read through play* (Aberdeen University Television, 1983) which shows nursery-school children playing with charts that show them how the printed word operates, and how the alphabet can be a compact filing system within which expanding knowledge can be mentally 'filed' to explain the variable relationship of sounds and print, and make first reading a clearly understood activity. It operates rather like natural spoken language learning – a network of comprehension is shown building up around the islands of knowledge that are at first the salient ones to the individual child – their own name, or a particularly salient letter or word or pages in a favourite book.

The potential of electronic media can be exploited to demonstrate a variety of reading strategies and their linking in efficient reading for meaning from the beginning – visual, phonic, semantic, lexical, context – to ensure that learners with difficulty in one mode have a safety net in the others, and all children develop maximum flexibility and fluency.

Pupils who have used information technology to gain rapid and efficient access to literacy can then use their books to help them to make sense of the otherwise bewildering rich world that looms at them continually from the TV screen. 'The basic function of a teacher is to reduce confusion and kindle enthusiasm' – teachers can help the students in their battle for intelligibility, by ensuring that they have a systematic foundation of knowledge about the world in space and in time, and a background realisation of 'real' life that can provide perspective to the 'exaggerated realism' (a film critic's phrase) of horrors real and imaginary on the screen. Video is already being developed to help parents ignorant of how to talk or play with or enjoy their children, so that children will not continue to grow up without the language skills and love of learning that can be nurtured best in secure relationships. Video can show adults ways to read books and tell stories and read *with* children rather than *to* them or 'hearing' them. So video can also be a way of ensuring that children learn about life itself from people, rather than from machines.

Teachers are now aware of the surprising proficiency with which even three to five year-olds can operate the new technology without prompting. I think we have yet to be aware of the surprising proficiency they will show in acquiring literacy when we are really making the most (rather than, in entertainment, the 'least') of our new horizons in media.

Basic technology – a reminder

It is important to remember that expense is not the main criterion of an effective literacy programme. It can be a great mistake to 'go for the best' judged in money terms of the higher cost. Much more can be made of resources that are not 'high-tec' as well – a stick in the dust may do some things more effectively than all 'bug-eyes and tap-a-tap'. Some of the most attractive play materials for reading can be made at home or by older children, and books remain the most essential item in 'learning to read by reading'. Again, cooperation is the game, for video can also demonstrate these 'non-tec' aspects of becoming literate too.

In considering information technology that is modern and developing in a way hard to keep up with, there is need also to consider the old familiar technology that needs a shake-up – the information technology of the writing system – including handwriting, the shapes of alphanumeric symbols, and spelling.

J. H. Martin's initial learning spelling has the advantage over systems such as i.t.a. in that it merges into present spelling, as a clue to reading it and an introduction to writing it. It is purely phonemic and close to how children tend to spell 'naturally', but we should also be thinking now about another possibility.

Could English spelling be improved so that it helped literate readers to read faster and more efficiently? It is quite possible that our elaborate orthography may handicap skilled readers too, with the additional visual processing required by the extra letters in words that appear to serve no function, either for pronunciation or for meaning. What is the basic structure of spelling that skilled readers rely on when they skim our elaborate orthography without the visual labour that others must employ? Chomsky (1972) has presented the notion of a 'deep' lexical structure for English spelling; it is demonstrated, by investigation of vocabulary lists that present spelling is far from exhibiting any such structure consistently (Yule, 1978) – but perhaps research could excavate what underlies the vagaries. The underlying 'form of the word' for good readers and spellers may be something that computers could handle without needing built-in dictionaries, and it might have affinities with the no-nonsense spellings that English words are given when adopted in other languages of the world.

One feature for experimentation with a 'Teach yourself to read' video-cassette would be the most effective form of structured initial learning spelling – which might later, by extension, not merely merge into present spelling, but remain as an acceptable co-existing alternative to it. It is possible that this first extension into public usage – already with some acquaintance with the shorter spellings used in commercial product advertising – would be via computer and TV screens, the newest media being the most hospitable to further new developments that followed their human-engineering principle of aiming to be 'user friendly'. Their operators often have more freedom than those in the print trade, and computer-regulated house-rules are easily modified.

Another medium of education that may be open to radical change through the new technology is the primary school – with the possibility of the 'Open Primary School' not too dissimilar from Open University, accessible to the same nationwide unsegregated audience with its television broadcasting.

It may be possible to have the social advantages of small primary and secondary schools, where children can grow up in real little communities that are integrated with their own home communities, and that are 'child-scale' according to the their developmental needs – rather than 'factory-scale' with all their depersonalisation, stress for teachers and parents, problems in accountability even extending to the need for constant guard over every belonging, and excessive overheads with minimum student participation in maintenance and innovation. Now the specialities that have made big schools seem economical can be taught through video, microcomputers and short introductory and concluding courses in centres that provide opportunities for educational travel trips, rather than the common wasteful long bus journeys daily through the school year.

The opportunities for individualised learning can also help trends away from 'Agism', that segregates people according to chronological age and can exact life-long penalties from those whose abilities do not develop within a twelve-month age-band of expectations, when they are expected to move up a 'grade' a year.

The renaissance of learning that ended the Middle Ages was limited to an élite aristocracy – but the increased possibilities for 'universal literacy' in the printed word as well as in other visual media, could now make possible an unrestricted flowering of the mind. Present searches for blind escapes and forms of violent sensation are poor substitutes for the excitement of discovery, invention, and 'raised consciousness' through wider interests and apprehensions, which are equally possible in the future for everyone.

We now have a Television Age. Let's use it, constructively. If we don't, we go under to it – and our books too.

References

ADULT LITERACY AND BASIC SKILLS UNIT (1983) *Literacy and Numeracy: Evidence from the National Child Development Study*. London: Kingsbourne House.
CHOMSKY, C. (1970) 'Reading, writing and phonology'. *Harvard Educational Review*, 40, pp. 287–309.
LABOV, W. (1972) *Language in the Inner City*. Philadelphia: Pennsylvania State University Press.
POSTMAN, N. (1970) 'The Politics of Reading'. *Harvard Educational Review*, 40, pp. 244–52.
YULE, V. (1978) 'Is there evidence for Chomsky's interpretation of English spelling?'. *Spelling Progress Bulletin*, 18(4), pp. 10–12.

Some relevant periodicals to watch:
Audio-Visual, Educational Computing, and educational issues of *Byte*.

For overviews of television research:

NATIONAL INSTITUTE OF MENTAL HEALTH IN USA (1982) *Television and Behaviour: Ten years of Scientific Progress and Implications for the Eighties.*

SINGER, J. (1983) 'Implications of Childhood Television Viewing', in J. Bryant and D. R. Anderson *Children's Understanding of Television*. New York: Academic Press.

SURGEON GENERAL'S SCIENTIFIC ADVISORY COMMITTEE ON TELEVISION AND GROWING UP (1972, and review 1982) *The Impact of Television Violence*. Washington D.C.: U.S. Government Printing Office.

Part III

11 Survey of teachers' opinions: Children's books and handwriting styles

Bridie Raban

Introduction

Between November 1981 and April 1982, 1500 questionnaires were circulated to infant school teachers throughout England and Wales. 270 completed questionnaires were returned from 31 local education authorities. The teachers included in this survey had a wide range of teaching experience in infant/first schools, with approximately 70 per cent of them having taught this age range for between six and twenty years. The survey also included teachers from a wide background of initial training courses, with over half of the sample holding a three-year certificate of education.

Choosing books for children

These 270 teachers were invited to rank order five features from a list of 14 which they considered most important as criteria when choosing books for young children. They were also asked to indicate any changes in their rank order across the ages five to seven years.

The story content of books was deemed to be most important at ages six and seven years. However, at age five years, this feature was seen as less important than the quality of the illustrations and a controlled vocabulary. These findings indicate that the motivation provided by good quality illustrations and the careful control of the vocabulary, which could be seen as ensuring success during a child's early reading experience, outweigh the other features of books for very young children. Nevertheless, quality of illustrations remained important at the level of third rank throughout the age range whilst the need for a controlled vocabulary dropped to fourth rank by age seven years.

Size of print was considered the fourth most important feature of books for five-year-olds, becoming less important for the six- and seven-year-olds, although still holding the position of fifth rank. The overall layout of the pages was considered to be more important for seven-year-olds, holding the position of seventh rank, while being placed at the fourth rank for six-year-olds and fifth rank for five-year-olds. Style of typeface was considered the sixth most important feature for five- and six-year-olds, holding seventh rank for seven-year-olds. It was the length of the book which took sixth position for seven-year-olds, this feature taking seventh rank for five- and six-year-olds.

Spacing between words, lines and then letters was considered important in that order for five- and six-year-olds, with the order being changed to spacing between lines first and then words and letters for seven-year-olds. The durability of books reached an equal rank of ten for all three age groups. The size of books was considered the next most important feature for five- and six-year-olds, while the quality of the paper was seen as more important for seven-year-olds. The least important of all the features ranked by these teachers was the cost of the book.

Table 1: Choosing books for children – 14 features arranged in rank order by age of child with percentage responses

	5-year-olds		6-year-olds		7-year-olds	
	Feature	%	*Feature*	%	*Feature*	%
1	Quality of illustrations	54	Story content	50	Story content	69
2	Controlled vocabulary	53	Controlled vocabulary	48	Layout of pages	38
3	Story content	42	Quality of illustrations	40	Quality of illustrations	32
4	Size of print	37	Layout of pages	38	Controlled vocabulary	25
5	Layout of pages	35	Size of print	30	Size of print	22
6	Style of typeface	25	Style of typeface	23	Length of book	19
7	Length of book	15	Length of book	15	Style of typeface	17
8	Spacing between words	13	Spacing between words	11	Spacing between lines	10
9	Spacing between lines	11	Spacing between lines	10	Spacing between words	10
10	Durability	7	Durability	10	Durability	9
11	Spacing between letters	7	Spacing between letters	7	Quality of paper	6
12	Size of book	6	Quality of paper	4	Spacing between letters	5
13	Quality of paper	5	Size of book	3	Cost of book	4
14	Cost of book	3	Cost of book	2	Size of book	4

61·5 per cent of the sample took the opportunity to reinforce the listed features, or to mention further features of books for young children not covered by the list of criteria mentioned above. Their comments fell into three main groups which are listed separately below. The percentages on these lists are calculated from the number of responses collected (N = 95). The three main groups of comments covered the physical features of books, their content and an assorted category.

Table 2: Physical features of books for young children
(in rank order of mention)
N − 95

	%
illustrations that match text	25
durability	13
{ attractive cover	12
print size	
{ length of book	9
layout of pages	
type of print	6
quality of paper	5
attention to line breaks	3
{ no print on illustrations	2
size of book	
quality of illustrations	
{ amount of print	1
laminated covers	
no split words	

With regard to the physical features of books a significant criterion mentioned by one quarter of this group related to the matter of illustrations which they maintained should match the text in books for young children. They also indicated their disapproval of text printed on top of illustrations, saying that this feature of books was very confusing for young children and should be avoided. They mentioned covers that should be attractive and laminated – in that order – and commented that care should be taken to regulate the amount of print in these books. Line-breaks should be carefully monitored and split words need to be avoided under all circumstances.

With respect to the content of books for young children, these teachers confirmed the earlier finding from the analysis of the ranking procedure, stressing that content was the most important feature that needed consideration. They also pointed out that they preferred the language of books to mirror speech forms and stressed the need for a graded vocabulary. They indicated the importance of variety in content, mentioning humour and non-fiction in particular. They also suggested guarding against stereotypes in books for young children.

14 per cent of this group of 95 teachers mentioned the need to keep the costs

Table 3: Content of books for young children
(in rank order of mention)
N = 95

	%
considered very important	25
language of books should mirror speech forms	8
graded vocabulary	5
variety of content	4
humour	3
inclusion of non-fiction	2
sexism	1

Other criteria mentioned
(in rank order)
N = 95

	%
low cost	14
{ check list of vocabulary inside back cover	2
supplementary books to those in schemes	
age suitability	
{ wide choice of books	1
reading age levels indicated	

down and a small minority wanted vocabulary checklists inside the back cover of books for young children. An equally small minority wanted more books at equivalent levels of difficulty, indications of age suitability and reading ages specified. They also stressed the need for a wide choice of books.

Styles of print in books for young children

Teachers were asked to decide which of two broad categories of typeface they would choose when using books with young children. These two categories of typeface were a serif typeface and a sans serif typeface, the latter being found most frequently in books for young children. Each category of typeface was exemplified with and without modified *a* s and *g* s as an additional criterion to bear in mind. They were also required to identify which of these categories would be most important in books for children at the three different age points: five, six and seven years of age.

These teachers clearly indicated their preference for the modified *a* and *g* in typefaces used in books for young children, although this preference was less marked in the case of seven-year-olds. There was also a clear indication that a sans serif typeface was preferred by two thirds of the teachers for books throughout the infant school stage.

126

150 teachers gave additional information concerning the styles of print in children's books and the percentages in the table below are calculated against that number.

Table 4: Styles of print in books (in rank order of mention)
(N = 150)

	%
didn't matter after seven years of age	54
print should match handwriting	39
modified *a* and *g*	14
size of print	11
letter shapes should be simple	10
didn't matter at all	5
{ consistency { spacing important	2
{ sans serif typeface { good story mattered more	1

More than half of these 150 teachers agreed that styles of typeface in books did not matter for children aged seven years and over, although 5 per cent suggested types of print did not matter at all. 39 per cent of them stressed the need for print in books for younger children to match the style of handwriting which was being taught, and large print and simple letter shapes were assumed to be more helpful for young children, particularly the letter shapes of *a* and *g* which should be modified to conform with the handwritten shapes. Consistency and spacing were also deemed significant while 1 per cent suggested that a good story mattered more than styles of typeface.

These teachers were also asked to indicate the importance they attached to the use of punctuation and capital letters in books for young children across the age range five to seven years. Approximately half of the teachers liked to see capital letters and punctuation used appropriately in books for five-year-olds, with this percentage increasing as the children moved from five to seven years of age, indeed the figure more than doubled in the case of punctuation. 29 per cent decided that capital letters and punctuation did not matter at five years of age; however, this group had practically disappeared by six and seven years of age. These teachers appeared to agree on the importance of capital letters and punctuation after the first stages of learning to read had been passed.

Alternative letter shapes

These teachers were asked to choose which letter shapes for ten letters they felt would be most suitable in typefaces for the three age groups specified. They were asked to tick more than one letter shape alternative where they felt this was necessary. There was a remarkable similarity among the choices made at each age range:

a g i j l I q (with a tail at 7 yrs) t u y

Teachers' comments on the teaching of handwriting

170 teachers volunteered further comments on the teaching of handwriting during the stage of infant schooling. The percentages shown in the table below were calculated as a proprotion of this sub-total.

Table 5.
(in rank order of mention)
(N = 170)   %
Ligatures should be added at 7 years of age   54
Handwriting should match print in books   31
Style should be consistent in school   22
q must have a tail   18
Letter shapes should be simple for young children   15
Letter formation more important than shape   13
Ligatures should be taught at 5 years of age   5
Style of handwriting should be personal preference   4
Ligatures should be taught at 6 years of age   1
School policy on handwriting
Handwriting should be taught
Lines to write on

Published programmes for the teaching of handwriting were mentioned by 12 teachers:

Marion Richardson, Nelson, Chris Jarman,
Macmillan and Ruth Fagg's style.

Handwriting styles

All 270 teachers agreed on the shape of four lower case letters: *c, g, p* and *s*. Other letters appeared in a variety of shapes with one dominant shape, although in the case of *e* there were two shapes as popular as each other. In the examples of upper case letters, these teachers agreed on the shapes of A, B, C, D, H, L, N, O, P, R, S, T, V, W, X and Z, except in the case of one teacher who used a script quite unlike the others, with capital letters represented as large lower-case letters in ten instances.

Summary

The teachers who took part in this survey showed a remarkable consistency in their opinions concerning important features of books for young children, placing matters of content before layout and design, and giving comparatively less consideration to factors such as cost and durability. Two-thirds of these teachers were convinced of the value of a sans serif typeface in books for children, although more importance was given to the need for modified *a* s and *g* s. This emphasis was reinforced later with the additional information that teachers wanted the print in books for young children to match the style of handwriting they were learning to master. However, with respect to these teachers' comments on the teaching of handwriting, they pointed out the need to teach a style of handwriting which should match the print found in books for young children.

In view of these two points of view there appears to be a circularity in the preferences of teachers which links better shapes through both recognition and formation. Simple shapes may well be easier to form, but can be quite confusing to distinguish. This latter point is made clear by these teachers when they object to I as a capital, and they also point out that q is too easily confused with p. Letters do indeed need distinguishing features to reduce such confusion. For instance, some printed *a* s can resemble *o*, and *g* s with limited curvature in the tail can be mistaken for *q*, even in the case of short descenders open *a* and *g* can become confused with each other, also *u* with *y*. Alternatively, handwriting needs to be quickly executed and legible, with the built in requirement that the letter shapes are amenable to the developmental progression from print to joined-up script. This developmental requirement highlights the needs to introduce ligatures at some stage, although exactly when this should happen appears to be uncertain.

Clearly, an amount of confusion remains concerning appropriate styles of typeface for use in books for young children, and this confusion extends to letter shapes taught during the early stages of learning to handwrite. Currently, the evidence is not available to clarify this confusion although further research based on children's reactions may well be helpful in providing guidelines for the solution to this problem. These teachers have provided useful information which indicates some general tendencies in their criteria and this in turn will lead to further illumination of the underlying assumptions behind much taken-for-granted practice. Ultimately such assumptions can be re-evaluated against further evidence and classroom practice will be able to benefit from this continuing cooperation between researchers and teachers.

12 Exploring the use of microcomputers in language and reading: breaking away from drills and programmed instruction

Frank Potter

Despite the fact that most primary schools will have a microcomputer by the end of 1984, we do not yet know how to make the most efficient use of this resource.

The immediate and natural reaction is to imagine children engaged in drill and practice, programmed instruction, or even playing games. It is also not uncommon for experienced teachers, whilst acknowledging the role it has to play in the teaching of maths, science and geography, to be rather sceptical about its use in the teaching of language and reading.

It may be that the micro's role will be limited in this area, but on the other hand we may discover a wide range of useful applications. The answer is that we won't know until we have explored and evaluated many different possibilities.

I should like to describe one possible use which I have been exploring, and which seems to have great potential.

My starting point was the language and reading curriculum: from a consideration of those needs of children that are difficult for a teacher to fulfil within the limitations of the classroom situation.

I shall first describe the activity I chose to explore, then describe the program, and finally discuss other possible applications of the microcomputer.

The activity

The effective reader has to be able to make good use of the context to help identify unfamiliar words. This is especially important for the reader with limited phonic skills. As I have discussed more fully elsewhere (Potter, 1983a) this use of context presupposes the ability to think divergently in a Cloze-type situation – that is, the ability to think of many different alternatives that would make sense in the context.

Unfortunately, traditional Cloze exercises do not encourage such divergent thinking – rather, they suggest that the child should think of only one answer.

An activity that does help is prompting children to produce as many 'guesses' (hypotheses) as possible when they come to a deletion (or an unfamiliar word), providing feedback as to the appropriateness of their responses (Potter, 1983b), and providing an explanation when necessary.

This is usually best done with a group of children, so that they can learn from the discussion.

However, this activity is time-consuming for the teacher: she or he has to work with a small group continuously to prompt and provide feedback. Because of the demands on time, it can therefore very rarely be undertaken.

The program

I therefore designed a program to enable children to take part in this activity with the minimum of teacher involvement. The program is simple in conception, its main task being to provide feedback concerning the acceptability of the children's responses – the program categorises their guesses as *good, possible,* or *poor*. A possible response is one which we cannot really say is wrong, but on the other hand we would not want to say is good: for example, a word that is extremely unlikely but not inconsistent with the context. This category is necessary partly because of the 'fuzziness' of language.

The primary features of the program are the following:

(1) It takes over the routine elements of the task – such as providing feedback as to the acceptability of the children's guesses. In this respect it is in fact *better* than the teacher: it has infinite patience, and does not try to lead children towards the 'right' answer, as it is so easy to do albeit unintentionally. It also makes the correct decision instantly, whereas even the best of teachers would take a bit of time to decide on the acceptability of a guess, and would make occasional mistakes. Of course, the only reason why the computer is able to respond at all is because some teacher has already told it what to do in the first place. But once told, it never forgets, never makes a mistake, and responds instantly and neutrally.

(2) It directs the group of children, choosing whose turn it is to use the keyboard, and giving directions at each stage so that the children keep on the right track. It is really quite interesting to see how they concentrate on the task in hand – partly because they are given immediate feedback, but partly because they are given directions at the appropriate moment.

(3) The children's guesses are stored by the computer and are reviewed by the teacher and the children together at the end. This enables the teacher to discuss and explain any points the teacher or children wish. This part is absolutely essential, and is when the teacher needs to be present – the computer cannot deal with the complexities involved. But the teacher and children together decide how long they spend on this part of the task – five minutes is often sufficient, after the children have spent about 50 minutes working on their own. In other words, the optimum use is made of the teacher's skills. The children have as educationally worthwhile an activity as if the teacher had been present all the time, but she or he has been free to teach elsewhere about 90 per cent of the time.

(4) The program is data-free, and can be used with any text. There is an option within the program to set up a data file with all the responses for a new

131

text. There is also another option to change or add to the current data file. Hence any teacher can produce a new version of the program, without any programming knowledge.

Other programs

From my experience it seems that the micro can be used to help classroom organisation, so that the teacher makes better use of her or his skills. It also appears that programming the computer to direct a group, by giving it clear instructions, is an essential part of the program. Further, if the same 'skeleton' can be used with different sets of data, then obviously it has far more potential than one which can only be used once by each child. This kind of content-free program also has the advantage that it can be linked by the teacher to specific materials she or he is using in class (such as a reading scheme).

Early examples of programs may seem limited, but some can be adapted to incorporate both these features. I have described elsewhere (Potter, 1983c) how a commercially produced program, namely *Word Sequencing Sentences* published by ESM, can be adapted so that it directs a group of children, and also how different sets of data can be fed in.

Other uses of micros

In these early stages I think we have to loosen our imagination, to avoid thinking along narrow paths. For example Papert (1980) sees a danger in our thinking solely in terms of micros being used to program children. He sees the greatest potential in children programming computers. By this he does not mean children learning BASIC or other such languages; he means children manipulating computers rather than being manipulated by them.

He gives an example (pp. 48–9) of a girl, through the experiences of 'programming' a computer to produce 'concrete poetry', *discovering* the purpose of the distinction between nouns and verbs. This is a far cry from a computer designed to 'stamp in' knowledge about nouns and verbs.

Another use which gets away from programmed instruction is the computer as word processor. Even though children can enjoy systematic drafting and redrafting (Binns, 1980), the mechanical process of writing is so slow for some children that they cannot get much experience at this. A word processor, on the other hand can transform drafting and redrafting: changes are made so easily and quickly, and the final product is error free, neat and tidy.

We should not limit ourselves to thinking of using word processors just with older children. With the addition of a 'concept board' as an input device, instead of a typewriter keyboard, it is possible for reception children to use a word processing system. A group of teachers in Southport, led by Elizabeth Crabtree, are doing just that. The result is another dimension to 'Breakthrough to Literacy'.

We may even find in the end that some of the best language development may come from programs in other areas, just as micros may improve children's spelling, not through spelling programs but simply because a wrong spelling of the correct answer is usually treated as a wrong answer. As computers require precise instructions for them to work, so they may incidentally teach children to be more precise in their use of language.

References

BINNS, R. (1980) 'A technique for developing written language', in M. M. Clark and T. Glyn: *Reading and Writing for the Child with Difficulties,* Educational Review Occasional Publication No. 8, University of Birmingham.

PAPERT, S. (1980) *Mindstorms: Children, Computers and Powerful Ideas.* Brighton: Harvester.

POTTER, F. N. (1983a) 'The reader's use of context: some implications for teaching'. *Reading,* 17(1), pp. 37–42.

POTTER, F. N. (1983b) 'Teaching children to use the linguistic context more effectively'. *Reading,* 17(2), pp. 95–104.

POTTER, F. N. (1983c) 'Evaluating microcomputer software: Word Sequencing Sentences; ESM'. *Primary Contact* (November).

Programs

Word Sequencing Sentences. Wisbech: ESM.
Divergent Cloze.

13 Developing a computer program to cater for children's special needs in reading

M. J. Carter

Computers are rapidly becoming familiar objects within many schools these days, their major function being to aid or assist learning – hence the term 'computer-assisted learning'. There is little doubt that this type of usage in schools is valuable, provided of course that all children of all ability ranges get the opportunity to benefit from this aspect of learning.

The use of computers in education is an extremely rapidly expanding field, with equipment and materials (known as hardware and software) becoming outdated almost as soon as they appear, or so it would seem. Teachers have a difficult enough task keeping up with the quantity of advertising material describing the latest innovations in this sphere of education, let alone trying to master the intricacies of the school's latest acquisition, the new 'micro', for them to be too concerned about extending the use of the computer.

In the main, the computer in school may well function entirely as a learning aid, yet it has the potential to be a powerful diagnostic and prescriptive tool, helping the teacher to provide individualised programmes of learning, thereby catering for each child's special needs.

For the purpose of this article an experience in developing a computer program to cater for children's special needs in reading will be described and discussed, giving not only the history of the development of this concept but also indicating future trends in development where the needs of individual schools are considered. The writer is not a computer expert, realising that there may well be idiosyncrasies in computer programming design; however, it is not the intention to dwell on the technicalities of programming, rather to demonstrate applications and the realisation of the potential of such machines by the 'inexpert'. The computer used for this program is the Sinclair ZX81-16K RAM, and although its programming language is slightly different from perhaps more conventional forms of BASIC, it is adequate to illustrate the principles involved.

Interest in the computer as a diagnostic aid arose out of a project the intention of which was to design a diagnostic profile of a reader's performance or ability which could (a) be compiled with relative ease by teachers as a means of recording a child's progress in reading and, (b) would lend itself to instant, almost diagrammatic interpretation displaying the reader's strengths and weaknesses in terms of relative proficiency using miscue analysis as the measure of assessment.

In itself, miscue analysis is a sterile form of diagnosis, merely indicating an individual's performance in reading related to a specific text. Where, however, miscue analysis becomes a profitable form of diagnosis is when it is understood that each miscue is but a revelation of the way the individual perceives the text and how he or she organises processing strategies to decode and extract meaning from the text. (Goodman's classic comment of 'miscue analysis . . . the window on the reading process'.)

Viewed in these terms miscue analysis can be seen to be a valuable classroom tool or aid, providing the teacher with the means to prescribe certain activities for individual children thereby enabling them to become more proficient readers. This presupposes an awareness on the teacher's part of what skills and strategies are characterised by various types of miscue, for the process of the analysis of miscues – as the term suggests   relies on an interpretation of performance.

The work of the Goodmans, and the way their thinking on linguistic performance is manifest in oral reading, has been interpreted for classroom use, most notably by Goodacre (1972), Clay (1979), Southgate *et al.* (1981) and Arnold (1982), but although these writers do give clear guidance on the way in which miscues can be interpreted, no positive indication is offered regarding the way in which teachers can relate the miscue-type to the characteristic form of behaviour it represents, to what can be done within the class to enable the individual to overcome the difficulties encountered when reading is typified by a particular miscue.

In attempting to devise a diagrammatic format that would provide teachers with a framework for interpretation, and which would indicate patterns of activities that could be devised for children encountering specific problems in reading, the seven major types of miscue were examined, their characteristics noted as being typical of certain forms of reading behaviour and from this appraisal, implications for prescription of activities that would check or strengthen weakness encountered.

A study of these seven major types of miscues – i.e. no-response; hesitation; reversal; repetition; insertion; omission; and substitution – suggested that some miscues were more typical of less proficient forms of reading ability, while others were more indicative of more positive forms. From this it appears possible to devise a format that would display a continuum of emerging forms of reading behaviour. This would then give the teacher not only a record of the child's performance as a reader (if that was required) but also a basis for interpretation which would also provide specific indication as to types of activities that could be utilised to increase reading proficiency.

Several attempts were made to devise a layout that would provide an instant almost 'at-a-glance' interpretation of performance. Specific reference was made to Southgate *et al.* (1981) and also to Arnold (1982) the final design being that shown in Figure 1 on page 136.

In construction, the profile indicates an emerging form of reading proficiency moving across the form from left to right. Miscues concerned with the manner in which the reader *perceives* the text – i.e. the no-response, hesitation, reversal, repetition, insertion and omission miscues – are kept to the top half of the form, whereas the manner in which the reader *interprets* the text – i.e. the most telling form of miscue, the substitution – is shown in the bottom half of the form. This form of layout is suggested by Goodman (1972)

MISCUE ANALYSIS PROFILE PATTERN

Child's name __John Smith__   d.o.b. __22.12.73__   date of analysis __10.10.82__

Class/teacher __Ms Jones__   Child's position in scheme/book __Level 7·5/8·0 yrs__

Title of passage/book read __Ladybird 'Beauty and the Beast'__ Page numbers __4-6__ Readability level __Fry ≈ 8.0y__

EMERGING FORMS OF READING BEHAVIOUR	MORE PROFICIENT FORMS OF READING BEHAVIOUR

NO-RESPONSE

INSERTIONS

2.5.

HESITATION

3.10.(12).(16).17.19.21.22.23.24

OMISSIONS

HESITATION & REPETITION

(13.)

REPETITIONS

4.9.

HESITATION & SUBSTITUTION

1.11.

WORD REVERSALS

PHRASAL/POSITIONAL ORDER REVERSALS

SUBSTITUTIONS

All SUBSTITUTION MISCUES must be entered in each of these levels – i.e. 3 times to show acceptability and appropriacy within the 3 levels of language.

	SOUND/SYMBOL MATCH	
Poor – bears no similarity to the text.	*Fair* – partial similarity to text – e.g. initial letter/sound.	*Good* – close similarity to text – e.g. sound/syllable match.
	8.(15).20	1.6.7.11.(14).18.25

	GRAMMATICAL	
Poor – bears no similarity to the text.	*Fair* – partial similarity to text – fulfils same purpose as original. up to and including miscue *only*.	*Good* – fulfils same purpose as text – on both sides of miscue – simile etc.
11.(15).	8.(14.)25. 1.	6. 7. 18. 20.

	SEMANTIC	
Poor – distorts meaning of sentence and passage.	*Fair* – makes sense up to and including miscue *only*.	*Good* – meaning is retained in sentence and passage – no distortion.
1. 11.(15).	6. 8.(14.)25.	7. 18. 20.

	SELF-CORRECTIONS	
Miscue self-corrected.		Miscue not self-corrected
11.	✓	

Devised by M. J. Carter (1982/3) ©

Fig. 1: An example of a completed profile of a reader's miscues.

and is to be found in Southgate *et al.* (1981), and demonstrates the way in which this particular form of miscue indicates not only degrees of proficiency but also how it is reflective of the way in which the reader uses the three linguistic cueing systems.

A point worth noting is the additional information provided as typified by the three varieties of hesitation miscue and the two forms of reversal miscue. In the case of the former, there is evidence to suggest a growing perception of the utilisation of reading strategies on the part of the reader in the way that a hesitation miscue becomes modified by repetition (demonstrating increasing use of scanning ahead and prediction) and by substitution (demonstrating more competent predictive strategies). (See Biemiller, 1970; Barr, 1972; Potter, 1981; and Southgate *et al.*, 1981.) Reversals tend to indicate a polarity of proficiency – in less proficient forms of ability tending to be word-reversals, while in more proficient forms indicative of competence in fluency and internalisation of the processing of meaning (D'Angelo and Wilson, 1979; and the Goodmans, 1977). On the profile, the emerging form of proficiency, characterised by the variants of the hesitation miscue, are shown in staggered arrangement moving from the least proficient form of simple hesitation to the arguably more proficient form of hesitation and substitution. The same is characterised by the polarity of the reversal miscue, showing it in its least proficient form on the left, whilst in its most proficient form on the right. In attempting to portray so complex a process as reading in diagrammatic form it is realised that in trying to simplify stages of development in an arbitrary form, such an interpretation is in itself open to interpretation. What justification there is of formulating such a design lies in the fact that it can and does provide a basis for discussion of what matters most – providing for the child's needs.

To complete the profile a teacher conducts an analysis of the reader's performance with regard to a specific piece of text. The reader's miscues are noted and coded – (see Southgate *et al.*, 1981 for coding). After the coding, each miscue is given a number – so that reference to specific miscues can be made. Certain miscues, explained above – i.e. composite miscues of the hesitation/repetition or hesitation/substitution variety – are identified as single miscues. The teacher then completes the profile form, entering the appropriate number from the coded text within the appropriate section on the form. An example of this is shown below:

Textual sample coded and numbered

12
'When his daughter asked him what was/the matter, he replied,
13   14 *not*   15 *fronton*
/"ALAS, I am no longer rich. I have lost my fortune. We must
   =====   16
all leave this/beautiful house and go to live in the country." '

From *Beauty and the Beast* – Ladybird Books (1980), page 5.

Miscue 12 = hesitation

Miscue 13 = hesitation *and* repetition (degree of repetition indicated as being 3 attempts before correct reading).

Miscue 14 = substitution

Miscue 15 = substitution (?word reversal)

Miscue 16 = hesitation

These particular miscues have been transferred to the profile form (Figure 1) and are noted in their appropriate places – shown circled.

A completed profile form is shown in Figure 1 and in this format it is arguably easier to interpret the reader's performance and ability than it is from just the coded sample of text – although this needs to be referred to in order to discover details such as the child's ability to carry over context, possible tie chains of meaning, span of scan, prediction and the way in which parts of the text have brought about miscues.

The profile, in effect, provides the teacher with a summary of the reader's performance, displaying patterns of ability – or the lack of it; strengths as well as weaknesses, thereby making diagnosis easier and prescription simpler.

In its present format, the profile sheet contains Figure 1 on one side with Figure 2 – the profile analysis – on the reverse. In design, the profile analysis echoes that of the profile form, attempting to display a developmental picture of emerging reading proficiency. Each miscue-type contains a description of its characteristics, a small checklist to enable the teacher to identify a pattern of behavioural characteristics and brief general suggestions (at present) for development or follow-up activities.

Pursuing the example given above concerning the number of hesitation miscues shown on the profile form (Figure 1) the teacher would locate the miscue-type on the profile analysis (Figure 2 – on the reverse side of the form) and find:

HESITATION

Child pauses for a brief time, then reads on.
Cue-gathering stage, characterised by 'voice-pointing'.
Too many hesitations will interrupt flow and impede facility to gather meaning.

CHECK

a) Why hesitation? Uncertainty regarding word attack?
b) Is there a pattern? i.e. before which words?
c) Afraid/unable to predict?
d) Material too difficult – readability/conceptually?

MISCUE ANALYSIS PROFILE

Reader's name __John Smith__   Reader's age __8-10__   Date of analysis __10.10.82__ Miscue rate ____

Title of passage read __'Beauty and the Beast'__   Readability level (Fry) __≈8.0__ yrs.

Bibliographic details of passage __Ladybird' (level in scheme 7.5 – 8.0 yrs)__

EARLY OR WEAK FORMS OF ABILITY

NO-RESPONSES
Child appears to make no attempt to read.
Allow child time to attempt word – may well be processing internally.

CHECK
a) What type of words not being read?
b) Is there a pattern of no-response types – e.g. certain phonic patterns?
c) Does child have sufficient experience to read material?
d) Is material outside child's conceptual experience?

FOLLOW-UP
a) Word attack skills – basic sight vocabulary.
b) Phonic training in types of rules shown up in diagnosis.

HESITATION
Child pauses for a brief time, then reads on.
Cue gathering stage, characterised by 'voice-pointing'
Too many hesitations will interrupt flow and impede facility to gather meaning.

CHECK
a) Why hesitation? Uncertainty regarding word attack?
b) Is there a pattern? i.e. before which words?
c) Afraid/unable to predict?
d) Material too difficult readability/conceptually.

FOLLOW-UP
a) Identify and remedy phonic weakness.
b) Encourage prediction using pictures and cloze.
c) Practice in word recognition.
d) Use easier material.
e) Use larger phonic units.

EMERGING PROFICIENCY

INSERTION AND OMISSIONS
Where these miscues do not distort meaning within the sentence or passage, they can be ignored as they are indicative of proficient reading. The reader is capable of scanning text rapidly but is being slowed down by oral reading.

CHECK
a) Is meaning distorted?
b) Do these miscues appear frequently?
c) Spacing between lines.

FOLLOW-UP
a) Slow down reading speed.
b) Emphasise accuracy as being important.
c) Mask-off reading as described for reversals.
d) Select text with wider spaces between lines.

DIRECTION OF PROGRESS   →

FROM   TO   →

LATER-PROFICIENT FORMS OF ANALYSIS

HESITATION AND REPETITION
Characterised by voice and finger pointing.

CHECK
As for hesitation miscues.

FOLLOW-UP
a) Word recognition of basic sight vocab.
b) Encourage reading-on to obtain clues.
c) Read along with tape.
d) Flash card work.
e) Go beyond literal level with comprehension.

REPETITIONS
Checks and follow-up similar to HESITATION & REPETITION.

Generally a 'marking-time' stage where reader is cue gathering.

REVERSALS
Early reading – rearrangement of letters in words to produce other common words e.g. WAS/SAW: ON/NO types

Later reading – phrasal reversals MOTHER SAID/SAID MOTHER type.

CHECK
a) Is this a particular problem – i.e. whenever potentially reversible words/phrases are encountered?
b) Is there a pattern? Or is this random behaviour?
c) Are only certain words reversed – certain grapho/phonic situations?
d) Are reversals nonsensical – POD/DOP? Is child aware of this?
e) Does child self-correct?

FOLLOW-UP
a) Emphasise directional order, tracing, copying.
b) Draw attention to different characteristics of reversible words, stress construction.
c) Provide phonic experiences that draws attention to similarities/dissimilarities of confusing letters and sounds.
d) Use cloze technique where reversible words appear.   e) Use a reading mask over the lines.

HESITATION AND SUBSTITUTION – see appropriate miscues above.

SUBSTITUTIONS
Most common form of miscue made by readers, yielding most information regarding the way in which reader processes text. Characteristic at all levels of reading ability and will indicate how reader uses cue gathering strategies within the 3 levels of language – e.g. grapho/phonic (sound/symbol), syntactic (structural), and semantic (meaning).

CHECK
Acceptability or appropriateness of miscue, phonetically, syntactically and semantically – i.e. HOW CLOSELY DOES IT FIT?
Depending on the above, strengthening weaknesses will become apparent.

SOUND/SYMBOL
Follow-up
a) Identify pattern and apply appropriate rule/programme.
b) Concentrate on maximising phonic information e.g. syllables.

STRUCTURAL
a) Look at word endings – indicative of tense changes.   b) Use cloze techniques for appropriate areas e.g. nouns, verbs etc.

SEMANTIC
a) Use of comprehension strategies.   b) Use of cloze procedure.   Developed by M. J. Carter (1982) ©

Fig. 2: An example of the profile analysis with suggested follow-up activities identified.

FOLLOW-UP

a) Identify and remedy phonic weakness.
b) Encourage prediction using pictures and cloze procedure.
c) Practice in word recognition.
d) Use easier materials.
e) Use larger phonic units.

(An extract from the profile analysis — see Figure 2.)

Space will not permit detail or elaboration regarding the information contained in the profile analysis (Figure 2). Granted, such generalisations as exemplified in the follow-up section of the example given too are all embracing, e.g. 'Identify and remedy phonic weakness'. Having said that, however, if the checklist has been followed closely, and if the teacher has given thought to interpreting the characteristics of the miscue-type, then such an example is perhaps justified as it should be possible to detect a pattern emerging which will then suggest or dictate the remedy.

In fact, it was this concern regarding the broadness of generalisation and the lack of specificity contained on the profile analysis that led to the consideration of alternative methods of presentation of this information. An expansion of information would necessitate an eventual proliferation of paper, with the result that it would not be an attractive approach for the majority of teachers, given that the process of miscue analysis is considered by many teachers to be too complex a classroom tool. Conversely, the format of the profile contains too scant information on follow-up activities for it to be of much appeal to perhaps all but the most interested and knowledgeable of teachers.

The advantage of using a computer to present the information contained in the profile form lies mainly in the fact that considerable amounts of data can be stored within the computer, but that the program controlling its use could be made to release small elements information, on the request of the user (teacher). In this way the necessary information could be stored in quantity, if required, being released only when 'requested'. Computerising the profile format would have the effect of making its use obsolete and this can be seen as an advantage not only in the sense that it reduces the amount of paper collected in the recording process, but also eliminates what could be seen as one of the profile's disadvantages, that of its apparent complexity regarding its completion in order to arrive at the interpretative and prescriptive stages.

In this computer-assisted approach towards the diagnosis of reading problems and the prescription of activities to increase proficiency, the teacher can move from the reader's response to the text to the necessary suggestions for prescription of follow-up activities on the computer without completing the profile form (the information contained on the profile analysis being incorporated in the computer program).

The teacher conducts an analysis of the reader's performance with regard

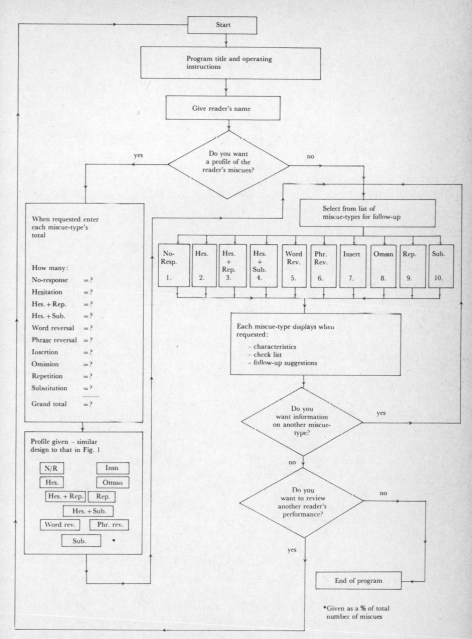

Fig. 3: Flow diagram of a computer program designed to indicate follow-up activities for increased reading proficiency based on the use of miscue analysis.

to a specific piece of text in the normal manner of recording miscues. The number of miscues is totalled for each type, e.g. 10 hesitations (see Figure 1). The teacher then runs the computer program and responds to the questions as they appear on the monitor. The questions are designed to elicit YES or NO responses, or to select from a menu of choices by deciding on the number of the choice indicated – for example, the selection of choice 2 would display information concerning hesitation miscues. Reference to Figure 3 will indicate the structure of the program displaying the appropriate stages within the program.

At this stage of its development, the program merely reproduces the information to be found in the profile analysis (see Figure 2). The potential of the computer to store large amounts of data has already been intimated so that the next stage of development will be that of devising additional and more specific activities related to each miscue-type – expanding the generalised follow-up notes on the profile analysis. Here again, the teacher will be in command of the situation, the computer program offering suggestions that can be accepted or rejected as the case may be.

An advance on this stage of development would be the ability to identify a trend in a pattern of reading behaviour so that the program is able to give precise guidance as to the nature of follow-up. To do this the program structure would require additional data from the individual concerning his or her responses to questions asked after reading the passage, such as types of comprehension questions; the individual's interpretation of what he or she thought such and such a word meant when he or she read it in the passage – e.g. the word 'fronton' contained in the extract. Such questions would be hard to quantify for the purpose of devising a program that would be able to identify linguistic strategies, but are surely not insurmountable.

It is envisaged that the use of such a program will considerably ease the teacher's task in the diagnosis of reading problems and the associated provision of suitable follow-up activities to cater for children's special needs. With teachers having to become more used to the idea of working with computers, such a program should ease the teaching load as well as dispensing with the need to keep bulky files of paper for recording progress. This particular program also contains commands to run a printer, if linked to the computer, so that if a profile of performance is required for record purposes it can be obtained. Similarly, the necessary follow-up activities can be obtained in print-out form as retainable information, if necessary.

An additional feature of this approach is that a school will be able to adapt the program to suit its own forms of prescribed activities. Suggestions as to how this may be effected will be contained with the instructions on the operation of the program. Where the program is to be used as a diagnostic and prescriptive aid, teachers will need to discuss what activities they consider most appropriate to meet the needs of certain reading behavioural characteristics – it is pointless to list specific materials within suggested follow-up activities in the program if the school does not have access to this particular material. Schools will therefore be able to insert particular lists of activities or materials within the program listing so that the program is suited to the needs and requirements of that particular school – reference to a specific set of texts, purpose-made materials, tapes, slide packs, worksheets, etc. Such an approach has implications for the resource management of the school, especially as there is the potential to develop the concept of individualised reading programmes with this method of diagnosis and prescription. The drudgery can perhaps be taken out of teaching using this approach of computer-assisted diagnosis and prescription, arguably leaving teachers better placed to use their professional judgement and expertise to cater for the special needs of the children within their care.

(Copies of the program listing and notes on the operation of this program can be obtained from the writer.)

References

ARNOLD, H. (1982) *Listening to Children Reading*. U.K.R.A. Monograph. Sevenoaks, Kent: Hodder and Stoughton.

BARR, R. (1972) 'The influence of instructional conditions on word recognition errors'. *Reading Research Quarterly*, 7, pp. 509–29.

BIEMILLER, A. (1970) 'The development of the use of graphic and contextual information as children learn to read'. *Reading Research Quarterly*, 6(1).

CARTER, M. J. (1982) *Towards implementing miscue analysis in school*. Unpublished B.Ed. In service dissertation, Worcester College of Higher Education.

CLAY, M. M. (1979) *Reading – the patterning of complex behaviour* (2nd edition). London: Heinemann.

D'ANGELO, K. and WILSON, R. M. (1979) 'How helpful is insertion and omission miscue analysis?' *The Reading Teacher*, 32(5), pp. 519–20.

GOODACRE, E. J. (1972) *Hearing Children Read*. Centre for the Teaching of Reading, University of Reading.

GOODMAN, K. S. and GOODMAN, Y. M. (1977) 'Learning about psycholinguistic processes by analysing oral reading', in L. J. Chapman and P. Czerniewska (eds) *Reading From Process to Practice*. London: Routledge and Kegan Paul.

SOUTHGATE, V. (1980) *Beauty and the Beast*. Loughborough: Ladybird Books.

SOUTHGATE, V., ARNOLD, H. and JOHNSON, S. (1981) *Extending Beginning Reading*. London: Heinemann.

14 Some issues in the teaching of spelling

Richard Binns, assisted by Ian Liddle

Introduction

The practice of teaching pupils to self-correct in spelling is reconsidered in these workshop materials. The materials relate to the discussions of a working party of Glasgow secondary school teachers. The purpose of the workshop is to discuss some of the issues involved in introducing pupils to a strategy for self-correction, if a visual approach to spelling is adopted.[1]

An attempt is made to answer teachers' questions about proofreading and revising activities during (re-)writing.[2]

1. As red-ink corrections are no longer recommended, how do you get children to deal with their 'spellings'?
2. What do you do if children fail to find their spelling mistakes?
3. Is it wrong to let the same word be mis-spelled in different ways in a piece of writing?
4. What is the best way to help children to identify the 'hard bit' of a word?
5. How do you get children to look hard enough at the spelling of a word for which they have asked?
6. When should pupils be given help to look up the correct spelling of a word in a class dictionary?
7. Why is it more effective in practice to pick some kinds of mis-spelling instead of others for self-correction?

Abstract

Some method must be found whereby children can with the least possible withdrawal of attention from their creative writing be faced with the correct spelling of a word they need

(M. Peters, 1967).

The problem in the teaching of spelling so aptly summed up in this quotation is first of all discussed broadly in terms of the teaching of written language (Peters, 1967). There follows a review of two different procedures for revision, as aids to self-correction in spelling during (re-)writing. Finally, miscues in spelling are seen to be significant for the purpose of assessment and intervention.

Theory and practice in teaching written language

The transition from the earlier to the later stages of writing is very demanding for children as young writers. This is primarily due to the demands on spelling brought about by the desire to express more complex ideas in written language. If these demands are to cause no more than a temporary setback, many children may require to be introduced to an effective strategy for self-correction in spelling (Cripps, 1983).

Demands on spelling in the process of (re-)writing

---

pause to reflect . . .   to read over work to check doubt about
the intended meaning . . .
the phrasing . . .

Spelling?
. . . rephrasing to avoid mis-spelling

The demands that generally cause strain in the process of (re-)writing are brought about by the element of rehearsal in the relationship between thought and language (Binns, 1980). For example, if children are asked whether they could have used a more appropriate word in a particular context, they may be often heard to say that the spelling was too difficult. As a pause for reflection may lead to confusion in wording part of a passage or in stringing together the letters of a word, care may have to be taken in leading children to assume greater responsibility for their (re-)writing. In the case of spelling, children may have to be alerted to the possibility of relying on their intuitive awareness of common letter patterns to see whether or not a word *looks right*.

The feasibility of teaching children at secondary level to read over and revise their written compositions has been considered to be for a long while very much an open question. In reading over work, common spelling mistakes are often overlooked. In trying out spelling, there may even be a tendency to fall back on the ineffective strategy of 'sounding out', as in reading a word aloud to deal with a difficult part of the letter string. The possibility of confusion between reading and spelling activities may even enter into the process of learning how to spell in the course of looking at a word. These difficulties suggest that proof-reading and revising activities may be too time-consuming for the majority of pupils. Consequently, it would appear to be more effective in the long run to give pupils the correct spelling of words for which they ask (D.E.S., 1975).

Revision as an aid to spelling

However, consideration has still to be given to those occasions when the teacher may not be available to give extra help with spelling. The advantages and disadvantages of two different procedures for proofreading and revising are now discussed. Particular regard is paid to the sequence of steps between drafts, as an aid to revision.

1. Traditionally, proof-reading and revising have been carried out on the following sequence of steps, in written composition.

Getting ideas from reading and discussion	Planning the topics for a composition	Building up detail – phrasing – in topic sentences and paragraphs	Writing out a final version	Proofreading and revising; making a fair copy.

The main advantage of this procedure lies in affording from the start of a composition an opportunity to ask for the correct spelling of a word. Thus spellings may be learned and used for writing about set topics.

A disadvantage is that children may suppose the importance of making a 'fair' copy to be paramount. Consequently, they may rely less on being able to spell a word that they were unsure of and more on copying out their work in order to get it handed in. The adverse effect is frequently that spelling mistakes may tend to occur in the process of (re-)writing due to miscopying.

2. A less conventional approach to written composition is to use the technique of drafting and re-drafting to accustom children to deal with the element of rehearsal in the process of (re-)writing (Binns, 1980).

Write a first draft (with/without using the original wording of any notes)	Read over draft for two main purposes; initially to see *where*; later on *how* to make alterations	Re-draft (a)part(s)/ the whole of a composition for a final version.

In this approach to revision, the proofreading activity of reading over work to deal with error and alteration may be introduced in two distinct steps between drafts. Frequent opportunities to read over and review work for different purposes in (re-)writing permit pupils to rely to a progressively greater extent on their visual awareness of common letter strings in checking for mis-spelling.

The advantage of this sequence of activities during drafting and re-drafting lies in the effect it has of slowing down pupils, as they read over their work to make alterations (Binns, 1978). In consequence, they begin to rely on the strategy of looking to see *where* a word has been mis-spelled and on 'sounding out' for the purpose of working out how to re-word.

The main disadvantage of this approach to revision is that children may find the strain of self-correction in spelling too great. Common spelling mistakes may be difficult to find in reading over work; homophones and other kinds of mis-spelling may appear to children to be reasonably plausible phonic alternatives. The number of 'new' words used for the first time in written language may be too numerous for checking in a class dictionary and learning, prior to redrafting. In this case, what is required at the intermediate steps of composition is a systematic procedure for assessing children's readiness to self-correct in spelling.

A procedure for assessment and intervention

Intervention to help with spelling depends on estimating the readiness of an individual pupil to self-correct. A useful starting point in planning intervention is to assess awareness of the English coding system (Peters and Cripps, 1980). For a reliable assessment it is necessary to find out what an individual pupil is capable of doing to improve the spelling of a passage without any extra help. This does not mean, for example, counting the incidence of spelling mistakes in one or two pieces of writing and planning a spelling programme accordingly.

This procedure is notoriously unreliable, as instances of the crossing out and the insertion of letters that are difficult to decipher may serve to create a greater impression of failure to spell than is revealed on closer inspection (S.E.C., 1977).

Neither has it been found to be very useful to regard the opportunity for revision between drafts as a testing situation. A more effective procedure is to introduce individual pupils to the various steps that may be taken in self-correction between drafts and then observe whether or not they are capable of studying how closely the spelling of a word approximates to its correct precedent (Fernald, 1943).

A comparison between drafts may permit a more reliable evaluation of the nature of difficulty in spelling to be carried out. General awareness of the *serial probability* of letters within words may be observed both in spelling errors and alterations (Peters and Cripps, 1980). In addition, the nature of any specific individual difficulty may be seen more clearly. The effect of sensory impairment in loss of hearing or sight, as well as physical difficulty in manipulating a pen, may be observed in the process of (re-)writing (S.E.C., 1977).

At this introductory stage, it has been found to be helpful neither to carry out 'red-ink' corrections nor to permit pupils to erase spelling mistakes (D.E.S., 1975). At the same time, every effort may be made to avoid the effect of any frustration at spelling by motivating pupils to write to the best of their ability. They may be encouraged to compose their ideas for a particular purpose and to realise in the process of reading over their work and re-writing, how certain spelling mistakes affect significantly the communication of meaning (S.C.R.E., 1961).

Questions for consideration at four steps in self-correction
during revision between drafts.

What kind of mis-spellings occur (in a first draft)? How aware is an individual pupil of miscues in checking to see if the spelling of words 'looks right'? Why do certain kinds of mis-spelling recur?	1. *Reading over work* silently/aloud to indicate doubt about spelling. 2. *Trying out spelling* on a blank page, facing a composition. 3. *Referring to a dictionary* to check/write out the correct spelling. 4. *Learning how to spell* by means of the (Look/Cover/Write/Check) × 2 routine.

In the process of self-correction, the application of a code to indicate spelling mistakes in the course of reading over work may reveal the kind of error that is causing real difficulty. The opportunity to try out the spelling of a word can even reveal that a child knows how to spell it correctly but was distracted during the process of writing. On the other hand, the trial of words may be used as a pretext to discuss the 'hard bits'. In this instance, it is possible to observe the extent of an individual pupil's awareness of the critical feature of English, that 'words look the same, irrespective of their sounds' (Peters and Cripps, 1980).

Composition page

Blank page	Double page of a jotter
Trying out spelling without the teacher	text of a composition the pupil indicates a possible mis-spelling . . . .
red . . . redy – – – – – – – – – – – – – –	'(reday)', with the aid of an agreed code; for example, by underlining or bracketing.

On the basis of these preliminary observations, the teacher may start to decide how ready a pupil is to self-correct. Further diagnosis may confirm that a mis-spelling, for example, 'redy' which is a reasonable phonic alternative, may be too difficult to check independently in a dictionary.

Diagnosis may lead to pupils being encouraged to read over their work to look only for mis-spellings which they are probably going to find. A visual cue in the margin may be used to signify the probability of both finding different kinds of mis-spelling in the text of a composition and checking them in either a class or a personal dictionary. A visual cue is in this case an agreed code. A further advantage of a visual cue in the margin to assist pupils to monitor their written language may lie in the encouragement it affords to write more deliberately.

Margin	Text of composition
(D) –	find mis-spelling; check correct spelling in a dictionary.
1. ( ) –	look for mis-spelling but refer to a personal dictionary at the back of the jotter to see where the teacher has written out the spelling correctly.

Margin	Personal dictionary
1.	ready with further words to aid visual discrimination; for example bead read ready readily

Finally, the Look/Cover/Write/Check routine may offer an opportunity to observe difficulty in revisualising and reconstituting the sequence of letters in a word (Peters and Cripps, 1980).

LOOK – doubt _____ (this routine may be used twice)
COVER
WRITE doubt
CHECK
doubt doubt

Difficulty in learning how to spell a word may be for two main reasons.
1. Failure to say over/look at a *whole* word, prior to writing it out (Peters and Cripps, 1980).
2. Lack of motivation to look intently enough, with the intention of using a word to write.
Miscue analysis at these four steps in self-correction may alert the teacher and the pupil to ineffective strategies in spelling.
A diagnostic and remedial spelling record may be kept of 'broadly three kinds of mis-spelling:

1. Reasonable phonic alternatives, e.g. 'rane' and 'rain'. These will gradually disappear if the teacher continues to keep alive the child's interest in words and adopts a rational correction procedure.
2. Unreasonable phonic alternatives, e.g. 'bukit' for 'bucket'. A child making these errors has not learned about serial probability and must be taught to look carefully at words containing the same letter pattern.
3. Unclassified words. These attempts are so remote that he needs to be given a remedial programme which is in fact a first spelling programme.'

(Peters and Cripps, 1980; Welch, Thornton and Aston, 1978.)

The workshop programme

The programme currently being tried out is intended to prepare for intervention to help with spelling in the context of ordinary classwork.

1. *Studying nonsense words* to draw attention to children's difficulty in learning how to spell by means of the (Look/Cover/Write/Check) × 2 routine, especially if they are not very familiar with common letter patterns in English.

   List 1. FINSTURBLAIT
   OLPHENSTOUR CHLOSTRAZINE
   HEPRADIGM CRUMBLEAZE

   List 2. ARMOSHREAN
   MYEROCHAN PRACKSYST
   BHORFORYL
   RHIZOGRONE

2. *Close reading of four pupils' first drafts of a story* to consider the nature of their difficulty in self-correction in spelling, prior to watching a video of first year, secondary, mixed-ability English classwork.
3. *Observing on video the introduction of* 'A Practical Approach to Writing and Spelling' (Peters, 1981) with an English and a remedial teacher present in a classroom.
4. *Reviewing the significance of miscues, as a guide to planning intervention.*

Record of error and alteration in developing written language – 'spelling'

Pupil's	Actual word	Error in text	Reading over work draft/re-draft coded	Dictionary reference tried out	Correct spelling written out
Colin	AUTUMN	autum			
	DUNGAREES		(dungarees)		
	AMONGST	a mon g s t	(amongst)	?	
John	BEGINNING	be g ing			
	DIGGING	di g ing			
	PIGEON	pidgoen	(pidgoen)		
	CAUTIOUSLY	cau i to usty		?	?
			(cauitousty)	causiousley	cauitously
	KETTLE	kettele		caushusley	cautiously
Teresa	DIGGING	diging	(diging)		
	READY	reday			
	THROW		(throw)		
	CHIRPING	ciping	(ciping)	?	
				ceping	
				cirping	chirping
	INSIDE	in side			

Record of error and alteration in developing written language – 'spelling'

Pupil's name	Actual word	Error in text	Reading over work draft/re-draft coded	Dictionary reference tried out	Correct spelling written out
	GREENWORTH	Crenworth?	(Crenworth)		
	COTTAGE		(cottage)		
	ABOUT		(about)		
	REEDS	reads	(reads)		
Thomas	SPOTTED	spoted	(spoted)		
	BROWNY		(browny)		
	COLOURED	cotherd?	(cotherd)	?	?
				colord	colour
				color	coloured
				colur	
	ABOUT	a but ?	(a) but		
	DETERMINED	determand			

Discussion points are based on miscue analysis.
a. All four pupils asked for help with a mis-spelling that significantly affected the meaning of their story about a nest in an old kettle (Meade and Kerry, 1976). 'a mon g s t', 'cau i to usty', 'ciping', 'a but'.
b. Reasonable phonic alternatives were harder to detect than mis-spelling with a visual gap in the letter strings – 'autum', 'diging', 'reday', 'determand', 'a mon g s t', 'cau i to usty', 'a but'.
c. Trying out the spelling of a word as a step to checking it in a dictionary was time-consuming, due to lack of familiarity with a letter pattern – 'causiousley, caushusley'.
d. Writing out the correct spelling of a word after looking it up was liable to error, due not just to omitting to turn over/cover up a dictionary but also to glancing back at the original mis-spelling in a jotter – 'cauitously'.

Conclusion

A judicious balance has to be maintained between the demands of writing and spelling. On balance, the importance is recognised of limiting self-correction during (re-)writing and of giving selective attention to certain words in a period of time set aside for spelling. The selection of words for attention in spelling is based on miscue analysis at the four steps in self-correction between drafts.

An element of distortion arises in the video, due to cutting a double period to a viewing time of 23 minutes. Writing time was edited out to focus on self-correction. Thus it appears as if too long is being spent on spelling during (re-)writing.

Readiness to self-correct is indicated, in Thomas's case, by the fact that he can be *heard* to pause then read on with appropriate intonation and stress at 'a but' as well as *seen* to code '(a)'. The deletion of '(a)' alters significantly the relation between grammar and meaning (Britton, 1975).

These workshop materials represent the transition from one set of notions about the teaching of spelling to another. They are not recommendations but observations on some of the issues that arise in introducing pupils to a predominantly visual approach to spelling.

Notes

1. Workshop membership:

Richard Binns, P.T.R.E.	St Pius Secondary School
Wilma Broughan, A.P.T. English	Kingsridge Secondary School
Norris Deeley, A.T. English	Possilpark Secondary School
George Hunter, P.T.R.E.	Possilpark Secondary School
Imelda McGrath, P.T.R.E.	Trinity High Secondary School
Philip Stockwell, P.T.R.E.	Kingsridge Secondary School
John Swan, P.T.R.E.	Whitehill Secondary School

with the assistance of Gordon Malone, Lecturer, Special and Remedial Education Department, Jordanhill College of Education; and Ian Liddle, Psychologist, Springburn Child Guidance Clinic, Glasgow Division.

2. Trial of the Workshop Materials: Acknowledgement is made here of the critical contribution to this paper from questions about issues related to the teaching of spelling put forward at meetings, by teachers, volunteer tutors, psychologists, members of the advisorate and the curriculum development service, between November 1982 and September 1983.

References

BINNS, R. (1978) *From Speech to Writing.* Edinburgh: S.C.D.S., Moray House College of Education.

BINNS, R. (1980) 'A technique for developing written language', in M. M. Clark and T. Glyn (eds) *Reading and Writing for the Child with Difficulties,* Educational Review Occasional Publication No. 8, University of Birmingham.

BRITTON, J. *et al.* (1975) *The Development of Writing Abilities 11–18.* London: Macmillan.

CRIPPS, C. C. (1983) 'A report of an experiment to see whether young children can be taught to write from memory'. *Remedial Education,* 18(3).

D.E.S. (1975) *A Language for Life* (The Bullock Report). London: H.M.S.O.

FERNALD, G. (1943) *Remedial Techniques in Basic School Subjects.* New York: McGraw-Hill.

MEADE, F. M. H. and KERRY, F. (1976) *Look, Think and Write.* Edinburgh: Chambers.

PETERS, M. (1967) *Spelling: caught or taught?* (Chapter 4). London: Routledge and Kegan Paul.

PETERS, M. L. and CRIPPS, C. C. (1980) *Catchwords. Ideas for Teaching Spelling.* New York: Harcourt Brace Johanovich.

PETERS, M. (1981) *Diagnostic and Remedial Spelling Manual.* London: Macmillan.

S.C.R.E. (1961) *Studies in Spelling.*

S.E.C. (1977) *English for Slower Learning Children in the Scottish Secondary School.* London: H.M.S.O.

WELCH, J., THORNTON, G. and ASTON, A. (1978) *Helping Pupils to Write Better.* London: I.L.E.A.

'A Practical Approach to Writing and Spelling'. A Videotape filmed and edited under the direction of Mr D. Gibson, Director of the Learning Resources Department at the invitation of Mr L. Howitt, Head of Special and Remedial Education Department, St Andrew's College of Education, Bearsden, Glasgow.

15 Children's needs in the reading curriculum

Ronald Mackay & Nick Pepin

The reading curriculum for children in the primary school must meet a wide variety of needs. It must prepare them to extract meaning from a text, to experience a variety of formats and to find enjoyment and pleasure in reading. Schools attempt to meet the needs of children in many different ways, whether it is through the carefully graded structure of an early reading scheme, the individualised approach to banding books according to levels of difficulty, training in information skills, group discussion activities to develop comprehension or the provision of a rich environment of children's fiction.

Schools often plan the reading curriculum to include the inter-related elements of reading for comprehension, reading for information and reading for pleasure. Such a division is not designed to compartmentalise the reading process but to ensure that there is adequate treatment of each aspect. There is no doubt that some children will read information text for pleasure and that comprehension is developed through the reading of fiction. However, it is helpful to devise strategies and approaches of many different types. Many schools assign first priority to reading for pleasure in children's fiction and it is children's needs in this area which we are going to consider, illustrating some approaches adopted by schools in the West of Scotland.

The heart of the reading curriculum in any school is the reading of fiction with all the opportunities it presents for motivation and interest. There is little point in devising elaborate programmes of work in reading if at the end of the day we fail to produce children who have experienced the joy, pleasure and excitement of stories. The Bullock Report highlighted the point that literature brings children into an encounter with language in all its rich variety, indicating the link between voluntary reading and reading attainment.

Again, more recently, the Schools Council Project 'The Effective Use of Reading' criticised the high incidence in schools of what they called 'short burst reading' and concluded that pupils in a classroom, 'have only a minimal opportunity to dwell on a substantial piece of reading'. The 'Extending Beginning Reading' Project, referring to younger children, strongly advocated more personal reading for children, arguing that 'the habit of reading is much more likely to become established if definite measures are taken early in the junior school not only to promote an interest in reading, but to set aside regular and increasingly lengthy periods when every child in the class reads in a quiet atmosphere without interruptions'. In the promotion of voluntary reading the school plays a vitally important role in that, if reluctant readers are not led to the pleasure of reading in the school, then it is difficult to imagine where this is going to happen in the world outside school.

Many arguments have been presented on the value of fiction in education.

From them emerge a number of common strands such as providing opportunities for understanding self, understanding others, and more particularly the extension of reading skills and the development of language skills.

When we come to look at some of the books which children might be reading, it is important to emphasise that the reading diet to be encouraged should be wide-ranging and varied. Just as adults enjoy a very wide range of different types, so too do children. Peter Dickinson has argued that he is always suspicious of people who advocate a diet of plums in reading, stressing that we all need a wide range of literature, including trivia, to suit our many moods and interests. This means that for some children comics would be a starting point while for others Ted Hughes or Alan Garner would be more apposite. It is the job of the teacher to ensure that the diet is well balanced, suited to the needs of the children and likely to motivate them to even more reading.

In devising a school programme to encourage the reading of fiction, there are two important aspects to take into consideration. First of all, there is the need to promote a fiction environment in which children are constantly stimulated to an interest in books. Secondly, there is need for a teacher to employ strategies which will ensure progress in the development of skills through clearly structured intervention. These principles will be illustrated through a discussion of book provision, authors' visits and fiction topic planning.

Book provision

One school started with a review of book provision in the school. The first step was to make books readily available to children; books which were relevant, stimulating and interesting. The school bookshop can prove a great advantage here especially at a time when few areas are well served by commercial bookshops catering adequately for children's books. It was decided to set up a paperback bookshop in the school.

A well stocked paperback bookshop located in the school and opening regularly enabled children to come along and browse even when they were not in a position to buy. They could see and examine the whole range of books available and could talk about them with friends, parents and teachers.

Parents and teachers too benefited greatly from this experience. For many parents it was only this exposure to books in the school bookshop that enabled them to appreciate the explosion in the variety and quality of books written for children that has occurred over the last few decades. Many parents commented on the improvement in their children's desire to read. Teachers were able, almost effortlessly, to glean a very useful knowledge as to current tastes among children, as well as usefully augmenting the deeper knowledge of children's books that is so essential to their success in motivating children to read and to helping them to develop their reading.

In the classroom also, the teachers made available a wide range of books for their classes. A regular financial commitment to purchasing books for personal reading was made by the headteacher. This enabled the stock to be built up and kept interesting. Care was taken to ensure that the entire range of reading ability was adequately catered for. Here the Cliff Moon individualised banding system for books helped pupils and teachers alike. Books were, of course, attractively and prominently displayed. Alongside them there were book posters, charts showing favourite books, comments on the books read, written by children to be read to others. Reading areas were made comfortable and inviting. Adequate time for personal reading was allocated as an integral part of the reading curriculum and the teacher herself acted as model of good reading behaviour by reading with the children at every opportunity.

The effect of the teacher who is both knowledgeable and enthusiastic about books can be dramatic as can be seen from this transcript of a filmed interview with some primary school children.

INTERVIEWER: A lot of people here said they like a particular kind of book. You like the supernatural books and you've liked other types of books. Do you sometimes pick a different book just for a change?

CHORUS: Yes.

CRAIG: I have read the series as well of Keill Rander and at the start I used to just read science fiction and then I started to reading things like *I am David* and that sort and then I started to really get into these kind of books.

INTERVIEWER: So you've got some science fiction too. What kind of book would you call that?

CRAIG: I'd call that a war book.

INTERVIEWER: It's set during the war isn't it?

CRAIG: Now and again I go back to science fiction.

INTERVIEWER: You still like them too.

JUNE: I started off reading war books. I read *When Hitler Stole Pink Rabbit* and I really enjoyed that and I read a few other war books and then I read *The Other Way Around*. I couldn't get into that one, but then I started reading these kinds of books and just left the war books. I can't go back to them.

INTERVIEWER: That's the kind you like?

STEVEN: I never used to read until I came into Mrs Houston's class and then everybody started reading and I started reading.

INTERVIEWER: You all caught the . . .

CHORUS: Reading fever.

INTERVIEWER: You caught the reading fever, did you?

CRAIG: There was only a few of us in the class that read before we came into this class.

STEVEN: I started with the war books and Mrs Houston told us about more books and everything like that, different kinds of books.

INTERVIEWER: How did you catch this fever, do you think?

STEVEN: Because everyone else started to read.

JUNE: Mrs Houston is very interested in books, she tells us about them.

CRAIG: With the teacher talking about them, we've got to get into them as well. You can't have the teachers talking about books when you don't read them.

INTERVIEWER: One last thing I was going to ask you about, it was – I wonder if you have any idea how many books you have read, say this term, since Christmas – it's nearly Easter now.

STEVEN: Well I haven't read very many books because I read *Lord of the Rings*.

INTERVIEWER: Yes, that was a long book.

JUNE: Round about twenty.

INTERVIEWER: You've read twenty books?

CRAIG: I've read about twelve.

STEVEN: I've read about twenty books.

INTERVIEWER: You've read about twenty, even though you read *Lord of the Rings*.

STEVEN: Yes, because once you have read *Lord of the Rings* when you go on to small books, you read them very quickly, because of the size of *Lord of the Rings*. There is something like a thousand pages in it.

INTERVIEWER: That's a hefty one. How many have you read do you think?

AUDREY: Sixteen.

JUNE: Eighteen.

INTERVIEWER: Eighteen, just since Christmas?

INTERVIEWER: So, it's about sixteen, twenty, thirty. It depends on the books and depends on how much you like and sometimes people say they wasted a bit of time because they didn't like a book. Well thank you very much for telling me about your books. That was very interesting.

Authors' visits

The book atmosphere within one school was further nurtured by a programme of events of 'happenings'. Exhibitions of books or illustrations were arranged and authors invited to the school. Advantage was taken of 'The Writers in School' Scheme sponsored by the Arts Council which provides financial assistance to schools wishing to use the various talents authors have to contribute. Over a period of three years, eight authors visited the school: some authors were excellent story tellers; others demonstrated how they illustrated their books; some involved children in dramatising parts of their books; one used puppets; and all talked to the children about the business of writing. In this excerpt from a film made during one such visit by the author, Alan Campbell McLean, he talked to a group of 11-year-olds about his work.

ALAN CAMPBELL MCLEAN: Oddly enough I had signed a contract in Germany for *The Hill of the Red Fox*. That's a Fifteen Hundred Book Club edition printed by Bertelsmann of Munich and selling like hot cakes there. Not a good book, that I must say. It's not really a good book, but it has never been out of print in this country since the 1950s when I wrote it. I made a note just before I came down here, *The Hill of the Red Fox*. I wrote 231 pages of it and the book ends at 254. So I had written everything but 23 pages, then I stopped and read it and I thought to myself, 'Who would ever read such utter nonsense as this?' and shoved it away in a drawer and it stayed in that drawer for the best part of three years. And I am being pressed for money by the bank and think, '23 pages'. I will bury Duncan Moore, which I proceeded to do and that is, I think, one of the best parts of the book, burying him off and the tinker's description earlier on.

Well that book was published in 1954, never been out of print in this country. There have been children's hour editions, six instalments. There is a television edition which was shown here, Australia, Saudi Arabia, Arabic translations, who knows, and it amazes me because really it is not a good book. I have spent the best part of twenty odd years in going round schools and telling children it isn't a good book, and whilst, often, writers are not the best judge of their own work, I think this book *The Year of the Stranger* is an infinitely better book and if the opportunity is afforded you, do read it.

Now I can stand here and yatter away but I don't know if that is of any great benefit to you so I am going to sit down and ask you to ask me any question of any kind what-so-ever about writing, books, films, anything.

LINDA: How long did it take you to write the book *The Hill of the Red Fox*.

ALAN CAMPBELL MCLEAN: It didn't take all that long. From the first page right up to page 231 then it sat for three years, nothing done, then I finished it. But, I mean, times can vary how long a book takes. *The Glass House* which was an extremely difficult book to write, took me four years and practically ruined me in the process until it was published. Another book *The Year of the Stranger*, I wrote in five weeks, would you believe, and that may have been the reason I had a stroke. But *The Year of the Stranger* – I'm always being pressed by my agents about when are you getting on with the next book and they were pressing me on this one and I wrote a 'wee white lie' and said. 'I've almost finished it' and just to assure them I said, 'I'll send you the first two chapters', which I did. And Sir John Vernie, who at that time edited *The Elizabethan*, was in my agent's office and said I am going to serialise it, which he started to do. The rest was unwritten, so like a lunatic I got to work and wrote it in five weeks. But it varies. On the whole about a year to write.

DAVID: What sort of books do you like best – mysteries, or science fiction?

ALAN CAMPBELL MCLEAN: Well I'll tell you what I like. I have a very wide taste. I like most of all, mysteries. I like Raymond Chandler, who was a great writer. I also like people like Robert Louis Stevenson. Stevenson wrote in an age when you had people like Scott, writing dreary turgid prose. Not Stevenson, he wrote sparely, pungent phrases that grip you from the start and also I'll tell you another book I like by Susan Crossland, *A Political Biography*, a great book that too.

ROBERT: What do you think makes a children's book different from an adult's book?

ALAN CAMPBELL MCLEAN: Nothing. Nothing of any description at all. A children's book is not different from an adult's. I defy anybody to say that a children's book is for children, not at all. A novel is like an onion, or whatever, peel off skins and there are different types. You can take a book and you can enjoy it at one level when you are twelve. Take that book at another level, read it when you are sixty. All the same book. The book is good, then it should stand reading at any age at all. I stand by that. I do not accept 'children's' books, 'adults'' books. Not at all.

Apart from stimulating interest in reading books, such encounters with authors greatly help to demystify the process of writing and encourage children to maintain their perception of themselves as writers. Alan Campbell McLean with his frank honest response to the children provided them with insights into both his books and the craft of writing.

Fiction topic planning

Using a novel as the basis for a project is an excellent strategy for intensifying children's experience of a book. Two possibilities are (1) to use the novel as a basis for a project and (2) to use it as an element in a project or topic. The richness of language from the use of fiction can counter the barren fact-amassing characteristics of many topics. Anna Davin highlights this point very well when she says the personalisation of history is the strength of the historical novel, enabling it to impart a richer historical understanding than formal history books can usually give. In (2), the emphasis should be on consideration of the key elements within the novel, the plot, incidents, characters, physical settings and changing moods. Through careful teacher intervention the relationships between people and incidents in the book and the children's own lives and experiences can be explored. John Cheetham expresses regret about the current situation in some schools when he says 'during the past decade an attitude seems to have been encouraged and developed in junior schools that to do other than read poetry and novels to children would sound the death knell of enjoyment: that children are so vulnerable and literature such a delicate thread in their lives that it cannot be used with the same rigour as other aspects of the curriculum. Perhaps this attitude sprang from the way poems and novels were analysed and dissected in schools a quarter of a century ago, and this form of teaching may be responsible for the present-day attitude which forbids close examination of poems and novels.' He also argues for the benefits of the novel-based project in these terms: 'What have the children gained? My hope would be that they have experienced the enjoyment of really knowing a book, a development of skills, a greater understanding of relationships between individuals, a desire to read other books with greater insights and development of imagination'.

A class of eleven-year-old children read, with their teacher, *The Snow House* by Nora Wilkinson and engaged in the following wide range of related activities.

1. The children made a large frieze of the square in the small Yorkshire village. They used the text of the first chapter to help them visualise what the village was like. Then individually or in pairs the children drew a building which they thought was suitable for the village by using pastels and white chalk and white sugar paper. These were then cut out and the children placed them on a white background. Finally when the frieze was completed spray snow was applied to the roofs on the white paper. The purpose of the frieze was to set the scene, build up the atmosphere of the story and help the children to feel they were part of the village.

2. A life-size painting of Aunt Jen was made and put on the wall. The children then used the picture and their first impressions of Aunt Jen to discuss words they felt described her. These were then put on labels and stapled round the picture. This work was done in order that children could see her character being built up and so that she would become a real person to them and they could form their own opinions about her.

3. In a small group discussion with the children they were given an opportunity to discuss snow. They talked about the words they thought described snow – its appearance in the field. From this wordbank they wrote a description of snow in a setting chosen by them. They then read an extract from the book and discussed the words the author used to build up a picture of the snow. Once this discussion was completed they made a finger painting illustrating the extract. The final part of this sequence of work was to look at their own writing about snow and see how successful they had been in representing snow in words and pictures.

4. The class gave their views as to what the mice in the story had to do about their predicament and it was established that they needed to escape. The children went on to talk about people they had heard about who needed to escape. Then in their social groups they invented a situation where escape was necessary. They then assumed a character and made up a short play which was subsequently taped.

5. The class re-enacted the escape of the mice from the Sundial to the Snow House. They planned out for themselves how they would organise their drama work in order to dramatise this incident in the story. Through the acting out of the incident the children further identified with the mice's feelings of fear and excitement.

6. The children made large-scale paintings of Fred, Alice, Willie, Benjamin, Uncle John and Fred's father. This helped them to identify with the characters, to make them real people and to make the whole book come alive for them. It also helped them to visualise the characters in a clearer fashion and also to come to a clearer understanding of their personalities.

7. The class discussed the rights and wrongs of the children looking after the mice and the responsibility they had taken on. This led them to discuss people for whom they had responsibility. They then wrote about looking after something or someone and all the responsibility this entailed. Through the discussion of an extract from the book describing the use of slates in the school, there ensued a discussion on the differences between the school described in the book and their own school. At the end of the

discussion the teacher read the poem 'Our School' by Gareth Owens and the children then wrote a poem about their own school.

8. Towards the end of the reading of the book, groups of children wrote character studies of Aunt Jen, Fred, Alice, Willie, Uncle John and Fred's dad. To do this they had to draw on their experience of the book and also their own impressions of these characters. This was left to the end of the reading of the book so that the children would have as complete a picture of the characters as possible.

Conclusion

In this account of aspects of school reading programmes the provision and use of children's fiction has been taken as the central focus for meeting children's needs in the reading curriculum. The examples presented here have attempted to demonstrate the need for positive attitudes in promoting fiction so that the atmosphere of the school is stimulating and exciting both in the provision of resources and in the way in which they are used by teachers and children. This approach cannot be seen as a peripheral and optional extra to more important aspects of the teaching of reading. It can only be regarded as a valuable opportunity for the development of a very wide range of reading skills and the promotion of positive attitudes to books and reading.

The authors are grateful to the pupils and staff of the following schools:
Arrochar Primary School, Tarbet.
Canberra Primary School, East Kilbride.
Glanmanor Primary School, Moodiesburn.
Wester Common Primary School, Glasgow.

References

CHEETHAM, J. (1976) *Quarries in the Primary School*, in G. Fox *et al. Writers, Critics and Children*. London: Heinemann.

DAVIN, A. (1978) *Historical Novels for Children*, in *Literature and Learning*. London: Ward Lock Educational.

D.E.S. (1975) *A Language for Life* (The Bullock Report). London: H.M.S.O.

DICKINSON, P. (1976) *A Defence of Rubbish*, in G. Fox *et al. Writers, Critics and Children*. London: Heinemann.

LUNZER, E. and GARDNER, K. (1979) *The Effective Use of Reading*. London: Heinemann.

SOUTHGATE, V., ARNOLD, H. and JOHNSON, S. (1981) *Extending Beginning Reading*. London: Heinemann.

16 Language demands of CSE examinations

Rosemary Threadgold

One of the results of studies like *The Bullock Report* (1975) and *The Effective Use of Reading* (1979) is an increased awareness among teachers of the complex language demands made upon their pupils by the school curriculum. Unfortunately, the extent of our appreciation is still far from complete and those of us teaching in secondary schools frequently lack significant knowledge of what happens outside our own subject area. We prepare our pupils for the hurdle of public examinations without knowing whether the language demands of the papers vary from subject to subject; whether those demands are recognised explicitly by the examiners; whether the skills required for English examinations are those needed in other subjects.

This study area grew out of a need to be better informed. As an English teacher in a comprehensive school, I was preparing students for CSE examinations without any knowledge of whether my coursework was relevant to the work my pupils did in other subject areas, or whether coursework elsewhere was reinforcing my own efforts. It seemed useful to know what emphasis was placed on language competence in subjects other than English.

Teaching full-time and researching in my spare moments required an easily manageable approach; I suggest that the methods of analysis used and the observations I made can be easily replicated by all teachers using material relevant to their own situation. It may be that others will be as surprised as I to find the extent to which language competence seems to be ignored in the setting and marking of questions in examinations at this level. There was also a poor correlation between the reading and writing needed in English examinations and that demanded in other subjects.

My raw material was the papers set by T.W.M.E.B. for CSE examinations in English Language, English Literature, History, Home Economics, Biology and Mathematics in 1980. Although originally I investigated the place of language competence in general within these examinations, I must restrict myself here to the nature of question types to be found on the papers and the variety of written responses elicited by those questions.

Question types

In order to make comparison of question types across different subject areas, some kind of objective assessment was required. The need was met by a hierarchy of question types based on Bloom's *Taxonomy of Educational Objectives*:

1. MEMORY: Answer repeats verbatim, recalling or recognising information.
2. TRANSLATION: Answer changes information into a different symbolic form or language, e.g. map symbols into words.
3. INTERPRETATION: Answer discovers relationships, but does not assess or judge.
4. APPLICATION: Answer solves problem by identifying issue and applying right method or skill, e.g. theorem.
5. ANALYSIS: Answer must consciously sort out specific parts or elements in order to solve problem.
6. SYNTHESIS: Answer solves a problem requiring original creative thinking, going beyond the information given.
7. EVALUATION: Answer makes a judgement according to rational standards and is, therefore, open-ended.

Using this table, it is possible to gain an impression of the overall demands of the examinations, as well as the range of questions on one paper.

One might expect the questions to reflect the stated aims and objectives of the syllabuses which indicate the importance of a range of learned capabilities. Examiners in History, Home Economics and Biology explicitly seek to encourage a lasting interest in the subject; to relate the subject to everyday life; to develop the intellect of the candidates. 'Encourage', 'stimulate' and 'develop' are key words in all three syllabuses, while History specifies its objectives:

To assess a candidate's ability:

i) to recall relevant facts
ii) to understand evidence
iii) to extract relevant material from more than one source
iv) to express ideas clearly and logically
v) to appreciate the views held by people of other times and places
vi) to understand historical extracts, maps and diagrams.

The aims and objectives cover the full range of learning tasks. As the question hierarchy used corresponds quite closely to Gagnée's hierarchy of learned capabilities, analysis of question types should reveal whether the papers fulfil expectations.

The first noticeable feature of the History and Home Economics papers is the preponderance of memory questions. Despite the stated intentions of the syllabuses, question after question requires no more than the reiteration of facts. Even questions which apparently demand higher order skills are frequently no more than memory questions because of the predictability of their appearance. Thus a question such as:

'Plan a menu for a meal which can be cooked completely in the oven.'
is likely to be memory rather than application because of the lack of variety in the papers from year to year. Well-prepared candidates will need only to recall their coursework.

There are a few interpretation questions on the Home Economics paper such as:

'Explain briefly how and why the diets of the following would differ:
  i)   a male car assembly worker
  ii) a typist, and
  iii) a woman during pregnancy.'

In general there is no evidence of any attempt to assess candidates' powers of discernment and adventure as claimed in the syllabus.

On the History paper the pattern is similar, though there is a greater variety of question type. From the candidate's point of view it is disturbing to find that the question types vary greatly from section to section. Thus a candidate may be required to respond to memory, translation and interpretation questions, belonging to the lower levels of the learned capabilities hierarchy, whereas a different choice may require a response to application and even synthesis questions, which are far more demanding. There is no indication as to whether the examiners are aware of these variations.

It may also be argued that questions which require essay answers, rather than short notes, in themselves constitute questions types which, in some candidates, involve synthesis and evaluation. This will be considered again later, but it should be noted here that there is no indication given to candidates or teachers as to whether the skills required in historical essay writing are allowed for or credited. It may be that only factual knowledge is assessed. What precisely, then, one wonders, is required or given credit when a question asks:

'Write short essays on the lives and works of any TWO of the following painters, poets, writers or musicians of the period . . .?

There were honourable exceptions. The Biology examination indicated that the paper would test: Knowledge (50 per cent), Comprehension (30 per cent) and Application (20 per cent) and these three qualities are catered for in the questions. Analysis reveals that a large proportion of the questions consists of memory and translation types. However, these show imagination and variety and take the form of multiple-choice questions, the labelling of diagrams and, interestingly, the completion of Cloze passages, selecting from a given vocabulary.

There are other imaginative approaches to question setting on the paper reflecting a genuine attempt to relate the subject to 'real life'. This is exemplified by one of the application questions which states:

'Some bleach/disinfectants advertised on television are said "to kill 99% of all known germs". Suggest experiments that could be carried out a) to test the claim, b) to find out the most effective but economical strength of solution to use in the home.'

It would be difficult to 'spot' such a question precisely.

Finally, mention must be made of the format of an interpretative question where success is surely grounded in reading fluency and mental agility, rather than solely in biological expertise:

> 'In each of the following questions you are given an *assertion* followed by a *reason*. Consider the assertion and decide whether, on its own, it is a true statement. If, and only if, you decide that both the assertion and the reason are true, consider whether the reason is a valid or true explanation of the assertion. Choose your answer as follows and on your answer sheet underline the letter of the answer you choose:
>
> A. If both the assertion and the reason are true statements and the reason is a correct explanation of the assertion.
> B. If both the assertion and reason are true statements and the reason is NOT a correct explanation of the assertion.
> C. If the assertion is true but the reason is a false statement.
> D. If the assertion is false but the reason is a true statement.
> E. If both assertion and reason are false statements.'

It is not difficult to see why this type of question has now been discontinued.

However, despite this, the Biology papers do show an interesting variety of question types and formats, testing a range of learned capabilities.

As far as Mathematics is concerned, the questions involve memory, translation and interpretation, but chiefly application. Candidates are expected to think about what they must do, and apply their knowledge in order to solve the problems set. Memory skills unaided serve very little purpose. This is perhaps one reason why candidates seem to find Mathematics such a problem.

Other than Mathematics, the significant differences in pattern are found on the English papers, both Language and Literature. No longer is factual information the main concern. The mode of analysis used here is not appropriate to the Composition paper, though the questions may be said to require skills of synthesis. It can, however, be applied to the Comprehension paper. Here, passages of prose are accompanied by questions which are mainly translation or interpretation. It is not acceptable to answer questions using the words of the passage. Put another way, the comprehension skills required are mainly reorganisational or inferential. However, there is some inclusion of more demanding or evaluatory comprehension, using an analytical approach: 'Why do you think Hampstead Hill was a favourite haunt of highway men?' The answer to this question is not provided directly by any of the information given in the passage.

The other two questions on the Comprehension paper require different skills. The letter writing is an example of application, while the report question demands something quite complicated. Here candidates are given a variety of subjective and objective evidence presenting information about a plane crash. They are asked 'to make a preliminary report on the basis of this information' and to write the report 'in the form of a short article'. Candidates must, therefore, make an imaginative leap to write in the persona of an investigator; they must adopt a style suitable for 'a short article' or 'preliminary report'. They must assimilate various pieces of information – verbal, visual and technical, evaluate their importance and synthesise them into a cohesive whole. To this extent such a question makes extensive demands of candidates in both reading and writing skills; there is no possibility of reproducing something that has been committed to memory.

On the Literature paper, the question types cover the whole range of categories under consideration. The rubric suggests the need for quotation to be used in answers and that requires memory. The questions themselves range from a comparatively straightforward translation type, such as:

> 'In your own words summarize Jo's attitude to life and in particular her pregnancy.',

through analysis:

> 'Write a careful character study of Ingrid and explain how you think she changes during the novel.',

to a question which demands an evaluative response:

> 'Much modern poetry deals with aspects of modern life and quite often the poet does not like what he sees happening. Choose a poem where this is true of the poet's attitude and write about it in detail saying whether you agree with the poet.'

This type of analysis reveals one reason why so many candidates find the poetry section difficult, for the questions it asks are higher in the table of skills. They demand evaluative and appreciative responses, rather than merely reorganisational or even inferential ones. It is also highly unlikely that candidates will have been specifically prepared for questions such as these, even though the general principles should have been covered.

The variety of question types on this paper means that selection can be important in governing the difficulty of question answered. However, the need to choose from prose, poetry and drama sections means that, in practice, candidates are likely to answer a cross-section of different types.

To conclude this section, it may be remarked that more attention should be paid to the kind of questions on the written examination papers by candidates, teachers and examiners. There is not always the balance of question that is desirable, nor are the question types always commensurate with the aims stated in the syllabus. The imaginative attempts to vary question format are to be commended, but such attempts could be extended to many other areas. Finally, it is important to realise that question selection is itself an important skill and that more attention should be paid to the particular reading demands required to cope with it.

Written responses

The types of question asked on the examination papers have implications for the kinds of written response they elicit. As we have already noted, essay questions have particular demands over and above their factual content: such demands should be recognised by candidates, teachers and examiners. An analysis of the types of written answers required by the various examinations reveals the demand for a wide variety of responses, though not always what one would expect.

The Mathematics papers naturally stand on their own as needing a numerical rather than a verbal response.

Biology and Home Economics concentrate on short answer questions. Both subjects have more than one paper. Home Economics uses a short answer paper which often does not require a candidate to write as much as a sentence, while the 'longer' paper demands no more than about a paragraph at a time of connected prose. The longest answer in 1980 was probably the response to:

'Describe the financial aid which is available for senior citizens from the state.'

This carried six marks. There was also a question asking:

'Write notes on FOUR of the following:
a) The Social Security benefits available to a mother for her children.
b) Preventing fire in the home.
c) Saving for holidays.
d) Caring for a young boy with a broken leg on his return from hospital.
e) Good relationships between teenage youngsters and their parents.
f) Leisure time facilities for young people which are available in your area.'

This kind of question raises the problem of what constitutes 'notes'. There is no further guidance on the matter.

The Biology papers show a very wide range of question styles. One paper consists entirely of a variety of multiple-choice questions which require no writing or words at all. There are also Cloze passages where the candidate has to select the appropriate words from a list provided. Many other questions require only one word or single phrase answers or, at most, a sentence or two. The longest questions carry six marks and even these do not require more than a paragraph. They involve the description of an experiment and, in another case, the description of the life history of a named creature.

One might expect more continuous prose on the History paper, particularly in view of the aims of the syllabus – 'to express ideas clearly and logically'. Here, however, we find an intriguing variety of questions. The majority require short answers, ranging from one word responses for one mark: e.g.

'Whose tomb in the Valley of the Kings was discovered intact in the 1920s?'

to paragraph length answers carrying up to eight marks: e.g.

'Flint mining played a vital part in the lives of Stone Age man. Draw and describe a typical flint mine.'

Such short answers are in line with the lower order question types of memory, translation, interpretation and application.

There are, however, longer essay questions on the History paper, but these are in the minority. Even here there is variation in style so that one question offers detailed advice on content, e.g.

'Consider, on the evidence of his reign, the suggestion that King John was a king who was unfortunate rather than incompetent. Deal with

i)   his military career
ii)   his problems with the barons
iii)   his relationships with the Church and the Pope
iv)   his difficulties with Stephen Langton
v)   Magna Carta
vi)   his attempts to overthrow that settlement.'   (20 marks)

But another question merely states:

'Write short essay on TWO of the following:

i)   the contrasts between life in Athens and Sparta
ii)   the ideas of Plato, Socrates and Aristotle
iii)   the war between Athens and Sparta
iv)   the Greek Colonies   (10 × 2 marks)

With such a variety of question types and complete freedom of choice, the matter of 'examination technique' in the selection of questions becomes significant. It is also difficult to see how the longer essay type of question can be assessed without reference to the capability of the candidate to produce logical, ordered answers, expressed in clear, careful English. Yet this cannot be a consideration in those questions where only one word answers are asked for.

No mention is made of this problem of assessment in the Examiners' Report, though the comment is made that the 'Imagine yourself' questions on the paper were poorly answered in general. It may well be that the kind of creative response generated by a question beginning 'Imagine yourself to be a soldier on Hadrian's Wall . . .' belongs more to English compositions than History essays. One wonders if examiners and teachers often stop to consider the problem from the point of view of the average CSE candidate, unfamiliar with the conventions of academic and imaginative prose. A more detailed discussion of the problem of register in these examinations can be found in Threadgold (1982).

The element of choice is not necessarily a problem. There is no significant difficulty on the Mathematics, Home Economics and Biology papers, nor in the various English examinations. However, the latter stand out from the other subjects by the volume of writing they require. Although the two comprehension passages require comparatively short answers, the other two questions on the paper demand a report of about 250 words and a letter. Added to this there is the Composition paper which asks for a piece of continuous writing extending to three or four sides of A4.

The Literature paper is even more demanding. Here, the candidate has to produce four essays, each long enough to gain a maximum of 25 marks. Although the questions are usually sufficiently detailed to give some help in the structuring of the answers, there is no other paper that approaches the complexity of writing required here.

In conclusion, it may be observed that the overwhelming impression gained from a study of examination papers is the lack of writing they require. With the exception of certain History questions and the English examinations, candidates may well avoid the need for continuous prose altogether. The dominant form is the short answer question where a word, phrase or sentence will usually suffice. Even where essay questions occur, they can be avoided by careful selection. Only in English is the demand for continuous prose compulsory.

This means that coursework either contains a great deal of writing and ignores the style of the examinations, or that pupils have little practice in continuous writing in their daily work. From the homework set in the fifth year in my own school, it would seem that much work is based on the examination format and that pupils' original writing is limited in extent. The exception is History where the essay is the dominant form.

It is important for English teachers to be aware of the difference in the demands of their subject. The problems of essay planning, sentence variety, punctuation and general fluency of expression are ones which every English teacher strives to overcome. Some pupils find immense difficulty in constructing a coherent, well-ordered composition of reasonable length. It seems possible that part of the problem lies in lack of practice. English teachers should not assume that these skills are being reinforced across the curriculum.

The other problem for English teachers – and for those teachers who require their pupils to organise their work into essay form – is that the writing skills tested in English examinations are unlike those encountered in other subjects. Imaginative narrative and descriptive prose are the sole properties of the English Language paper, as is letter writing and the kind of comprehension and synthesis required by the summary question. On the Literature paper, the style of essay is highly specialised and is unlikely to have any transference value to another subject. It is only the basic mechanical skills of spelling and punctuation which may reinforce each other from subject to subject.

Such conclusions are not encouraging, particularly when the problem appears to be unacknowledged by the examiners. There is virtually no mention of language competence anywhere in syllabuses or Examiners' Reports, yet it seems inconceivable that spelling, handwriting and clear expression can be separated from content assessment. The research findings of Scannel and Marshall (1966) would appear to substantiate this. Question choice and difficulty add another dimension. It would be a positive step towards improvement if teachers themselves became aware of the difficulties so that they can help their candidates and speak out to the examiners.

References

D.E.S. (1975) *A Language for Life* (The Bullock Report). London: H.M.S.O.

LUNZER, E. and GARDNER, K. (1979) *The Effective Use of Reading*. London: Heinemann.

SCANNEL, D. P. and MARSHAL, J. C. (1966) 'The effect of selected composition errors on grades assigned essay examinations'. *American Educational Research Journal*, 13(2), pp. 125–30.

THREADGOLD, A. R. (1982) 'The problem of register in selected CSE examinations across the curriculum'. *Reading*, 16(3), pp. 169–80.

17 Modelling: an approach to reading comprehension

Patricia McCall & Sue Palmer

Introduction

Teachers have always recognised the need to develop and assess children's comprehension of written material. Once children have attained a reasonable degree of fluency in reading, comprehension usually becomes the key word in primary reading programmes, and considerable time is devoted to it. The most widely adopted procedure is the setting of comprehension exercises, in which children are required to read a passage thoroughly and then answer (in sentences, please) a number of questions on its content. Such an exercise is intended to have a two-fold purpose: it is designed to encourage children to read attentively (thus, it is hoped, developing their powers of comprehension), and it provides material for teachers to assess their pupils' progress.

Publishers have, of course, seen the potential for sales of books purveying such exercises, and a very wide range of comprehension text books exists. The following extract is from a widely-used language text book (Oxford Junior English) aimed at 10–11 year-old children. It is part of a longer passage on heraldry.

> A coat of arms and the surrounding parts is called an achievement of arms and consists of up to seven parts: shield, helmet, wreath, crest, mantling, motto and supporters. The helmet rests on top of the shield, except when the coat of arms belongs to a peer. (A peer has a coronet above the shield and the helmet is placed above the coronet.) The wreath fits round the top of the helmet and just below the crest. The mantling is an array of ornamental drapery around the shield. The motto, written on a scroll, is usually found below the shield. Supporters, if any, are usually placed one on each side of the shield.

The following questions, relating to the paragraph, are included in the comprehension exercise:

What name is given to a coat of arms and its surrounding parts?
Where does the helmet rest?
Where does the wreath fit?
What is the mantling?
Where is the motto usually found?

These questions are, like the others in the exercise, of the literal recall type. Although, since the popularisation of 'Higher Order Reading Skills' text books have begun to include more inferential, predictive and evaluative questions, in a factual passage of the type above it is genuinely difficult not to rely heavily on literal questioning.

Perhaps we should acknowledge at this point two broad areas within what teachers call 'comprehension'. There is, firstly, the element concerned with readers' emotional and intellectual response to a text, and how language is used to express ideas. This is the comprehension necessary for the critical appreciation of literature. Many text books (e.g. *Scope for Reading*) now cater for this type of comprehension with questions requiring inference, prediction and evaluation. The other area of comprehension is, quite simply, that of understanding what a piece of writing means. It is this area with which we are concerned in this paper. The passage and questions above show an attempt to provide children with material which will develop this capacity to extract meaning from print.

The effectiveness of traditional comprehension exercises

As has been pointed out by John Merritt (1978), such exercises may not test the reader's understanding of the text at all. The following example illustrates the point:

The jerrybobs impleeded hobdontily on the zapdons.
1) Who impleeded on the zapdons?
2) Where were the jerrybobs when they impleeded?
3) How did the jerrybobs impleed?

It is possible to answer gobbledegook questions 1–3 (and in sentences, too!) without an understanding of anything other than the syntactical patterns of the English language. It would seem, then, that much that is done in the name of reading comprehension is merely an encouragement to children to reproduce, albeit in real sentences, words and phrases which they do not fully understand. It is an encouragement to them to skim the surface of the text not, as Bullock would urge them, to 'interrogate' it.

And interrogation of text is vital. Throughout the educational process and in the real world beyond school, children will be required to read and understand often quite complex ideas embedded in print, and to process these ideas into a form of their own. In particular, they will have to learn to take notes and summarise information in their own words – a task with which even the most able children have great difficulty, as teachers well know. When confronted with these tasks, children are inclined to copy wholesale sections from the text with which they are working. One does not need to look far to see one reason for this. The type of comprehension exercise quoted above actually trains them to do so: it trains them to over-value the text in the book and to under-value themselves as thinkers and processors. Not only is literal questioning inefficient in teaching children to read for meaning, it can also have effects which, in terms of information-handling, are positively counter-productive.

An alternative approach

The teacher's task, then, must be to find other ways of encouraging children to read for meaning (and real understanding) and to guide them away from mere parrotting of the words in the book. But how is this to be done? What helpful strategies can the teacher give children to facilitate interaction with the text?

One very helpful strategy, introduced to many teachers through the Open University PE231 Reading Development course, is known as 'modelling' or 'diagrammatic outcome'. It involves children putting the information they have acquired from reading into a graphic or diagrammatic form. The passage from Oxford Junior English, for example, lends itself to the modelling technique. Using the information contained in it (and with help from illustrations accompanying the original passage) the 'picture model' of Figure 1 can be produced:

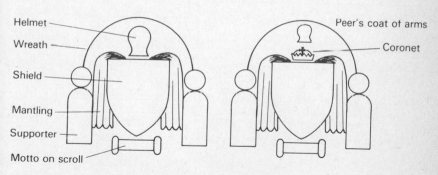

Fig. 1: 'Picture model' of a coat of arms.

In producing such a model, the reader has to:

1. read the text carefully with a purpose in mind;
2. identify a graphic form in which the meaning can be represented;
3. perceive semantic relationships ('above', 'below', etc.);
4. select the relevant material embedded within the text and dismiss irrelevant material;
5. reorganise information to meet his or her requirements.

All of which adds up to understanding and the successful processing of information. As a bonus, the reader is also alerted to inadequacies within the text (in this case, what exactly is the 'crest', and where is it?).

There are many other structures in which information extracted from print can be represented in graphic form: cycles, hierarchies, time-lines, graphs, matrices, Venn diagrams, keys, cross-sections, diagrams and flow diagrams of various types. Children can be introduced to such structures and taught to apply and interpret them when reading for meaning.

For example, children familiar with the concept of the cycle would be able to process the information from the following passage on the seasons of the Egyptian year into a cycle model similar to the one shown below in Figure 2.

Fig. 2: Cycle diagram of the Egyptian year.

THE EGYPTIAN YEAR

Life in Ancient Egypt depended on the River Nile, which watered the land so the people could grow their food. The seasons of the year were decided by the behaviour of the Nile. There were three seasons:

Inundation, from June to October, when the land flooded, because the Nile was full and burst its banks;

Emergence, when the level of the Nile went down and the fields were free of the waters (October to February);

Drought, when the Nile was very low, from February to June.

The annual rhythm of the seasons led to a regular pattern of work and activity for the farmers of Egypt. During Inundation, most of them went to work on the great building projects of the Pharoah – hauling huge stone blocks to build pyramids or tombs. During Emergence, they went back to their lands, dug irrigation ditches and planted and tended their crops. When Drought came they harvested the crops and threshed the cereals, to store grain for the year ahead.

174

The effectiveness of modelling

The benefits of this sort of interaction with text (as far as comprehension is concerned) have been outlined. But there are other benefits. One is that modelling gives experience in the organisation and processing of information into a reader's own summarised form. In application, therefore, modelling techniques are not only appropriate to a primary school reading programme, but also to the teaching of information-handling across the whole curriculum. The production and interpretation of models is a learning strategy which is particularly valuable in the area of Environmental Studies, where it not only teaches information-processing, but also aids the internalisation of concepts and the memorisation of factual material. Through their involvement in making the model, readers come to understand and then, as Frank Smith puts it, 'comprehension takes care of memorisation' (*Reading*, 1978).

And modelling is a thinking strategy. When this workshop was being prepared, one of the authors' flats was undergoing 'temporary elements of refurbishing' – a joiner was busy fitting shelves in a box-room. To help him with his work he had produced a plan and a cross-section of what had to be done. He explained that he had learnt to construct such models at college and found them valuable to his thinking, not only his work: 'It makes you look at things differently. It helps you plan and work things out in your head.'

Finally, it can be argued that the skill of modelling is becoming an evermore important part of our modern competence. In a world which relies increasingly on the graphic representation of information, we are neglecting our pupils' education unless we equip them to produce and interpret graphic information for themselves.

Introducing the technique

We have seen that modelling can be a valuable strategy for helping children with their reading for meaning across the curriculum, and also with their learning, their critical skills, their thinking processes and their dealings with the world beyond school. But how, in practical terms, is the technique to be employed in the primary school classroom?

The first decision to be made by teachers wishing to use modelling is how to introduce the technique to their pupils, and to familiarise them with the various types of model available in which to represent their reading. There are two main choices open to teachers: they can either teach the skills in isolation, or they can teach them in an existing context. If they choose to teach the skills in isolation they can do so by means of a published text book of modelling exercises; or through suitable material culled from other text books; or by using material they have written themselves. Of these possibilities the first is probably the most convenient and the last is the ideal, in that it allows teachers to tailor material to suit the situation, interests and abilities of their pupils. It does, however, involve teachers in a great deal of extra work. (As the writers of a purpose-designed text book of modelling exercises, the authors would offer teachers wishing to write their own material the following advice:

work backwards. Produce the model first and then use it to help you write the passage you wish the children to interpret. In this way you are less likely to be unintentionally unclear.)

If teachers choose to teach the skill in context, they must find or write material from which to work which is connected with the existing language or Environmental Studies activities being undertaken in class. As with all learning, it is ideal for children to meet a new skill for the first time in a context which demonstrates its usefulness. Of the two approaches, therefore, teaching through context is probably more educationally sound than the teaching of the skill in isolation. In practice, however, the context method is more difficult for teachers, and a good compromise can be achieved by the initial teaching of skills in isolation and their subsequent application in context.

Conclusion

Once a battery of modelling skills has been acquired, children can be expected to use the technique whenever it is appropriate in their reading throughout the curriculum. Children who have learnt to model seem to find conventional note-taking considerably easier. They no longer over-value the text as children do when reared on traditional comprehension exercises. Instead they are able to select information, identify the structures of meaning underlying print, and reorganise and represent information in their own summarised forms. The teacher is also provided with a very useful means of assessing children's comprehension of written material – a graphic outcome can often be very much more revealing than a written one.

As acknowledged earlier in this paper, though, the technique is appropriate only for dealing with the *meaning* embedded in print. It does not cater for evaluative and appreciative aspects of comprehension.

The authors would like to thank the members of the workshops at the 1983 U.K.R.A. Conference for their valuable contributions to the investigation of this topic.

References

BARRETT, T. C. (1972) 'Cognitive and affective dimensions of reading comprehension', in A. Melnick and J. Merritt *Reading: Today and Tomorrow*. London: University of London Press.
KILPATRICK, A., McCALL, P. and PALMER, S. (1983) *I See What You Mean*. Edinburgh: Oliver and Boyd.
MERRITT, J. E. (1978) 'Who is literate?', in C. M. McCullough (ed.) *Inchworm, Inchworm: Persistent Problems in Reading Comprehension*. Newark, Del.: I.R.A.
SMITH, F. (1978) *Reading*. Cambridge: Cambridge University Press.

18 Don't close the door on Cloze

Eleanor Anderson

Introduction

At the 1976 U.K.R.A. Conference, Peter Pumfrey drew our attention to the suggestion that 'the appreciation of the theoretical and practical value of any new scientific technique passes through five stages.' (p. 205.)

Stage 1: no-one, other than its inventors, is particularly interested. Indeed workers in allied fields may be hostile.
Stage 2: The technique begins to gain support on the basis of its promise.
Stage 3: This is characterised by extensive and even indiscriminate use by those working in the field, often irrespective of whether or not they are competent to assess its value.
Stage 4: The reaction that occurs in the fourth stage leads to a disillusionment with the technique without the critical examination logically demanded in such circumstances.
Stage 5: This occurs when both the strengths and weaknesses of the technique are acknowledged and it is applied appropriately.

(based on Pumfrey 1977)

Five stages in the appreciation of the theoretical and practical value of Cloze Procedure

With reference to Cloze Procedure, the first stage occurred in the 1950s when Wilson Taylor developed the technique.

The second stage was reached ih the 1960s with a number of American doctoral studies making use of the technique and culminating in the National Reading Conference symposium on Cloze Procedure in 1968. For those interested in the development of Cloze Procedure during the period 1953–70, probably the most thorough general treatment is contained in chapters 2 and 3 of J. Anderson, *Psycholinguistic Experiments in Foreign Language Testing* (1976).

Stage three began in the U.K. in the mid 1970s with references to Cloze Procedure in the Open University *Reading Development* course, Christopher Walker's *Reading Development and Extension* in 1974, the Bullock Report in 1975, while the proceedings of the 1976 U.K.R.A. Conference (Gilliland, 1977) contained one paper by Harrison (1977) on Cloze Procedure in assessing the readability of school texts, one paper by Davies and Vincent (1977) on the development of Cloze reading tests and one on its use in developing reading ability (E. Dolan, 1977). Further fuel was added to the fire of enthusiasm for the use of Cloze Procedure in teachers' centre publications such as that of Jenny Senior for south-west Herts. Teachers' Centre and in two Schools Council Project Reports, *The Effective Use of Reading* (Lunzer and Gardner, 1979) and *Extending Beginning Reading* (Southgate *et al.*, 1981).

A hint that the fourth stage had been reached in this country was present in Alastair Hendry's presidential address to the 18th U.K.R.A. Conference in 1981, when he referred to Cloze Procedure being viewed popularly as the knight on horseback who would overcome all the evils of reading problems.

Disillusionment with Cloze Procedure may have been due to unrealistic expectations, but it may also have been due to the fact that the practical value of the technique was presented with little or no discussion of its theoretical value nor indeed of its theoretical origins; a point also made by Rye (1982) in his recent, very practical and theoretically explicit book on Cloze Procedure. Part of the difficulty is that Taylor presented two explanations for the ability to complete Cloze deletions. The first derives from the *Gestalt* concept of 'closure' and is compatible with a view of reading as principally a perceptual activity. The second draws on a communication model and is compatible with a psycholinguistic view of reading as a complex cognitive and linguistic activity. Where theoretical explanation has been provided it has tended to be the first and simpler rationale.

Disillusionment with Cloze Procedure may also have been due to the gradual dissemination of Jongsma's 1971 review in which he stated that most studies failed to show any improvement in reading due to the use of Cloze. Or it may have been due to claims that Cloze items are only sensitive to contexts of about five to ten words on either side of a blank. However, Oller (1979) asserts that 'these claims have been shown to be generally incorrect' (p. 347) and goes on to support this stance with reference to his own work.

A similar process of disillusionment with Cloze seems to have been at work in the U.S.A. At the 1982 International Reading Association World Congress, Constance McCullough, H. Alan Robinson and Robert Pehrsson saw fit to redress the balance by presenting a symposium on 'Cloze Procedures as Instructional Strategies'. Pehrsson's contribution, 'Developing Context Cue Competence with Sequential Cloze Procedures: A Case Study', to be reported in a volume by Robinson and Pehrsson due to be published this year, should be of special interest to those working with children or adults with severe language or reading difficulties.

On this more cheerful note I would suggest that stage 5 is dawning 'when both the strengths and weaknesses of the technique are acknowledged and it is applied appropriately'.

I am optimistic because unrealistic expectations have probably run their course. Cloze Procedure should be considered a panacea no longer.

There are also a number of recent publications which provide guidance in the appropriate application of Cloze Procedure. The chapter on Cloze in Harrison's *Readability in the Classroom* is as good an introduction to the subject as any. Rye's (1982) consideration of how to use Cloze as a teaching strategy more effectively is particularly welcome in the light of Jongsma's (1980) conclusion from his second review that Cloze is as effective as traditional methods for developing reading comprehension. Chapman (1983) provides guidance on a simple analysis of text structure which may help out understanding of how textual cues function.

This is of particular significance when we consider Oller's (1979) statement about the distinguishing quality of Cloze tests:

> . . . they require the utilization of discourse level constraints as well as structural constraints within sentences. Probably it is this distinguishing characteristic which makes cloze tests so robust and which generates their surprisingly strong validity coefficients in relation to other pragmatic procedures. (p. 347)

In the work in progress by Chapman and reported in Chapman (1983b) and J. Anderson (1982, 1983) the items deleted were not randomly chosen, but were items from the chains which Halliday and Hasan (1980) claim are devices by which we keep track of people, objects and places in text, by which parts of text are joined together and by which the content domain of the text is defined.

In this case what is being employed would seem to be a very powerful tool indeed, and one that permits consideration of socio-cultural elements as well as psycholinguistic ones (Steffensen, 1981). The classroom implications of this particular approach have been considered by Anderson (1983), Winchester (1983) and by Wishart (1983).

Conclusion

So if you have not reached state of awareness stage 5 in the 'Clozural Revolution' at least acknowledge that Cloze Procedure has strengths as well as weaknesses and 'Don't close the door on Cloze'.

References

ANDERSON, E. (1983) 'Cohesion and the teacher'. *Australian Journal of Reading*, 6(1), pp. 35–42.

ANDERSON, J. (1976) *Psycholinguistic Experiments in Foreign Language Testing*. St Lucia: University of Queensland Press.

ANDERSON, J. (1982) 'The measurement of the perception of cohesion'. Paper presented at the International Reading Association Ninth World Congress on Reading, St Patrick's College, Dublin.

ANDERSON, J. (1983) 'The writer, the reader and the text', in B. Gillham (ed.) *Reading Through the Curriculum*. London: Heinemann.

CHAPMAN, L. J. (1983a) *Reading Development and Cohesion*. London: Heinemann.

CHAPMAN, L. J. (1983b) 'A study in reading development: A comparison of the ability of 8-, 10- and 13-year-old children to perceive cohesion in their school texts'. in B. Gillham (ed.) *Reading Through the Curriculum*. London: Heinemann.

DAVIES, P. and VINCENT, D. (1977) 'The development of cloze tests', in J. Gilliland (ed.) *Reading: Research and Classroom Practice*. London: Ward Lock.

D.E.S. (1975) *A Language for Life* (The Bullock Report). London: H.M.S.O.

DOLAN, E. P. (1977) 'A programme to develop reading for learning in the secondary school', in J. Gilliland (ed.) *Reading: Research and Classroom Practice*. London: Ward Lock.

GILLILAND, J. (ed.) (1977) *Reading: Research and Classroom Practice*. London: Ward Lock.

GILLHAM, B. (1983) *Reading Through the Curriculum*. London: Heinemann.

HALLIDAY, M. A. K. and HASAN, R. (1980) *Text and Context*. Sophia Linguistic Working Papers in Linguistics No. 6. Tokyo: Sophia University.

HARRISON, C. (1977) 'Assessing the readability of school texts', in J. Gilliland (ed.) *Reading: Research and Classroom Practice*. London: Ward Lock.

HARRISON, C. (1980) *Readability in the Classroom*. Cambridge: C.U.P.

HENDRY, A. (1981) Presidential Address to the 18yh U.K.R.A. Conference, Edinburgh (unpublished).

JONGSMA, E. (1971) *The Cloze Procedure as a Teaching Technique*. Newark, Del.: I.R.A.

JONGSMA, E. (1980) *Cloze Instruction Research: A Second Look*. Newark, Del.: I.R.A.

LUNZER, E. A. and GARDNER, K. (1979) *The Effective Use of Reading*. London: Heinemann.

McCULLOUGH, C. C., ROBINSON, H. A. and PEHRSSON, R. (1982) 'Cloze procedures as instructional strategies'. Symposium presented to the World Congress on Reading, Dublin.

OLLER, J. W. (1979) *Language Tests at School*. London: Longman.

PUMFREY, P. D. (1977) 'Reading measurement and evaluation', in J. Gilliland (ed.) *Reading: Research and Classroom Practice*. London: Ward Lock.

ROBINSON, H. A. and PEHRSSON, R. (in press) *Teaching Reading and Writing to Children with Special Language Needs*. Newton (Mass.): Allyn and Bacon.

RYE, J. (1982) *Cloze Procedure and the Teaching of Reading*. London: Heinemann.

SENIOR, J. (1980) *Cloze Procedure*. S.W. Herts: Teachers' Centre.

SOUTHGATE, V., ARNOLD, H. and JOHNSON, S. (1981) *Extending Beginning Reading*. London: Heinemann.

STEFFENSEN, M. S. (1981) *Register, Cohesion and Cross-Cultural Reading Comprehension*. Technical Report No. 220, Center for the study of Reading, University of Illinois at Urbana.

TAYLOR, W. L. (1953) ' "Cloze Procedure": a new tool for measuring readability'. *Journalism Quarterly*, 30, pp. 415–33.

TAYLOR, W. L. (1954) *Application of 'Cloze' and Entropy Measures to the Study of Contextual Constraint in Samples of Continuous Prose*. Doctoral dissertation, University of Illinois.

WALKER, C. (1974) *Reading Development and Extension*. London: Ward Lock.

WINCHESTER, S. (1983) 'Characteristic features in the development of coherent writing'. Paper presented to the 20th U.K.R.A. Course and Conference, Worcester.

WISHART, E. (1983) 'Textual cohesion and effective reading: a teaching strategy'. Paper presented at the 20th U.K.R.A. Course and Conference, Worcester.

19 Handwriting: meeting children's special needs

Peter Smith

It is generally accepted that there is a need for a school policy with regard to the teaching of handwriting. In *A Language for Life* the Bullock Committee had this to say:

> If a child is left to develop his hand-writing without instruction he is unlikely to develop a running hand which is simultaneously legible, fast-flowing and individual and becomes effortless to produce.

It follows, therefore, that agreement must be reached by all teachers involved so that instruction and examples provided shall be consistent. Such an agreed policy must be based on decisions regarding the shapes and methods of making letters initially and, in preparation for the later stage, a decision as to the choice of style for joined writing.

There are several important aspects to consider in formulating a school policy for handwriting. The first question that should perhaps be clarified is whether the aim of the school is to attempt to train calligraphers or whether the concentration should be on the achievement of a satisfactory running hand by all children. The latter goal would appear to be more realistic, particularly if the style of joined writing chosen is one which allows children to enjoy some appreciation of the aesthetic qualities of handwriting and also for some leaves open the door for the development of calligraphy at a later date. Although attractive handwriting is a joy to behold and a pleasure to produce, few teachers would argue that aesthetics should have priority over the achievement of an efficient mastery enabling fluent written communication.

Given a sensible and consistent policy for the teaching of handwriting there is good reason to expect that most children will learn to write adequately. The energies of class teachers and/or supplementary remedial teachers can then be used to meet the special needs of children with difficulties.

The majority of children begin to learn to read and write during their first year in the infant school and infant teachers are aware of the importance of ensuring that their pupils come to understand the function and purpose of print and writing. Whether the teaching is incidental or through a structured programme, children are helped to realise that thoughts can be communicated through symbols on paper. Often the first direct experience of this process occurs when teachers and/or children label drawings with words, phrases or sentences and the school policy should be operative from this beginning. It is customary for reception class teachers to provide activities and experiences that parallel those featured in the reading scheme and to encourage the children to compare the captions produced through the language experience approach with the print in the basal readers. For this reason many teachers choose to employ modern reading schemes that use more natural language structure to comment on situations that are both interesting and within the experience of the children. However, I must not digress, this is not the place for comparison of reading schemes. Reference to this aspect of early literacy learning is made solely to draw attention to the need for consideration of the kind of letters to teach at this stage. Clearly, early reading and writing are, in a sense, complimentary and there should be maximum correspondence between letters for early writing and those in the reading schemes.

At this point, mention must be made of the concept of 'Readiness'. Although, as already stated, most children make a start with literacy learning during the first year at infant school, all are not ready to commence at the same time. 'Readiness for writing' is a similar concept to that of 'readiness for reading' and equally it is not a stage to be waited for passively. To begin formal instruction too soon may be harmful but there are many sub-skills that should be consciously developed in preparation for handwriting and provision for these should be included in the programmes of nursery and reception classes. The three main areas of development – visual discrimination, motor control and memory recall – are discussed, together with suggestions of helpful activities, in Chapter 2 of *Developing Handwriting* by Peter Smith.

Hopefully the case has been made that maximum correspondence between forms of letters for early writing and the print in reading schemes in use is one major criterion in deciding a policy for handwriting. The other main criterion that must be borne in mind is that the letter forms chosen for the initial stage must facilitate progress to the chosen cursive style with minimum change and relearning. In the author's experience it is impossible to find a form of print that leads into any form of cursive writing without some degree of relearning and there is need for compromise between the demands made by the two major criteria discussed. In Chapter 4 of *Developing Handwriting* many alternative styles of cursive writing are reviewed and the author describes a personal recommendation.

The recommended sequence of print-script followed by Marion Richardson or Nelson is one which accords with the criteria discussed above but decisions as to the exact forms of the print-script letters must be made in each school or group of schools in the light of individual circumstances. It is important to emphasise that, whatever form is decided for the print-script, all letters must be correctly made, starting at the correct point with pencil movement in the right direction otherwise problems will occur at the time of learning to join. Handwriting patterns give a good basis for development of correct habits in this respect and they should be practised throughout the learning stage. The practice of making letters from separate round and straight strokes, i.e. 'ball and stick', should never be allowed and although roundness may be encouraged at the beginning stage there should be a gradual change to more oval shapes with increasing maturity. Procedures for teaching print-script are discussed in some detail in Chapter 3 of *Developing Handwriting*.

Just as there is need for recourse to a range of techniques and strategies for the efficient teaching of print-script, so must teachers develop a programme for teaching the cursive style. It is widely accepted that the first requirement is a fresh emphasis on pattern making. Some teachers, in the absence of training and guidance themselves, have then distributed the publishers' books or cards as models and invited the children to attempt to copy them. Not surprisingly many pupils find this approach less than helpful and produce imperfect versions of the style at the same time as developing harmful writing habits. The time of introducing the cursive style, which I suggest may be in the eighth year of life for most children, is necessarily a time for teacher direction and demonstration. Since cursive writing depends on a continuous left to right flow of correct movement it is essential for the teacher to master the style and to be competent at demonstration on the blackboard and elsewhere.

It is also necessary to be aware of the nature and logic of the various joins employed in Marion Richardson and Nelson styles of handwriting, and in Chapter 5 of *Developing Handwriting* and in the Teacher's Book to the New Nelson Scheme I have described a method of classifying the letters into sets as a way of involving children in thinking about the characteristics of different ligatures. Children benefit from practice in making the basic joins and then in using them in the process of copying words, phrases and sentences before being required to produce original composition in cursive writing. Therefore it is recommended that, during the two or three months devoted to learning the rudiments, all other writing tasks should continue to be executed in print-script. Once the children achieve a sufficient mastery of the joined style they should be encouraged to gradually adopt the style for all writing purposes and, at this stage, the published specimen cards provide excellent material for occasional revision practice when the concentration can again be on technique rather than on content. This is also the stage at which the children should be encouraged to begin to develop some degree of individuality in their writing although it must continue to be soundly based on the fundamental principles taught. Examination of the writing of a class of ten- or eleven-year-old children shows quite clearly that individuality does develop and it is usually possible to identify the writer of each script from the writing.

As evidenced by the published books and cards there is a tendency for children to be taught to write large at the beginning of the course and, as it progresses, to gradually reduce to a size appropriate to the individual. This practice seems helpful as it accords with the needs of developing maturity. By the age of nine or ten many children, when using lined paper, limit the size of their writing to two-thirds of the line height. This has the advantage of avoiding clashes between ascenders and descenders as well as resulting in what appears to be an appropriate size. The mention of lined paper here should not be misinterpreted as a recommendation for the exclusive use of lined paper. The author feels strongly that the great majority of children should commence writing print-script on plain paper and that all children should continue to have some experience of unlined paper throughout their schooling.

Throughout the primary and middle schools children should be made aware of the importance of spacing, layout, and presentation and, particularly in the later years, opportunities should be seized or created to provide motivation for really careful presentation. Suitable opportunities might occur in connection with projects when reports for display could justifiably be prepared in draft form and then reproduced as a handwriting exercise after correction.

While the children are learning to write and later when they use the skill, attention should be paid to such matters as posture, pencil grip, position of paper and suitability of furniture, etc. This is not to suggest that a narrow view should be taken and conformity demanded in these matters but there do appear to be certain criteria for success that should be followed within reasonable tolerances. Left-handed children in particular will benefit from sensible advice in the early stages and, hopefully, will be prevented from adopting any of the extremely awkware solutions to their problems which they frequently evolve when left to their own devices. Detailed advice on methods and materials for helping children with special needs are to be found in *Developing Handwriting*.

It is to be hoped that the need for good handwriting instruction is readily accepted by the reader. That written communication must be legible, that flow of thought is hampered when the writer cannot keep pace with the processes of the mind and that pleasure is experienced from producing well-formed writing are all undeniable reasons for paying adequate attention to the teaching of the skill. There are, however, two other justifications, if justification be needed, that are less widely considered.

Spelling and writing are quite clearly linked. The confidence and fluency of the writer may be hindered by lack of confidence in spelling ability while spelling ability is greatly influenced by good writing habits. As Dr Margaret Peters explains in her *Diagnostic and Remedial Spelling Manual*:

The two areas in which the child is most vulnerable, as far as spelling goes, are the motor and visual areas. In other words, he must have been taught a consistent, economical and swift form of handwriting and he must learn to look at words with every intention of remembering and being able to reproduce them. In this way he will learn the probabilities of certain letters occurring together.

This point of view is reiterated by Marie Clay who in *Reading, The Patterning of Complex Behaviour* writes:

The details of words involve knowing precisely which letters occur in what order, and such discriminations and attention to sequence are consolidated by the acts of constructing these words in creative writing. Discrimination and an awareness of the sequential probabilities of letters and letter clusters in English are sharpened by the act of writing.

In a series of three books of spiritmasters published by Holmes McDougall Ltd in 1981, under the title of 'Writemasters', I am attempting to provide practice in writing the Marion Richardson style while, at the same time, drawing attention to patterns of spelling and helping children develop motor and visual memory of probable letter clusters.

The final justification for attention to handwriting is discussed in a report on an investigation into the influence of handwriting on assessment by Dennis Briggs of the Open University. Writing in *Education Research* Vol. 13, No. 1, Nov. 1970, he describes an interesting experiment in which 50 teachers were asked to assess ten essays which were each reproduced in ten different writing styles. As a result of this research there seems little doubt that, particularly in the case of anonymous marking, there is an unconscious tendency to mark students down for poor handwriting. The possible significance of this tendency in the case of a borderline pass/fail situation in an important examination is obvious.

In conclusion, it must be emphasised that for the many reasons discussed here, a school policy for handwriting is essential. Because of the interrelation between the various aspects of literacy, any improvement in standards of handwriting will make a contribution to the achievement of the aim of this conference – 'Reading: Meeting Children's Special Needs'.

References

D.E.S. (1975) *A Language for Life* (The Bullock Report). London: H.M.S.O.

SMITH, P. (1977) *Developing Handwriting*. London: Macmillan.

RICHARDSON, M. (1935) *Writing and Writing Patterns*. London: Hodder and Stoughton (Previously U.L.P.).

PETERS, M. (1975) *Diagnostic and Remedial Spelling Manual*. London: Macmillan.

CLAY, M. M. (1972) *Reading, The Patterning of Complex Behaviour*. London: Heinemann.

BRIGGS, D. (1970) 'The Influence of Handwritting on Assessment'. *Education Research*, 13(1).

SMITH, P. and WILLIAMS, J. (1981) *Writemaster* (6 book series). Edinburgh: Holmes McDougall Ltd.

SMITH, P. and INGLES, A. (1984) *The New Nelson Handwriting* (Teachers' Handbook and 6 books plus 2 books of spiritmasters). London: Nelson.

20 An experiment in teaching cohesion in expository texts to nine- to ten-year-old children

Sylvia Winchester

Until about 15 years ago, children were taught conventional English 'grammar', especially in the grammar schools, in the belief that an understanding of the rules of sentence analysis and construction would develop language competence. Then, in the last two decades, research began to indicate that performing 'autopsies' on dismembered fragments of text did not necessarily lead children to an appreciation of how living language works.

It is now generally agreed that, in creating or comprehending written language in particular, the features which contribute to coherence and continuity of meaning are not only to be found within individual sentences, but more especially in links created between sentences and longer stretches of text. For it is these links which maintain the network of relationships throughout a text, and it is these relationships which are its meaning. In order to create or comprehend coherent text, the writer or reader uses not only the structures of within-sentence syntax, but also the devices of inter-sentential cohesion.

If this is how real language works, then teachers of language need to be developing children's awareness of text as an integrated whole. We must draw their attention to the features which interrelate successive elements of meaning in the texts they read, and encourage their use of such features when they write. We can now replace the sterile 'autopsy' which was traditional English grammar with a study of the 'physiology' of language, a careful and continuous examination of how language 'moves and grows', that is, how meaning is made.

Also during the last ten to twenty years, there has been a revolution in the basic assumptions of linguistics, and linguists such as M. A. K. Halliday have begun to examine language in terms of the user's choice from a range of available options, and the influence of context and function upon that choice. A speaker or writer is aware of the audience, the situation and the purpose for which he or she is speaking or writing, and that awareness is an integral part of making meaning, giving the text appropriate register, the hallmark of authentic language.

Therefore, those aiming to develop children's competence, in either creating or comprehending written texts, now realise that this includes developing their awareness of register and its influence upon the choice of appropriate language for a wide variety of contexts. From infancy, or at least from the infant school, children receive continuous exposure to narrative registers, and are given opportunities in the primary years to practise telling and writing stories in varied styles. But comparatively little preparation is given for the more formal expository registers in which most of their subsequent education will be conducted, and in which information will be presented to them most frequently in adult life.

It is therefore essential that, in the later years of the primary school, children are presented, across the curriculum, with texts which are at an appropriate conceptual level, but which are also written in a register beginning to approximate the formal expository styles of secondary school text books. Many history, geography and science books, designed for and used in primary schools, are suitable for this purpose. Some either make no concessions to the inexperience of children, or use a narrative register which denies children the early experience they need. When suitable materials are not available, teachers either produce their own, or rely almost completely on oral language, thus contributing to the 'retreat from print' observed by the Lunzer and Gardner 'Reading for the Learning' project.

But the presentation of suitable texts is only a beginning. It is a common experience of many teachers to find that children may be able to read a text aloud quite competently, and can deal with the concepts involved when they are paraphrased orally for them, but are nevertheless unable to comprehend unaided the unfamiliar form of 'text-book language' in which those concepts are presented. To give 'comprehension' questions on the text does no more than reveal the inadequacy of the child's comprehending; to paraphrase the content into more accessible oral language does not extend the child's experience or competence.

It is at this point, confronted with a difficult text related to on-going work, that the child needs the teaching of 'language across the curriculum' to be focused into a study of 'the language *in* the curriculum'. The meaning and language of the text need to be studied together, so that the child can understand not only *what* the text is saying, but also *how* it is said. An analysis of the features of cohesion and register in a text can greatly clarify and underline its meaning. Experience of such analysis applied to a variety of increasingly demanding texts in the later primary years is likely to make 'text-book language' more familiar and accessible before children reach the heavily text-based secondary learning situation. Furthermore, comprehension and composition seem to draw on the same fundamental language resources. It is likely, therefore, that a growing understanding of how expository texts are framed and integrated will encourage the development of control and coherence in their own non-narrative writing.

The above observations serve as an outline of the context and the purpose of a small project conducted in a Birmingham primary school in the summer term of '83. This was prompted by involvement in Dr J. Chapman's Cohesion Research Survey and by his early findings. The project was an experiment in teaching the properties of cohesion in expository texts to a class of average third-year children in the course of their work on 'The Industrial Revolution'. Teaching methods were developed from earlier work by E. Anderson in a Cambridgeshire primary school. A small-scale experiment cannot be expected to provide quantifiable evidence or universal rules, but only to indicate some areas of difficulty or promise for future investigation. This chapter gives a <u>How a lock works</u>

When a boat comes to a lock the first gates open and the boat goes into the lock. Then the first gates are closed. As soon as the gates are closed the sluices in the upper gates start to open so that the water starts to flow in. The water level rises and so does the boat. When the water is the same level as the water beyond the upper gates, they open and the boat can continue on its way.

b The boat goes into the lock and the gates shut. Somebody has to wind the windlass and the water comes through the sluices and fills the lock and the boat goes up. Then the outer gates open and the boat goes out of the lock.

Fig. 1

188

an account of some of the procedures followed, reproductions of a few of the materials devised, and a summary of the issues which emerged as significant.

Figure 1 shows two accounts of the same process, how a canal lock works, written by different children of the same age, 10 years. The response of most teachers to these two accounts has been that the first seems to show a greater degree of control and precision than the second. A closer analysis of the two texts shows that the first includes: four appropriate sequential connectives – *when, then, as soon as, when*; four comparative terms – *first, upper, the same as, beyond*; a number of lexically related pairs – *open/close, comes to/continues, start to open/start to fill, level rises/same level*; appropriate use of pronomial reference – *they*, and verbal substitution – *so does*. These are examples of cohesive elements which create meaning links within and between sentences and which contribute to the impression of coherence, albeit elementary, in the text. The second text uses; one sequential connective – *when* ; two lexically related pairs – *goes into/goes out, shut/open*; one attempt at a comparative term – *outer*. While the difference between the two texts may be considered marginal, any contrast is increased by the knowledge that the writer of the second text was a child who would generally be considered to have the advantage of considerably greater language resources.

In fact, the second text was written spontaneously after reading and discussing relevant information sheets and diagrams. The writing of the first text, on the other hand, was supported by additional procedures which focused attention on the specific language demands of the task. It was considered that the significant features in the process were the sequence of events and the need to distinguish between similar things. A procedure was therefore designed to draw children's attention to sequential and comparative language features. First, illustrated information sheets about canals and locks were given out to provide content vocabulary and stimulate discussion. One sheet included a short 'Cloze'-type passage to initiate the search for a variety of sequential connectives. This was completed in small groups and checked by class discussion. Then the diagram shown in Figure 2 was presented and, with this as the only support, the class together composed an oral account of how a boat goes through a lock. As individuals volunteered sentences and improved on each other's suggestions, the sequential and comparative terminology which would be useful was collected, (or provided), and the children were directed to write each term alongside the appropriate section of the diagram, as in Figure 2. This annotated diagram was the 'notes' from which the children, again working in groups of two or three, produced their accounts. Several of the joint accounts produced were fuller and more impressive than that given in Figure 1, since they included more of the technical terminology from earlier worksheets, (balance beams, paddles, etc), and also made appropriate use of more of the sequential and comparative terms provided. All the texts showed a greater degree of precision and organisation than could reasonably have been expected without the support given.

The suggestion being made here is not that the writing competence of these children had instantaneously improved, but that the support given in this and subsequent procedures has features which could be applied to a variety of

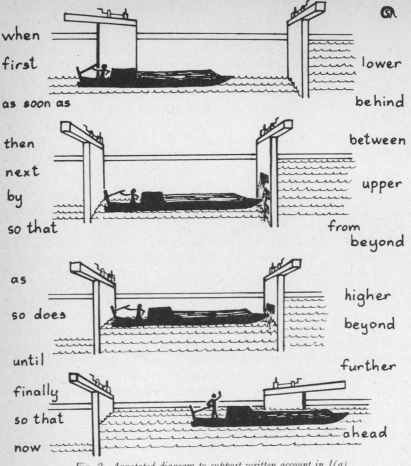

when
first
as soon as
then
next
by
so that
as
so does
until
finally
so that
now

lower
behind
between
upper
from
beyond
higher
beyond
further
ahead

Fig. 2. Annotated diagram to support written account in 1(a).

comprehension and writing tasks. Such directed language activities could be expected to contribute over a period of time to a growing mastery of expository registers. Features of this procedure which might be considered valuable in other contexts are as follows:

1. The writing task was related to on-going class work, a history project which, incidentally, had included a school visit to the Iron Bridge Gorge Museum. Any language work involved was therefore integral to the investigation and recording of information, and did not take the form of 'English lessons'.

2. Specific language demands of the task were assessed in advance and support was focused here, rather than on the 'content vocabulary'. Often, in the organising and recording of information, it is not the content which presents difficulties, but the 'framework language'. For this task, sequential

and comparative vocabulary was assembled and related to a diagram. The method is flexible but requires careful preparation by the teacher.

3. There was continual emphasis on oral 'testing'; 'Read it aloud and see how it sounds', 'Does another word or another way of putting it sound better?'. Similarly, in text comprehension tasks, there was continual 'imprinting' of correct intonation. Passages were read, difficult sections re-read, *to* the class, using the rhythms and stresses of intonation to underline meaning, without paraphrasing. Children began to verbalise stretches of text in group activities and when justifying their interpretations. This was taken as evidence that children were beginning to deal with the actual language features of the expository register with more confidence.

4. No clear distinction was drawn between text processing and text production. Most procedures, like the one outlined above, included a combination of reading, interpretation, discussion, selection from alternatives, completing or reorganising disrupted texts, focusing on particular aspects of language, and producing individual or joint texts.

5. There were three underlying assumptions implicit in the whole approach to the work; first that there is an appropriate register for the effective presentation of information in written form, second, that mastery of this register has to be worked towards steadily, and third, that children can recognise for themselves, with satisfaction, when they begin to achieve it.

The reconstruction of disrupted texts is not an original strategy. Figure 3 shows such a text, both as given out to the class with sections extracted and placed below, and also with those sections pasted back into their original positions by the children. However, it is less common for this strategy to be followed up by an analysis of the specific language features which enabled the children to carry out the reconstruction. Such an analysis can reinforce meaning at the same time as highlighting the integrating devices in the text. It is helpful, especially for the average child of primary age, for implicit meaning devices, which will be taken for granted by the mature reader, to be made explicit in the context of on-going work. The worksheets shown in Figs 3 and 4 were devised for this purpose.

The whole of each text was read aloud *to* the class before and after the re-positioning of extracted sentences. Then, working in pairs or threes, the children were asked to identify, and mark on one child's copy, the meaning links, or cohesive ties, which enabled them to allocate the missing sentences. (Needless to say, this task was presented without reference to the terminology used here.) Figure 3 shows how one example of Demonstrative Reference, 'of this' in the first strip, is tied to the whole of the preceding sentence. In a similar way, 'do this' in the second strip was tied to a large portion of the preceding three sentences, and the pronouns 'he', 'this' and 'it' in the third strip were tied to their presupposing noun-groups and so on.

Then followed a discussion of what the text was 'about', and themes of 'coal', 'the mine', 'children in mines' and 'cruelty/suffering' were collected. Using different coloured crayons on the second child's text, the groups were then directed to ring and link every reference to a chosen theme, every item contributing to a chain of meaning.

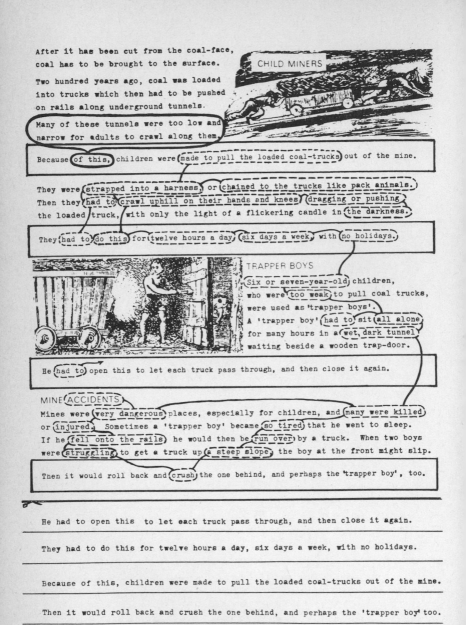

After it has been cut from the coal-face, coal has to be brought to the surface.

Two hundred years ago, coal was loaded into trucks which then had to be pushed on rails along underground tunnels.

Many of these tunnels were too low and narrow for adults to crawl along them.

Because of this, children were made to pull the loaded coal-trucks out of the mine.

They were strapped into a harness, or chained to the trucks like pack animals. Then they had to crawl uphill on their hands and knees dragging or pushing the loaded truck, with only the light of a flickering candle in the darkness.

They had to do this for twelve hours a day, six days a week, with no holidays.

CHILD MINERS

TRAPPER BOYS

Six or seven-year-old children, who were too weak to pull coal trucks, were used as 'trapper boys'. A 'trapper boy' had to sit all alone for many hours in a wet, dark tunnel waiting beside a wooden trap-door.

He had to open this to let each truck pass through, and then close it again.

MINE ACCIDENTS

Mines were very dangerous places, especially for children, and many were killed or injured. Sometimes a 'trapper boy' became so tired that he went to sleep. If he fell onto the rails he would then be run over by a truck. When two boys were struggling to get a truck up a steep slope, the boy at the front might slip.

Then it would roll back and crush the one behind, and perhaps the 'trapper boy', too.

He had to open this to let each truck pass through, and then close it again.

They had to do this for twelve hours a day, six days a week, with no holidays.

Because of this, children were made to pull the loaded coal-trucks out of the mine.

Then it would roll back and crush the one behind, and perhaps the 'trapper boy' too.

Fig. 3. Disrupted text reconstructed and analysed.

192

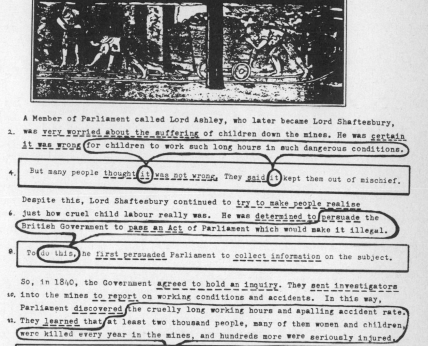

A Member of Parliament called Lord Ashley, who later became Lord Shaftesbury,
2. was very worried about the suffering of children down the mines. He was certain it was wrong for children to work such long hours in such dangerous conditions.

4. But many people thought it was not wrong. They said it kept them out of mischief.

Despite this, Lord Shaftesbury continued to try to make people realise
6. just how cruel child labour really was. He was determined to persuade the British Government to pass an Act of Parliament which would make it illegal.

8. To do this, he first persuaded Parliament to collect information on the subject.

So, in 1840, the Government agreed to hold an inquiry. They sent investigators
10. into the mines to report on working conditions and accidents. In this way, Parliament discovered the cruelly long working hours and apalling accident rate.
11. They learned that at least two thousand people, many of them women and children, were killed every year in the mines, and hundreds more were seriously injured.

14. As a result of these discoveries, Parliament passed the Mines Act of 1842.

15. This Act made it illegal for women, girls or boys under 10 to work underground.

A. To do this, he first persuaded Parliament to collect information on the subject.

B. This Act made it illegal for women, girls or boys under 10 to work underground.

C. But many people thought it was not wrong. They said it kept them out of mischief.

D. As a result of these discoveries, Parliament passed the Mines Act of 1842.

Fig. 4. Disrupted text reconstructed.

For clarity, only the 'cruelty/suffering chain', as identified by the children, is marked in Figure 3. Some of the vocabulary ringed here would not be classified as ties on a cohesive chain according to the precise definitions of Hasan's model, (Hasan, R., 1980), but the children were searching for the meaning relations which are expressed in those chains of ties, and precision was not important.

It was interesting that 'surface' was excluded from the 'mine' chain, but 'darkness' was included in both the 'mine' and the 'cruelty' chain by some children. At least one child suggested that 'it' in the first line was the first member of the 'coal' chain. After discussion, 'pack animals' was recognised as a simile for the children's experience and included in both the 'children' and 'cruelty' chain. The Nominal Substitution, 'the one behind' was recognised as contributing to the 'children' chain.

The children received a lot of stimulus from each other and seemed to enjoy the exercise. In the course of discussion and decision-making, they were making semantic and linguistic judgements for themselves, if at an elementary level, and in this way much of the implicit meaning became explicit for them. It seems likely that this type of procedure in a variety of contexts would foster an awareness of text as a network of inter-related meaning.

With the companion text, shown in Figure 4, a similar initial procedure was followed. The only cohesive ties shown here are the Verbal Substitution 'do this', two examples of Demonstrative Reference, 'these' discoveries and 'this' Act, and double use of Pronominal Reference, 'it', in the first strip. When asked what this text was 'about', the children found it more difficult to be specific, but, with help, the themes of 'changing people's minds' and 'changing the law' were agreed upon. Vocabulary relating to these themes was then underlined, as in Fig. 4, and copied out as a framework for subsequent writing. In the event, time allotted for this work was curtailed, but it may be evident that the underlined vocabulary would provide support for written work, perhaps by older children, on how social change was brought about.

Two important aspects of comprehension of written texts can be defined as, first an appreciation of the author's precise choice of vocabulary, and second an awareness of the relation between the words chosen and earlier or later sections of the text. Similarly, when constructing his or her own texts, the child needs to be encouraged to choose words carefully for the way they can support and carry forward the meaning he or she is making. Figure 5 shows a worksheet on 'Climbing Boys' designed to foster this 'meaning search' approach to text in average third year children. After the text, with all its alternatives, had been read aloud, the children were asked to work in pairs or threes to select which of the alternatives, all or any, made sense. Then stretches of text were read aloud again and children were asked to justify their decisions. The discussion which followed raised many points of information and clarified terms, but the most significant feature was the extent to which children were relating their selections to earlier or later sections of text. 'It was because they were too "twisting" that they couldn't be "cleaned by a brush".' 'It must be "the picture below" because there it's "opened out" and "being

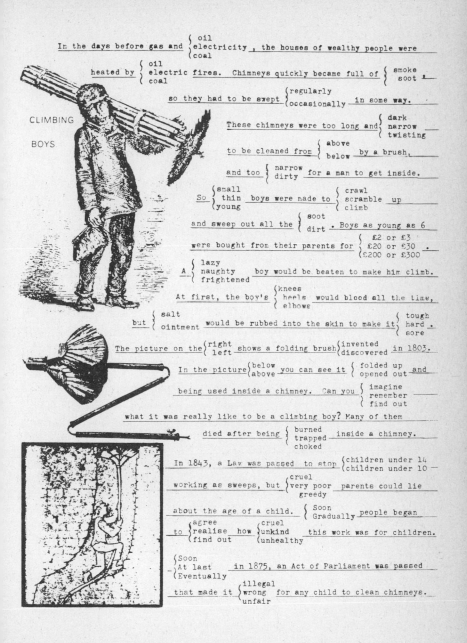

Fig. 5. Multiple-choice worksheet.

used in a chimney".' ' "Two or three pounds" was a lot of money to "very poor" parents who might be starving.' 'The last one must be "illegal" because it says "an Act of Parliament, was passed".' Reference back to the surrounding text did not seem to be a spontaneous strategy and had to be encouraged frequently at first. Most of the meaning relations involved were contained within sentences, and the exercise may seem simplistic. Nevertheless, it proved to be a useful method of open-ended questioning which led the children back to the text to search for meaning relations beyond the immediate context of the alternatives.

Language which concerns change and contrast, for instance in processes and physical movement, is often significant in history, geography or science texts. This became evident in the course of studying early and modern blast furnaces after the visit to Iron Bridge. After reading and working on preliminary texts and diagrams, the children were presented with the worksheet shown in Figure 6. The task was to use their prior knowledge and the information on the sheet, working in pairs, in order to paste the title, the three small and four larger labels in their correct positions on the diagram, and then to justify their decisions. The exercise was designed to draw attention to contrasts such as mixes/separates, lighter/heavier, floats on top/sinks to the bottom, and required the children to select from a density of information characteristic of certain kinds of expository text. The whole procedure was also designed to serve as a preparation for written descriptions of the similarities and differences between early and modern blast furnaces, giving children the opportunity to use for themselves the language which had been highlighted.

A characteristic feature of expository texts is the form of Verbal Substitution, 'do it', 'do this', 'do so', 'do the same' etc, which is termed Verbal Reference. This is a useful form of linguistic 'shorthand' whereby a preceding and possibly lengthy statement can be related succintly to a following statement while retaining its full meaning. Figure 7 shows a Cloze-type worksheet which was devised to familiarise the children with the form and implicit meaning of this device, at the same time as introducing the topic of The Coming of Steam Transport. The forms of Verbal Reference cited above were first written on the blackboard, and familiar oral examples provided. Then the worksheet was given out and read aloud to the class, with rhythmic pencil taps in place of deletions. The children were told to look out for opportunities to use this form of 'shorthand' in completing the gaps. Examples of Connective, Comparative and Lexical cohesive devices were also included in the text. The language was intended to approximate to that of text-books, with perhaps an overloading of Verbal Reference for practice. The first two examples were worked as a class oral activity, and the exact meanings substituted by 'do this' and 'does this' were identified and marked by the children as indicated on Figure 7. Then the children worked in groups, with much oral testing, to complete the gaps.

Most of the class began to be able to use the substitution device appropriately with the support of the blackboard and each other, and seemed to find satisfaction in doing so. Acceptable alternatives were found for several

A blast of hot air is sent up through the mixture and the coke burns fiercely. The iron ore melts. The molten iron separates from the parts of the ore which cannot be used.

Hot gases are removed from an outlet in the top of the furnace.

Skips carry a mixture of iron ore and coke and limestone up to the top of the furnace. A supply of this mixture is dropped into the top of the furnace all through the smelting process.

Slag is lighter than iron, and so it floats on top of the molten iron. Slag is drained from the slag notch every few hours. It is taken away in trucks, and used to be piled into slag heaps.

Every few hours, the molten iron is drained from the bottom of the furnace through the tap-hole. From the Old Furnace, it ran into sand moulds to cool into pig iron. Today, it goes to the steel works.

Molten iron and slag trickle downwards. The iron is heavier so it sinks to the bottom of the furnace.

HOW IRON ORE IS SMELTED IN A BLAST FURNACE

In the intense heat, the limestone mixes with the parts of the ore which are not used. This makes slag.

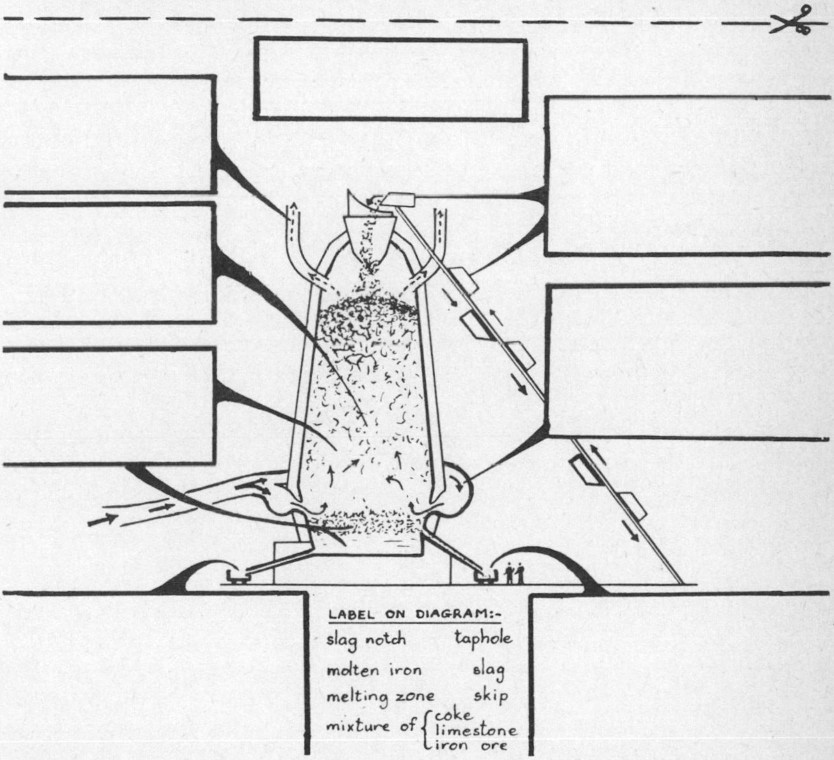

LABEL ON DIAGRAM:-

slag notch   taphole

molten iron   slag

melting zone   skip

mixture of { coke
             limestone
             iron ore

Fig. 6. Labelling exercise.

THE COMING OF STEAM TRANSPORT.

1   The first steam engines were used to ⟨pump water,⟩
or to ⟨power machines⟩ or to ⟨wind heavy loads uphill.⟩
But they had to be stationary to __do this__ , that is,
they were fixed in one place.

2.   Robert Trevithick was the first to build a
steam engine which ⟨moved along a track on wheels.⟩
An engine which __does this__ is called a locomotive.
This picture shows Trevithick's locomotive on display
in London in 1809. He said it was 'mechanical power
subduing animal speed' and called it 'Catch me who can'.

Trevithick's circular railway set up
near Torrington Square the combination of railway and steam engine
used here as a pastime was to change
the face of civilization

3.   In __those days__ , coal was transported from mines on tramways, that is,
horse-drawn trucks running on rails. A mine engineer called William Hedley saw
Trevithick's engine. He realised that the power of steam could be used to move
coal trucks along the tramways of his colliery in Wylam, Northumberland.
__So__ in 1813, he built a locomotive called 'Puffing Billy' to __do   this__ .

4.   The Wylam tramway ran past the childhood home of __another__ mining engineer
called George Stephenson, and he visited Wylam to see 'Puffing Billy' at work.
He was so impressed that he returned to the mine where he worked and told the
mine owner how Hedley had converted his colliery tramway into a steam railway.
Stephenson persuaded the mine owner to let him __do__ the __same__ . He built
a __similar__ locomotive and called it 'Blucher' after a famous Prussian general.

5.   __But__ Stephenson knew that steam locomotion was not just an improvement
for the mines. He realised that it was an important new method of transport.
Not only coal, __but also__ people needed to move from one place to __another__ ,
and he could imagine a time when steam railways would be used to __do   this__ .
__So__ he set about persuading Parliament to give permission for a railway line
to be built from Stockton to Darlington. __At   first__ Parliament did not agree,
__but__ after a great deal of argument, they __did   so__ , and Stephenson set to work.

Opening of the
Stockton and
Darlington Railway
27 September 1825

6.   It took several years to lay the track and build the
locomotive. __But__ at last, in 1825, the world's first
public steam railway was opened. The very first 'train'
was made up of 12 trucks of coal and 21 wagons filled with
__passengers__ . It travelled at the __amazing__ speed
of 15 m.p.h. and was pulled by Stephenson's latest engine
called 'Locomotion No.1! A group of young men on horse-back
tried to outrun the smoking monster, __but__ they were
unable to __do so__ . The age of the horse was over.

The Age of __Steam__ had arrived.

Fig. 7. Cloze-type passage.

198

of the Temporal Connectives and Lexical items. The Comparatives, 'another' and 'similar', were more difficult. But it was apparent in this and other worksheets that Adversative Connectives caused the most difficulty. While the conjunction 'but' may be familiar in the narrative context, in expository texts, its crucial function of introducing contrasting, contradictory or unexpected elements of meaning seems to be much more problematic. It has been a consistent finding of this project and of the Cohesion Survey, that the significance of Adversative Connectives such as 'but', 'although' and 'however', together with Causal Connectives, seems to be less readily appreciated by primary and early secondary children than other cohesive relations. This suggests that, where such connectives are met in text-based study, their full meaning needs to be emphasised and elaborated to ensure continuity of comprehension.

The project as a whole was an illuminating and satisfying experience, for the investigator greatly enhanced by the consistent support and good humour of the staff of the school, and the lively spirit of the children. The timespan of the experiment was too short for great significance to be attached to objective measures indicating improvement. But a subjective impression remained that many members of the class, especially some in the middle of the average range, were beginning to show greater interest, skill and confidence in dealing with expository texts.

The materials devised for the project, including those illustrated here, had many shortcomings which were immediately apparent in the hands of a class of children. But failure can be as instructive as success, and the experience of both in this experiment gave rise to the following general conclusions:

1. Teaching children to perceive and apply the cohesive properties of language is a valid and supportive literacy development strategy which would justify much more investigation and experiment by teachers.

2. In helping children to deal with formal 'text-book language', teachers' most valuable resources are their own linguistic understanding and ability to anticipate and prepare for the demands such unfamiliar language will make upon children. Teachers need time and opportunity to develop and apply their own resources.

3. Cohesion and register, like phonics and syntax, can be seen as examples of language as a code-making process. When presented appropriately, analysis of these more subtle language features can provide children with the stimulus and satisfaction of code-breaking and puzzle-solving activities.

4. Many 'average' children seem to possess a facility with language which emerges in the kind of oral work on written texts included above, but which may not be reflected in their reading or writing performance as normally assessed in school. If this linguistic 'common sense' could be activated and nurtured more effectively by our language-teaching strategies, it is likely that more children would fulfil their educational potential.

5. The majority of primary school children are not initiated into 'the language of learning' by literary or academic backgrounds, and it is therefore seen as an important function of the primary school to de-mystify 'establish-

ment' language. This de-mystification process must include strategies which make implicit meaning explicit, which clarify the encoding devices involved, and which enable children to use these devices for themselves.

References

HALLIDAY, M. A. K. and HASAN, R. (1976) Cohesion in English. London: Longman.
HASAN, R. (1980) The Texture of a Text, in Sophia Linguistica Number 6, Sophia University, Japan.
CHAPMAN, J. (1983) Reading Development and Cohesion. London: Heinemann.

List of contributors

Eleanor Anderson
Lecturer in Education
Hertfordshire College of Higher
    Education

Professor Richard Bamberger
President
Austrian Reading Association

Richard Binns
Principal Teacher of Remedial
    Education
St Pius' Secondary School, Glasgow

Mike J. Carter
Headmaster
Monkswood Infant School, Worcester

Dr L. John Chapman
Faculty of Education Studies
The Open University

Roger Cocks
Lecturer in Education
Worcester College of Higher Education

Professor Christian Gerhard
George Washington Univeristy (D.C.)

Nigel Hall
Senior Lecturer in Education Studies
Didsbury School of Education
Manchester Polytechnic

C. Morag Hunter
Lecturer in Education
School of Education
University of Leicester

Ian Liddle
Educational Psychologist
Springburn Child Guidance Clinic

Ronald Mackay
Principal Lecturer in Primary
    Education
Jordanhill College of Education,
    Glasgow

Patricia McCall
Assistant Head Teacher
Morningside Primary School,
    Edinburgh

Dr Joyce M. Morris
Educational writer, consultant and
    researcher
London

Chris Nugent
Teacher and writer
East Kew, Victoria, Australia

Sue Palmer
Head Teacher
Caddonfoot Primary School
Borders Region

Nick Pepin
Headteacher
Arrochar Primary School
Tarbet, Dunbartonshire

Dr Frank Potter
Senior Lecturer in Education
Edge Hill College of Education

Bridie Raban
School of Education
University of Reading

Peter Smith
Primary Adviser
London Borough of Hillingdon

Rosemary Threadgold
English Teacher
The Chase High School, Malvern

Nicholas Tucker
Lecturer in Developmental Psychology
University of Sussex

Sylvia Winchester
Marlborough Junior School
Birmingham

Valerie Yule
Department of Psychology
University of Aberdeen